Ho
Pea

2020

with
World Peace Directory

67th Edition ISSN 0957-0136

Published and distributed by

HOUSMANS BOOKSHOP
**5 Caledonian Road, Kings Cross, London N1 9DX, UK
(tel +44-20-7837 4473; email diary@housmans.com)**

ISBN 978 0 85283 281 3

Editorial co-ordination — Albert Beale
Cover design & month illustrations — Soofiya Andry
Dates & quotations compilation — Bill Hetherington
Historical research — Bill Hetherington
Lay-out & production — Chris Booth, Form & Function

Directory from Housmans Peace Resource Project,
editor Albert Beale (www.housmans.info)

Copyright © 2019 Housmans Bookshop Ltd

Printed by iPrint (UK) Ltd, Leicestershire

Personal Notes

Name

Address

Telephone

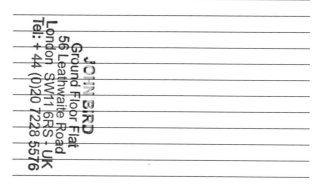

JOHN BIRD
Ground Floor Flat
56 Leathwaite Road
London SW11 6RS · UK
Tel: + 44 (0)20 7228 5576

EXPLANATORY NOTES

National public holidays in the UK, Republic of Ireland, Canada and the USA
are noted by the abbreviation HOL, followed by abbreviations for relevant
countries: ENG – England, NI – Northern Ireland, SCOT – Scotland,
W – Wales; UK – United Kingdom (ie all the preceding four); IRE – Republic
of Ireland; CAN – Canada; US – United States. We regret that we are not
able to show holidays in other countries.

Dates of moon phases, solstices and equinoxes are for GMT; users in other
time zones will find that the local date is different in some cases.

ORDERING INFORMATION

Copies of the Diary may be ordered from:
Housmans, 5 Caledonian Road, Kings Cross, London N1 9DX, UK
(tel +44-20-7837 4473; email orders@housmans.com)

Introduction

Welcome to the 67th edition of *Housmans Peace Diary*, intended – as always since its inception – as both a resource and an inspiration for campaigners around the world.

The feature in this edition looks at the various Peace Days – and similar "special" Days and Weeks – which we include in the *Diary*. Many of them have been established by bodies such as the United Nations, but not exclusively so. We explain when they were established and give some of the political context; the human cost of peace-making and the defence of human rights is clear. We also look briefly at the rationale for – and uses of – the daily anniversaries included throughout the *Diary*.

Among the anniversaries included this year are the tercentenary of the birth of John Woolman, war tax resister; the bicentenary of the birth of Susan Brownell Anthony, feminist slavery abolitionist; the centenaries of the coming into force of the Versailles Treaty, of the establishment of the League of Nations (forerunner of the UN), and of the birth of pacifist writer Alex Comfort.

We also, amongst much else, mark: 90 years since the birth of Harold Pinter, conscientious objector and playwright; 80 years since Women's Peace Day in WW2 Britain; the 75th anniversary of the founding of Pax Christi; 70 years since the death of Carl Heath, pacifist activist; 60 years since since the death of Toyohiko Kagawa, Japanese pacifist; 50 years since a school of peace and conflict theory was established for conscientious objectors in Norway; 40 years since members of the 5th International Nonviolent March for Demilitarisation were arrested in Romania; 30 years since the dedication of the Peace Pagoda, Milton Keynes; and 20 years since the festival of national reconciliation and peace, Cambodia.

The Diary and the Directory are both non-profit services to fellow activists, depending on much voluntary labour. We welcome promotional help – leaflets are available from Housmans Diary Group, 5 Caledonian Road, Kings Cross, London N1 9DX, UK (fax +44-20-7278 0444, email diary@housmans.com). We are grateful to all who have helped in many ways over the past year.

HOUSMANS DIARY GROUP

Peace Days and anniversaries – their origins and uses

A distinctive feature of the *Housmans Peace Diary* is that it notes, in the same way as "conventional" public holidays and similar dates, a number of widely-recognised Days – and some Weeks – of special significance to campaigners who use this diary. This year's feature article explains why, how and by whom they were first designated, at their historical context, and at ways in which people have engaged with them. These Special Days and Special Weeks include ones designated by official bodies such as the United Nations, as well as others declared and adopted by major peace organisations.

We also look briefly at the daily anniversaries – "for celebration or protest" – which we note against each date during the year.

World Day of Peace

The World Day of Peace was designated by Pope Paul VI (1963–78), in a message dated 8 December 1967, addressed to "all men of good will", exhorting them

> to celebrate The Day of Peace throughout the world on the first day of the year, **1 January** 1968, ... and every year ... as a hope and as a promise, at the beginning of the calendar which measures and outlines the path of human life in time, that Peace with its just and beneficent equilibrium may dominate the development of events to come ... The proposal ... is not intended as exclusively ours, religious, Catholic. It would hope to have the adherence of all true friends of Peace, as if it were their own initiative, to be expressed in a free manner, congenial to the character of those who are aware of how beautiful and important is the harmony of all voices in the world for the exaltation of this good, Peace, in the varied concert of modern humanity.

However, buried in the rich rhetoric was a gratuitous attack on the "cowardice","flight from responsibility" and "base and slothful concept of life" of "those who fear it may be their duty to give their life for the service of their own country ... peace is not pacifism". By this he presumably meant conscientious objectors, entirely misconstruing that what conscientious objectors fear is not losing their own lives, but taking the lives of others *(see the quotation for week 33)*. Fortunately, such a digression has not been repeated in later annual papal World Day of Peace messages.

Since the institution of the UN International Day of Peace in 1982 (later established as 21 September), the special significance of the World Day of Peace may have marginally lessened, but it is worth recalling that from as far back as the 1880s a practice developed in Britain of observing the fourth Sunday in Advent (the last Sunday before Christmas Day) as Peace Sunday *(see the event recorded on 21 December)*, when relevant prayers would be said and sermons preached. That practice was unable to survive the First World War.

Martin Luther King Day

Martin Luther King Day marks the birth of the Reverend Dr Martin Luther King Junior, in Atlanta, Georgia, USA, on 15 January 1929. Following his father into the ministry of the Baptist Church, he became increasingly conscious of the urgent need to preach and act against the racial segregation entrenched in what became known as the "Jim Crow" laws of the Deep South of the United States.

When, on 1 December 1955, Rosa Parks was arrested for sitting in the designated "White" section in the front of a bus in Montgomery, Alabama, and refusing to move to the arbitrarily separated African American section at the rear,

King speaking to an anti-Vietnam war rally at the University of Minnesota, 1967   photo: Minnesota Historical Society

King – as President of the Montgomery Improvement Association – organised a mass bus boycott by the town's 50,000 Blacks, lasting 381 days, until the segregated seating ordinance was rescinded. In 1957 King joined with other church leaders to form the Southern Christian Leadership Conference, offering training and assistance for local efforts to confront segregation, emphasising nonviolence as its central tenet and means. A campaign in Birmingham, Alabama, in 1963, including sit-ins at shops, lunch-counters and other facilities, kneel-ins in churches, and a march urging blacks to register to vote, was given prominence by the brutal repression by the police, and a court injunction against such protests. In defiance, King was among those arrested on 12 April 1963, leading to his celebrated "Letter from Birmingham Jail". Intervention by the embarrassed Federal administration of John Kennedy led to his release. At the conclusion of the march on Washington DC, 28 August 1963, King shared his dream:

> I have a dream ... deeply rooted in the American dream ... that my four little children will one day live in a nation where they will not be judged by the colour of their skin but by the content of their character ... that little black boys and little black girls will be able to join hands with little white boys and little white girls and walk together as sisters and brothers ...

President John Kennedy was spurred into submitting a Civil Rights Bill to Congress, passed into law the following year and signed by his successor Lyndon Johnson, after the former's assassination.

Awarded the Nobel Peace Prize in 1964, King was himself assassinated on 4 April 1968, the day after a prophetic speech at Memphis, Tennessee.

In 1970 the US Congress ordained a Federal public holiday in honour of King's birthday, but to be observed on the **third Monday of January** rather than always on 15 January.

When the Direct Action Committee Against Nuclear War was formed in Britain in 1957, it acknowledged inspiration from the direct action against segregation in the US Deep South. From 1982 peace groups, such as the Peace Pledge Union in the UK, and others elsewhere, have observed **15 January** to mark the life and work of King in nonviolent resistance to artificial segregation of people, and his less well known but steadfast resistance to the incipient Vietnam War.

International Holocaust Memorial Day

On 1 November 2005, the UN General Assembly declared **27 January**, anniversary of the 1945 liberation of Auschwitz/Oswiecim Extermination Camp, Poland, as International Holocaust Memorial Day, observed from 2006. It commemorates not only the 6 million Jews killed during the Holocaust – the so-called "Final Solution" – but the many others, political dissidents, religious groups, gays, physically and mentally disabled or ill, "undesirables", slaughtered en masse in many different ways and places in Nazi-occupied Europe before and during WW2. It needs to be remembered also that although the scale and mechanical organisation of the Nazi's slaughter was unprecedented, there had been other previous mass slaughters, and there have been more since.

Nuclear-Free and Independent Pacific Day

In the southern hemisphere, Nuclear-Free and Independent Pacific Day (known in Japan also as "**Bikini Day**") has since 1984, apparently by common assent of the people, commemorated the second US Hydrogen Bomb test "Castle Bravo" on **1 March** 1954 on Bikini Atoll in the US-owned Marshall Islands. The largest manufactured explosion at that date seriously affected the crew of the Japanese fishing vessel *Lucky Dragon*, which was plying its ordinary business, killing one of them. Three days later the islands Rongelap and Utirik were evacuated. The people who had been affected by the test explosion were treated as if they were "human guinea pigs" in nuclear experimentation.

International Women's Day

The commemoration of International Women's Day stems from a women's march in the USA, on **8 March** 1908, for suffrage and against child labour. The Day was first observed in 1910, by 100 socialist women from 17 countries in conference in Copenhagen, Denmark. It is now a day for

German poster for International Women's Day, March 8, 1914 (banned by the German Empire)

general celebration and assertion of women's rights and women's contribution to society, and has now been adopted by the UN as one of its official International Days.

International Day for the Elimination of Racial Discrimination

This Day was proclaimed by the United Nations General Assembly on 26 October 1966 in commemoration of what had become known as the Sharpeville Massacre on **21 March** 1960. Sharpeville was a township in Transvaal, South Africa, which, since the coming into power of the Nationalist Party in 1948, had endured an increasingly repressive regime of apartheid. The population was rigidly divided into three categories – White (of British or Afrikaans descent), Coloured (of mixed White & Black descent), and Non-White (of essentially Black descent).

Apartheid operated in two particular dimensions. The three population groups were required to live in separate designated areas. All public facilities were provided separately for the three groups, so even a public bench in the street might be labelled "Whites Only". The second dimension of apartheid was that all political power was vested in the Whites, with the right to vote, let alone to stand for office, completely excluded from Blacks (who formed the far greater proportion of the population).

Despite these artificial divisions, the economy necessitated Blacks travelling into "White areas" to work. To control and limit such movement, Blacks were required to carry a "pass" (essentially an identity card), which was clearly discriminatory and a public emblem of repression. Growing discontent by Blacks led to a demonstration by some thousands centred on the Police Station at Sharpeville, where they openly declared themselves as being in public without their passes. The demonstrators were unarmed, although a few may have thrown stones at the police. Suddenly the police began firing guns, causing the demonstrators to turn round and run away, but the police continued firing, evidenced by demonstrators being shot in the back.

Altogether 69 were killed, including 10 women and 8 children; 180 were wounded, including 31 women and 18 children. Nonviolent resistance nevertheless continued – Albert Lutuli was awarded the Nobel Peace Prize in 1960, and Bishop Desmond Tutu in 1984 – but apartheid was

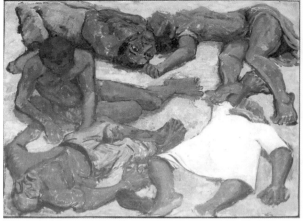

Painting of victims of the Sharpeville massacre by Godfrey Rubens, currently in the South African Consulate, London

not dismantled until President Frederik de Klerk released Nelson Mandela (imprisoned since 1964) in 1990, and negotiated with him the writing of a new constitution. This led to the first free and fair elections ever in South Africa, in 1994. Mandela and de Klerk shared the Nobel Peace Prize in 1993.

International Conscientious Objectors' Day

International COs' Day was first observed in 1982 by West European objectors to compulsory military service, as a focus both of campaigning for the right of objection to be established where it was lacking, and of support for objectors everywhere. The date **15 May** was chosen simply because it happened to be mutually convenient in 1982, but was retained for renewed activity in 1983 and 1984. Then in 1985 it was formally adopted by the European Bureau of Conscientious Objectors, and soon received worldwide recognition – being adopted by War Resisters' International (WRI) – and changed from being European Conscientious Objectors' Day to International Conscientious Objectors' Day.

Ever since, it has been marked by vigils outside prisons or barracks where COs are held, by demonstrations at Embassies of states where COs are not recognised and/or unfairly treated, by street theatre, and by ceremonies

where names of conscientious objectors past or present are read out and publicly honoured.

The ambiguous word "hero" is not normally associated with conscientious objection, but it should be recalled that conscientious objectors have been executed for maintaining the right to refuse to kill. Maximilian in 295 AD resolved as a Christian not to serve in the Roman army, and was summarily beheaded with the sword his father had intended to give him on taking the oath as a soldier. More than two hundred conscientious objectors were shot by firing squad or beheaded by guillotine in Nazi Germany in the Second World War. As late as 1949 two conscientious objectors were shot by firing squad in Greece; the international scandal led to a reprieve for a third. Between the World Wars a French objector was held for twenty years on the notorious penal colony, Devil's Island, off French Guiana. Three conscientious objectors have been imprisoned continuously since 1994 in Eritrea. In 1916, 35 British conscientious objectors were formally sentenced to death by firing squad, though immediately reprieved; on the other hand more than 100 British WW1 objectors are known to have died prematurely as a result of their treatment in prison or the army.

International Women's Day for Disarmament and Peace

This Day originated in 1981, when 30 women from 11 countries in Europe met to announce a day of women's peace and disarmament actions. They declared, "A powerful way of attacking a system that threatens to kill you is not to co-operate with it, but, instead, to spend that time co-operating with each other and providing the kind of life we as women would like." No record survives as to the reason for the choice of **24 May** for the Day.

As the Day developed, it was particularly supported in Britain by Women for Life on Earth, whose initiative led to the setting up of the Women's Peace Camp at Greenham Common RAF/USAF cruise missile base, Berkshire, on 5 September 1981. In 1983 one million women around the world took part in actions relevant to their communities.

International Day for Children as Victims of War

This Day is a natural amplification and generalisation – by the producers of the *Peace Diary* – of a declaration of the UN General Assembly on 19 August 1982. They resolved to commemorate **4 June** each year as "the International Day of Innocent Children Victims of Aggression". Since it is clearly no function of a *Peace Diary* to exclude, by implication, "naughty children" who are victims of military "defence", we have modified the title of the Day to accord with humanitarian reality. There have been, thus far, no complaints about our redesignation.

Numerically, children are most at risk in modern warfare, and the risk is not only as direct victims of violence. Children clearly have no place in war either as victims or participants. Recruitment of children (including girls) as soldiers, even as young as ten or eleven by guerilla groups in some developing countries, is a continuing scourge. By international protocol the minimum age for military recruitment is 18 but – to its eternal shame – Britain demanded a special exception; it is now the only country in Europe to recruit children into the military from their 16th birthday. It is as recently as this new millennium that Britain finally stopped sending under-18s into battle. Two 17-year-old members of the British forces were killed in the Falklands War in 1982, and two more in the first Gulf War in 1991.

International Day in Support of Victims of Torture

The International Day in support of Victims of Torture was designated by the UN General Assembly on 12 December 1997 as **26 June**, to draw attention to the UN Convention against Torture and other Cruel, Inhuman or Degrading Treatment or Punishment. The necessity for an international standard in the treatment of prisoners or those suspected of crime is illustrated by the US use of "waterboarding", or the methods used by Britain in treating some suspects in Northern Ireland only a generation ago. Apart from the evil of torture as a practice, it is notoriously unreliable in obtaining information, as victims may well succumb to telling interrogators what they apparently want to hear, rather than the truth.

The use of electrical shock, particularly to the genitals, is well known. Less well known is forcing the arms in an unnatural position behind one's back. Another method not requiring physical force is sleep or rest deprivation by waking a person in the small hours for further interrogation and even doing this repeatedly; this was used in Northern Ireland.

Hiroshima Day, Nagasaki Day

Hiroshima Day commemorates the first of two deliberately planned uses of nuclear weapons against living people. A uranium "atom bomb", developed in the USA with British assistance, was dropped by a USAF plane on the Japanese city Hiroshima, on **6 August** 1945 – killing some 150,000 – at a stage when it was already known that the Japanese government was making overtures towards surrender.

A second, plutonium, bomb was dropped on Nagasaki on **9 August**; 100,000 were killed.

The use of the two atomic bombs is frequently "justified" as effectively ending the Second World War, as the Japanese surrendered on 14 August, five days after the destruction of Nagasaki. However, this interpretation ignores the fact that Japan had already begun soundings for surrender before the Hiroshima bomb – an obvious factor being intensive bombing of Tokyo by "conventional" high explosive weaponry. A more realistic, if truly awful, interpretation of the dropping of the two bombs was the desire of the US military to discover the effect of an atomic explosion on a living target. Haste was of the essence, lest a Japanese surrender obviated the opportunity, and the haste extended to the different – plutonium – Nagasaki bomb, so that a comparison could be made between the two types of bomb.

The first formal observance of Hiroshima Day was in Hiroshima itself, where 10,000 rallied in 1947; but in 1948 a move began to call it "World Peace Day", with demonstrations around the world – including at the War Resisters' International conference in Shrewsbury, Britain. However, in 1949 "Hiroshima Day" became established under that name, including with a rally in Hyde Park, London, Britain. In 1950, the Peace Pledge Union played a leading part in a "No More Hiroshimas" demonstration in Trafalgar Square, London, famously the venue for the final rally of the Aldermaston Marches of 1959–63. In later years a pattern developed of planting Japanese cherry trees in public parks, where flowers could be laid on Hiroshima Day.

International Day Commemorating Victims of Acts of Violence Based on Religion or Belief

On 28 May 2019 the UN General Assembly declared **22 August** to be the International Day Commemorating Victims of Acts of Violence Based on Religion or Belief; there appeared to be no significance in the choice of date, although the context of establishing the day was the attacks on mosques in New Zealand on 15 March 2019 and on churches in Sri Lanka on Easter Day 2019.

In necessarily condemning such violence, we mustn't fail to bear in mind that any such violence needs to be as strongly condemned – and eradicated – whatever the perceived motive.

United Nations International Day of Peace

On 30 November 1981, the UN declared the day of the opening of the annual session of its General Assembly, always the **third Tuesday of September**, to be the UN International Day of Peace. First observed in 1982, it was to be "devoted to commemorating and strengthening the ideals of peace both within and among all nations and peoples".

Some years later, however, a private individual – who presumably didn't use a *Peace Diary* and had difficulty in calculating the third Tuesday in September – spent much time and money campaigning to persuade member states of the UN to agree a variation in the Day's definition. Eventually, on 7 September 2001, the UN changed the designation from the third Tuesday to **21 September** (the latest possible date under the "third Tuesday" rule, and – as it happened – the date on which it fell on first observance in 1982). The change came into effect on 21 September 2002. As part of the change of date, the UN declared that the Day should "be observed as a day of global ceasefire and non-violence; an invitation to all nations and peoples to honour a cessation of hostilities for the duration of the Day". There is no record of any ongoing hostilities having actually ceased for the duration of any 21 September.

Unfortunately, there has been a tendency by some people to shorten references to the International Day of Peace by calling it "World Day of Peace", or "World Peace Day", without regard to the World Day of Peace, on 1 January each year, established in 1968 by Pope Paul VI.

International Day of Prayer for Peace

At a meeting in 2004 between the UN Secretary General and the General Secretary of the World Council of Churches, it was agreed to establish an International Day of Prayer for Peace, observable on the **nearest Sunday** (or other convenient day) **to the UN International Day of Peace**. It is promoted among member churches of the World Council of Churches.

International Day for the Total Abolition of Nuclear Weapons

On 5 December 2013, the UN General Assembly declared **26 September** to be the International Day for the Total Abolition of Nuclear Weapons (no reason for choosing that particular day was given). Clearly, while the focus on Hiroshima and Nagasaki Days is the victims of the two atom bombs, the focus on 26 September is the need for abolition of the many nuclear weapons which have continued to be made, by several countries, since 1945.

International Day of Nonviolence

On 15 June 2007, the UN General Assembly declared **2 October** to be the International Day of Nonviolence, commemorating the birth of Mohandas Karamchand Gandhi in India in 1869. He was an early apostle of non-violence in the struggle, first for civil rights for Indians in South Africa before the First World War, and then for Indian independence between the two world wars and during and immediately after WW2.

He learned from Leo Nikolaevich Tolstoy (1828-1910), as Martin Luther King later learned from Gandhi in his turn. And like King, Gandhi suffered assassination, on 30

January 1948, five months after Indian independence in August 1947.

The very word "nonviolence" in English was a coinage of Gandhi in translating his own writing into English. It is a direct translation of the Sanskrit *ahimsa*, literally "non-harm", and is to be distinguished from "non-violence". The latter refers to a mere absence of violence in an incident, whereas "nonviolence" refers to a positive mental engagement in dealing with potential opponents:

Gandhi collecting salt in protest at colonial law which gave a monopoly on salt collection to the British.

> Nonviolence is not a garment to be put on and off at will. Its seat is in our heart and and it must be an inseparable part of our being…

> Practise nonviolence not because of weakness, practise nonviolence because of strength and power; no training in arms is required for realisation of strength.

Gandhi also coined *satyagraha*:

> *Satyagraha* was a term I coined because I did not like "passive resistance" … Its root meaning is "holding on to truth", hence "force of righteousness". I have also called it love-force or soul-force … the mighty power of truth to be set against the evil of falsehood.

United Nations Day

United Nations Day, **24 October**, commemorates the coming into force of the United Nations Charter on that date in 1945, and thereby the formal establishment of the UN (formally, the United Nations Organisation, distinguishing it from "the United Nations" which had been used by the Allied side to describe themselves during the later stages of the Second World War).

This was the first International Day to be designated by the UN, on 31 October 1947. This early and lone designation led to its sometimes being treated as a "peace day", rather than focussed on the UN *per se*, and this potential confusion has not entirely dissipated, despite the subsequent formal establishment of the International Day of Peace. On 6 December 1971 the UN General Assembly recommended it as a public holiday for all member states, but it is not known that any state has adopted it.

World Science Day for Peace and Development

In 1988, UNESCO designated the week including 11 November as the International Week of Science and Peace, but in its 31st session, 15 October – 9 November 2001, changed this to proclaiming **10 November** each year, from 2002, as World Science Day for Peace and Development. It considered that "science affects peace and development, and must be used for peaceful and sustainable societies".

Remembrance Day

For more than a century, the eleventh hour of the eleventh day of the eleventh month has had a special significance,

A white poppy wreath at the Cenotaph in Whitehall, London, in 2018, the centenary of the end of the First World War.

photo: Ethan Doyle White

marking the cessation of hostilities (the Armistice) in the First World War – though not of course that war's official end. After the Second World War the emphasis shifted to Remembrance, and in Britain it's now formally observed on **the Sunday nearest 11 November**; however in Canada and the USA (where it is **Veterans' Day**), it is maintained on **11 November**.

From the 1920s, the newly burgeoning international peace movement struggled to establish a means of asserting the idea of what eventually became known as Alternative Remembrance – alternative, that is, to state commemoration, and frequently celebration, of the military dead. In 1921 there was a demonstration in Berlin under the slogan *Nie Wieder Krieg (No More War)*, not on 11 November but on 31 July, looking back to the beginning of the war on 28 July 1914, when Austria declared war on Serbia, and Germany joined in on 1 August. This pattern continued until 1923, when there were No More War rallies in 23 countries on 29 July.

The pattern then seems to have dissipated until 1933, when there was a different development. Because of their prevalence in the trenches of Flanders in the First World War, red poppies had become, since 1921, a symbol for commemorating the British military dead, and artificial red poppies were sold to raise funds for widows, orphans and the maimed. The new development in 1933 was that the Women's Co-operative Guild (the women's section of the British Co-operative movement and strongly pacifist-oriented), decided that an alternative symbol was needed to commemorate *all* the dead of *all* "sides", civilians as well as military. This symbol would also represent a meaningful determination that war must not happen again. They chose a white poppy, with Alternative Remembrance ceremonies until 1938, and the week leading to 11 November becoming celebrated as "Peace Week". There were occasional attempts at revival after the Second World War and finally, in 1980, Alternative Remembrance and white poppies were permanently re-established.

Universal Children's Day

The UN General Assembly first promoted the concept of Universal Children's Day on 14 December 1954, to be observed from 1956, but – because of differing customs – left it to member states to designate an appropriate day, with a default option of the first Monday in October.

After the UN had adopted the Declaration of the Rights of the Child on 20 November 1959, and the much stronger Convention on the Rights of the Child on 20 November 1989, it was decided that Universal Children's Day would regularly and internationally be on **20 November**.

International Day for the Elimination of Violence Against Women

On 17 December 1999, the UN General Assembly declared **25 November** to be the International Day for the Elimination of Violence Against Women. It recognised that "violence against women is a manifestation of historically unequal power relations between men and women which have led to domination over and discrimination against women by men and to the prevention of their full advancement, and that violence against women is one of the crucial social mechanisms by which women are forced into subordinate positions … human rights of the woman and girl child are an inalienable, integral and indivisible part of human rights"; and the General Assembly invited governments and agencies to organise activities to raise public awareness of the problem of violence against women.

As was commented in the case of the commemoration of victims of violence based on religion or belief, drawing attention to a particular context of violence in the case of women does not derogate from the need to eliminate all such violence, whoever the victims may be.

Prisoners for Peace Day

From the Second World War there developed a practice of sending greeting cards in December to imprisoned conscientious objectors. This system was formalised in 1956, when War Resisters' International declared **1 December** each year to be Prisoners for Peace Day, and began to publish an Honour Roll of names and prison addresses for prisoners in various countries, so that

Prisoners for Peace day poster from South Korea.
credit: World Without War

cards could be sent, sometimes by a group of people collectively signing them. On occasion this has extended to sending cards to those imprisoned for peace activities other than conscientious objection to military service. Sometimes recipients of such cards have responded movingly in terms of the impact of receiving such support.

Human Rights Day

On 4 December 1950 the UN General Assembly declared **10 December**, the anniversary of the signing of the UN Declaration of Human Rights in Paris in 1948, to be Human Rights Day. It invited all states and interested organisations to celebrate the Day by making increasing efforts in this field of human progress.

Turkish journalists protesting against imprisonment of their colleagues, Human Rights Day 2016

Week of Prayer for World Peace
Second Sunday in October – Third Sunday in October

The Week of Prayer for World Peace began in 1974 as a Christian initiative by the Reverend Dr Edward Carpenter, sometime Dean of Westminster. It soon became an interfaith activity, and now welcomes people of all faith traditions and none, under the guiding principle, "The peace of the world must be prayed for by the faiths of the world".

At the time of its inception, the World Day of Peace (1 January) was not well established, and the International Day of Peace had yet to come into being, so United Nations Day (24 October) had by default begun to be regarded as a principal Peace Day. This led to the week including 24 October being designated the Week of Prayer. However, with the launch of One World Week in 1978, also based around UN Day, there was a clash, and it was eventually decided a few years ago to permanently define the Week of Prayer as running from the 2nd to 3rd Sundays in October, thereby breaking the direct connection with UN Day.

The International Day of Prayer for Peace, associated with the International Day of Peace, remains an entirely separate initiative.

One World Week

One World Week began in Britain in 1978 as an initiative by the World Development Movement (renamed Global Justice Now in 2015). The aim is to establish the Week as a nationally recognised annual event, during which organisations hold local activities on global issues, involving all parts of society and all communities – including diaspora and refugee communities.

As in the case of the Week of Prayer, United Nations Day was deemed a default Peace Day when One World Week was established. It is now defined as taking place in the week **Sunday–Sunday which includes UN Day (24 October)**. If 24 October is a Sunday, the week starts on the 24th.

International Disarmament Week

This was called for in the Final Document of the Tenth UN General Assembly Special Session on Disarmament, 30 June 1978. "The Members of the UN are fully aware of the conviction of their peoples that … general and complete disarmament is of utmost importance." Disarmament Week, always beginning on UN Day – hence taking place during **24–30 October** – is a time for pressing on all governments and arms manufacturers the urgent need for disarmament of all kinds of weapons.

Daily anniversaries – for celebration and protest

The *Peace Diary* notes an appropriate anniversary for every day of the year – with a new selection being made for each edition. It is clear, from feedback, that people often use the anniversaries given here as a reliable reference source.

The are many factors in each year's choice of anniversaries: frequently a "round number" anniversary is chosen; there might be dates relating specifically to the theme of the feature pages at the beginning of the Diary, or to something politically topical; and they are often linked to the quote given at the beginning of each week. It is hoped they serve as a simple way of spreading the history of peace, war, and resistance to war.

They are also a potential spur for action of one kind or another. A particular past demonstration may inspire fresh action on the same or even another cause. An anniversary of the birth or death of a significant activist may encourage looking again at what the person was able to do and what can be learned from it. And as to protest, the 70th anniversary of NATO on 4 April in the 2019 Diary – for example – was a reminder that it is still there needing dismantling, while its erstwhile counterpart, the Warsaw Treaty, was dissolved on 25 February 1991, as was celebrated in the 2011 Diary.

We must acknowledge that – as with much of the Diary – assembling and researching the information for the anniversaries is partly a co-operative effort. Suggestions – and criticisms – from Diary users are always gratefully received, especially if ideas sent in are validated with clear and accessible references.

We also know that the increasing ease and speed of communication – not least via so-called "social" media – enables the message of the Diary to be spread even wider: "Ten, twenty, fifty years ago such and such happened", or "Today is so and so International Day". When users share the information in such ways – which we warmly encourage – a credit to *Housmans Peace Diary* would always be welcomed.

Technical note

The places of historical events referred to in the *Peace Diary* – whether in articles or in anniversary notes – are as at the date of the event, regardless of subsequent changes in name, frontiers etc.

Similarly, the dates are recorded in the form that was applicable at the relevant period in that place, that is in Old Style where relevant, New Style being disregarded – hence in some cases we are noting nominal anniversaries rather than mathematically correct ones.

Probably every generation sees itself as charged with remaking the world. Mine, however, knows it will not remake the world. Its task is even greater: to keep the world from destroying itself.
Albert Camus, 1913–1960

MON

30

TUE

31

NEW YEAR'S EVE

WED

1

NEW YEAR'S DAY
(HOL UK/IRE/CAN/US)
WORLD DAY OF PEACE

1995 - Abolition of
military conscription
comes into force,
Belgium

THU

2

2000 - World Peace Bell rung, France

FRI

3

2000 - Festival celebrating unity, national reconciliation and peace, Angkor, Cambodia

SAT

4

1960 - Death of radical writer Albert Camus, France

SUN

5

1990 - 50 demand taxes for human needs, not Israeli occupation, at Israeli Embassy, Washington DC, USA

JANUARY

Any war or threat of war, whether immediately affecting any of the Members or not, is hereby declared a matter of concern to the whole League... It is also declared to be the friendly right of each Member... to bring to the attention of the Assembly or of the Council any circumstance which threatens to disturb international peace...

League of Nations Covenant, Article XI, 1919

WEEK 2

MON

6

1950 - Franco-German parliamentary conference, the first step towards EU - Basle, Switzerland

TUE

7

1920 - 5 socialists expelled from State Assembly for opposing WW1, New York, USA

WED

8

1995 - Mothers' March for Life & Compassion to Grozny, Chechnya, leaves Moscow, Russia

9

1950 - Destructive
hunt for alleged
Communists among
political & cultural
establishment begins,
USA

10

1920 - Versailles
Treaty comes into
force, establishing
League of Nations

11

2000 - Self-styled
Islamic Salvation
Army agrees to
disband, Algeria

12

1991 - 200,000
demonstrate against
Gulf War, Germany

JANUARY

The means by which we live have outdistanced the ends for which we live. Our scientific power has outrun our spiritual power. We have guided missiles and misguided men.

Martin Luther King, *Strength to Love*, 1963

MON

13

1980 - Founding meeting of German "Greens", Karlsruhe, W Germany

TUE

14

1980 - Nej til Atomvaben founded, Denmark

WED

MARTIN LUTHER KING DAY

15

1929 - Martin Luther King, born, USA

16

1920 - First meeting
of League of Nations
Council, Paris, France

17

1991 - Allied aerial
bombardment
begins, Iraq

18

1990 - Azerbaijan
declares war on
Armenia

19

1960 - 59 arrested in
civil rights sit-in,
Chattanooga,
Tennessee, USA

JANUARY

I noticed that the control levers [of a means of total destruction] were in the hands of people who, though talented in their own ways, were cynical.

Andrei Sakharov, nuclear physicist, *Sakharov Speaks*, 1974

MON

MLK DAY OBSERVED
(HOL US)

20

1920 - Civil Liberties
Union founded, USA

TUE

21

1980 - Women for
Peace founded,
Norway

WED

22

1980 - Andrei
Sakharov, Nobel
Peace laureate, sent
into internal exile at
Gorky, USSR

23

1920 - Allied War
Council is refused
handing-over of ex-
Kaiser Wilhelm II, in
voluntary exile in
Netherlands

24

2000 - 2000
Albanians
demonstrate for
release of hundreds
detained by Serbs,
Pristina, Kosovo

YUAN TAN
(CHINESE NEW YEAR 4718)

25

2000 - Government
agrees to return
Jewish property
seized under Nazi
occupation, Czech
Republic

26

1950 - UN Relief &
Works Agency
established for
refugees from
Palestine

JAN-FEB

Our language lacks words to express this offence, the demolition of a man.

Primo Levi, 1919–87, *If This Is a Man*, 1958, writing of a year in Auschwitz

MON

INT'L HOLOCAUST MEMORIAL DAY

27

1945 - Extermination camp liberated, Oswiecim/ Auschwitz, Poland

TUE

28

2000 - NATO promises assistance to modernise armed forces of Ukraine

WED

29

1950 - Series of demonstrations against apartheid begins, Johannesburg, S Africa

30

1970 - US Polaris
submarine runs
aground in fog,
Charleston,
S Carolina, USA

31

1950 - President
Harry Truman
ordains development
of hydrogen bomb,
USA

1

1960 - Sit-in against
segregated lunch
counter,
Woolworths,
Greensboro,
N Carolina, USA

2

1920 - Russia
recognises Estonian
independence, Tartu,
Estonia

FEBRUARY

There can be no peace so long as hunger and want are found among millions of working people and the few who make up the employing class have all the good things of life.

Preamble to the constitution of the Industrial Workers of the World (the "Wobblies"), 1905

MON

3

1960 - UK Prime Minister Harold Macmillan forecasts "wind of change" in southern Africa, Parliament, S Africa

TUE

4

1860 - Bill Haywood, founder of anti-militarist Industrial Workers of the World, born, USA

WED

5

1970 - USA invades Laos

6

1869 - Following
Ottoman ultimatum,
Greece agrees to
withdraw troops
from Crete

7

1990 - Communist
Party cedes primacy,
USSR

8

1819 - John Ruskin,
social critic, born,
Britain

9

1981 - Army General
takes over as Prime
Minister, Poland

FEBRUARY

The people must take over — you must take over. The leaders of all the parties are waiting, as they always wait, on any issue of principle, to follow public opinion. We can coerce them.

Alex Comfort, Launch of CND, London, 17 February 1958

MON

10

1920 - Alex Comfort, pacifist author, born, Britain

TUE

11

1990 - Nelson Mandela released after 26 years in prison, S Africa

WED

12

1909 - National Association for Advancement of Colored People founded, USA

13

1920 - First
international
administration by
League of Nations,
Saar

14

1950 - 30-year
USSR-China alliance
signed, Moscow,
USSR

15

1820 - Susan
Brownell Anthony,
feminist slavery
abolitionist, born,
Adams,
Massachusetts, USA

16

1995 - 2000 leave on
peace train to
Vavunia from
Colombo, Sri Lanka

FEBRUARY

Women's Peace Campaign — join the demand for Peace Negotiations Now.

Slogan lead banner of Women's Peace Day march, Liverpool, 17 February 1940

MON

PRESIDENTS' DAY
(HOL US)

17

1940 - Marches in several towns mark Women's Peace Day, Britain

TUE

18

1961 - In Committee of 100's first demonstration, 4000 sit down at Ministry of Defence, Whitehall, London, Britain

WED

19

1921 - General Frank Crozier resigns command of auxiliary police in protest against corruption, Ireland

20

1895 - Death of
Frederick Douglass,
black abolitionist,
USA

21

1971 - International
march in support of
Spanish CO Pepe
Beunza leaves
Geneva, Switzerland

22

1971 - Government
breaks UN embargo
by approving sale of
helicopters to
S Africa, Britain

23

1945 - Mass
bombing by RAF,
Pforzheim, Germany

FEB-MARCH

The moment the slave resolves that he will no longer be a slave, his fetters fall. He frees himself and shows the way to others. Freedom and slavery are mental states.

Mohandas Gandhi, *Nonviolence in Peace and War*, 1949, vol 2

MON

24

1981 - Nuclear-Free
Pacific Week begins,
Melbourne, Australia

TUE

25

2000 - Jury decides
police killing of
unarmed man with
volley of 42 bullets is
not murder, New
York, USA

WED

ASH WEDNESDAY

26

1980 - Exchange of
ambassadors for first
time by Egypt &
Israel

THU

27

1920 - Allies announce international control for the Dardanelles

FRI

28

1919 - Gandhi launches satyagraha campaign, India

SAT

29

2000 - 6-year-old boy shoots dead girl in his primary school class, Michigan, USA

NUCLEAR-FREE AND
INDEPENDENT PACIFIC DAY

SUN

1

1991 - Women for Peace protest against militarism, Belgrade and Ljubljana, Yugoslavia

MARCH

Many people say that government is necessary because some men cannot be trusted to look after themselves, but anarchists say that government is harmful because no man can be trusted to look after anyone else.

Nicolas Walter, *About Anarchism*

MON

2

1807 - Import of
slaves prohibited,
USA

TUE

3

1998 - Two friends,
Protestant and
Catholic, shot dead,
Poyntzpass,
Co Armagh,
N Ireland

WED

4

1950 - Death of Carl
Heath, pacifist
activist, Britain

5

1990 - First World
Conference on
Education for All,
Jomtien, Thailand

6

1960 - 400
demonstrate at
USAF base,
Lakenheath, Britain

7

2000 - Death of
Nicolas Walter,
nonviolent anarchist,
Milton Keynes,
Britain

INT'L WOMEN'S DAY

8

1910 - 100 women
from 17 countries
meet to declare
their right to be
treated as equal to
men, Copenhagen,
Denmark

MARCH

Nationalism is an infantile sickness. It is the measles of the human race.
Albert Einstein, quoted by Helen Dukas & Banesh Hoffman,
Albert Einstein — The Human Side, 1979

MON

9

1945 - "Foodless
lunch" for hungry of
Europe, Waldorf
Hotel, London,
Britain

TUE

10

1945 - 100,000 killed
in US bombing of
Tokyo, Japan

WED

11

1990 - Independence
from USSR declared
by Lithuania

THU

12

1930 - Mohandas
Gandhi begins civil
disobedience with
"salt march" to coast
from Ahmedabad,
India

FRI

13

1945 - Pax Christi
founded, France

SAT

14

1879 - Albert
Einstein, pacifist
physicist, born, Ulm,
Germany

SUN

15

2019 - As act of
"white supremacy",
lone gunman kills 50
at two mosques,
Christchurch, New
Zealand

MARCH

Nonviolent revolutionaries do not think that the nation state is the "foundation of world order"; they think it is the active promoter of disorder, and fear that various rival agents will one day start throwing nuclear bombs at each other and destroy the only civilisation we have.

Geoffrey Ostergaard, *Resisting the Nation State*

WEEK 12

MON

16

1961 - Parliamentary
Labour Party
withdraws whip
from 5 members
who voted against
"defence" estimates,
Britain

ST PATRICK'S DAY
(HOL NI/IRE)

TUE

17

1920 - General
strike overcomes
Kapp Putsch,
Germany

WED

18

1969 - USA begins
bombing Cambodia

19

1970 - First meeting
of heads of
government of E &
W Germany, Erfurt,
E Germany

EQUINOX

20

1987 - Vietnam
Veterans for Peace
begin march to
Wicuili from
Jinotega, Nicaragua

INT'L DAY FOR ELIMINATION OF
RACIAL DISCRIMINATION

21

1990 - Ploughshares
2 disable F-111
bomber, Upper
Heyford USAF base,
Britain

SAKA
(INDIAN NEW YEAR 1942)

22

1990 - Death of
Geoffrey Ostergaard,
gentle anarchist,
Britain

MARCH

We have continuously to repeat, although it is a voice that cries in the desert, "No to violence, yes to peace".
Archbishop Oscar Romero, El Salvador

MON

23

1950 - World Meteorological Organisation established

TUE

24

1980 - Archbishop Oscar Romero assassinated at Cathedral altar, San Salvador, El Salvador

WED

25

1990 - Soviet tanks encircle parliament, Vilnius, Lithuania

26

1979 -
Israeli/Egyptian Peace
Treaty signed,
Washington DC,
USA

27

1961 - 3 members of
Polaris Action Group
board Polaris
submarine, Holy
Loch, Scotland

28

1981 - Child hostage
on Indonesian
airliner killed by
"rescue"
commandos,
Bangkok, Thailand

BST BEGINS

29

1970 - Death of Vera
Brittain, pacifist
author, Britain

MARCH-APRIL

Politics are usually the executive expression of human immaturity.
Vera Brittain, *The Rebel Passion*, 1964, written to celebrate the 50th
anniversary of the founding of the Fellowship of Reconciliation

MON

30

1995 - Appeal Court
recognises
conscientious
objection, Bermuda

TUE

31

1985 - 3000 take
part in peace rallies
countrywide,
Australia

WED   ◑

1

1950 - Death of
Alex Wood, pacifist
physicist, Britain

THU

2

1951 - NATO Supreme HQ becomes effective, Paris, France

FRI

3

1970 - US bomber crashes on landing, Ellsworth Air Force Base, Michigan, USA

SAT

4

1961 - Direct Action Committee march to Holy Loch leaves London, Britain

SUN

5

1940 - Death of Charles Freer Andrews, Gandhian disciple, India

APRIL

I will not kill nor hurt any living creature needlessly, nor destroy any beautiful thing, but will strive to save and comfort all gentle life, and guard and perfect all natural beauty upon the earth.

John Ruskin's St George's Company, 1871, Rule 5

MON

6

2000 - 93 states and
1500 organisations
sign up to Abolition
2000

TUE

7

1990 - DFG/VK
established,
Magdeburg,
E Germany

WED

○

8

1970 - 30 children
killed in Israeli
bombing of primary
school, Nile delta,
Egypt

THU

9

1980 - Israeli troops
enter Lebanon

GOOD FRIDAY
(HOL UK/CAN)

FRI

10

1900 - Victor Yates,
antimilitarist
parliamentarian,
born, Britain

SAT

11

1950 - Plane carrying
"unarmed" nuclear
weapon crashes into
mountain, Marzano
USAF base, New
Mexico, USA

EASTER DAY

SUN

12

1980 - World
Disarmament
Campaign launched,
Central Hall,
London, Britain

APRIL

Can it be that statesmen in the nineteenth century believe that they who sacrifice human lives in bloody wars do more for the sum of human happiness and development than they who try to save the multitude and teach them how to live.

Elizabeth Cady Stanton, Matilda Joslyn Gage and Susan Brownell Anthony, *History of Women's Suffrage*, 1882

WEEK 16

EASTER MONDAY
(HOL ENG/W/NI/IRE/CAN)

MON

13

1945 - Liberation of
Belsen &
Buchenwald
concentration
camps, Germany

TUE

◑

14

1975 - Coup d'état
by Khmer Rouge,
Cambodia

WED

WAR TAX RESISTANCE DAY (US)

15

1960 - 1000 take
part in first anti-
nuclear Easter
March, Bergen-
Hohne, W Germany

THU
16
1980 - Fire in
nuclear reprocessing
plant, France

FRI
17
1960 - 140 black stu-
dents found Student
Nonviolent
Co-ordinating
Committee, Raleigh,
N Carolina, USA

SAT
18
1960 - 100,000 in
final rally of
Aldermaston March,
Trafalgar Square,
London, Britain

SUN
19
1990 - USSR
violently represses
independence
movement, Lithuania

Nie wieder Krieg! [No more war!]
Text of celebrated Käthe Kollwitz drawing of a women shouting a slogan, 1924

MON

20

1999 - 2, exercising right to bear arms, shoot dead 12 fellow pupils and a teacher, Columbine High School, Colorado, USA

TUE

21

1945 - Death of Käthe Kollwitz, artist of peace, Germany

WED

22

1970 - First observance of Earth Day

23

1960 - Death of
Toyohiko Kagawa,
Christian pacifist,
Japan

24

1930 - Abdul Ghaffar
Khan, Pathan
nonviolent activist,
arrested, Risalpur,
India

ANZAC DAY (AUS)

25

1945 - Founding
conference of United
Nations
Organisation opens,
San Francisco, USA

26

1995 - First UN War
Crimes Tribunal
opens, The Hague,
Netherlands

APRIL–MAY

Our love widens until it includes not all humanity but all created things... In the marvellous design of the universe, not even a sparrow can fall to earth meaninglessly.

Toyohiko Kagawa, *Meditations on the Cross*, 1936

MON

27

1945 - 3 anarchist editors gaoled 9 months for "incitement to disaffection" of soldiers, London, Britain

TUE

28

1980 - European Nuclear Disarmament launched, Brussels, Belgium

WED

29

1958 - UN Economic Commission for Africa established

30

1920 - WWI
conscription
abolished, Britain

1

1830 - Mary Harris,
"Mother Jones"
anti-war activist,
born, USA

2

1960 - 13 gaoled 6
months for refusing
binding-over after
sit-down at Foulness
AWRE, Essex, Britain

3

1960 - European
Free Trade
Association comes
into effect

If the masses in all lands would refuse to manufacture arms, there would be no more war.

George Lansbury, *My Quest for Peace*, 1938

MON

4

1970 - National Guard kill 4 students protesting against US invasion of Cambodia, Kent State University, Ohio, USA

TUE

5

1990 - National Pilgrimage for Abolition of Death Penalty leaves for Atlanta, Georgia, from Starke, Florida

WED

6

1980 - 15,000 demonstrate against public swearing-in of 1700 army recruits, Weser Stadium, Bremen, W Germany

7

1940 - Death of
George Lansbury,
pacifist former
Leader of Labour
Party, London, Britain

VE DAY
MAY DAY HOL OBSERVED (UK)

8

1945 - End of World
War 2 in Europe

9

1995 - 12 Buddhists
& Quakers protest
against war in
Chechnya by walk to
Kremlin, Moscow,
Russia

10

1920 - Dockers
refuse to load
armaments for use
against Russia, Britain

CHRISTIAN AID WEEK 10–16 MAY

Christian Aid is the aid and development wing of the Council of
Churches in Britain. The week focuses on the need for helping the
self-development and achievement of justice of people suffering
from poverty, famine and war in many parts of the world.
Contact: Christian Aid, 35-41 Lower Marsh, London SE1 7RL,
Britain; tel +44-20-7620 4444; www.christianaid.org.uk

MON

11

1995 - Nuclear Non-
Proliferation Treaty
extended indefinitely

TUE

12

1970 - UN Security
Council condemns
Israeli military action
in Lebanon

WED

13

1930 - Death of
Fridtjof Nansen,
advocate for
refugees, Norway

14

2000 - Million
Mothers' March,
Washington DC, is
one of 65 events
calling for gun
control, USA

INT'L CONSCIENTIOUS
OBJECTORS' DAY

15

1970 - Millions of
students strike
against Vietnam War,
USA

16

1995 - 2 gaoled 3
months for sit-in at
Defence Force
recruiting office over
complicity with
invasion of E Timor,
Australia

17

1980 - The only
W European
demonstrator
admitted distributes
antimilitarist leaflets,
E Berlin

All states should put aside mutual suspicion and unite in one sole society, or rather family, of peoples, both to guarantee their own independence and to safeguard order in the concert of peoples.

Pope Benedict XV, *Pacem*, 1920

MON

18

1979 - Kerr-McGee found guilty of contaminating employee Karen Silkwood's food and person with plutonium, USA

TUE

19

2000 - Ethnic Fijian gunmen storm parliament and kidnap ethnic Indian government, Suva, Fiji

WED

20

1989 - To quell pro-democracy movement, martial law ordered, Beijing, China

21

1961 - Direct Action
Committee march
from London arrives
Holy Loch, Scotland

22

1970 - Apartheid-
based S African
cricket tour
cancelled, Britain

23

1920 - Pope
Benedict XV issues
encyclical *Pacem* on
Christian restoration
of peace, Vatican

INT'L WOMEN'S DAY FOR
DISARMAMENT

24

1959 - First radiation
fall-out domestic
shelter built, USA

If nations could overcome the mutual fear and distrust whose sombre shadow is now thrown over the world and could meet with confidence and goodwill to settle their possible differences, they would easily be able to establish a lasting peace.

Fridtjof Nansen, 1861–1930, Nobel Peace Prize acceptance speech, Oslo, 1923

MEMORIAL DAY (US)
(HOL UK/US)

MON

25

2000 - After 18 years Israel withdraws troops from Lebanon

TUE

26

1980 - 50 clergy arrested after protest march against detention of fellow minister, Johannesburg, S Africa

WED

27

1980 - 2 killed by army in 200,000-strong protest against dictatorship, Kwangju, S Korea

28

1930 - British army
burns down offices
of nonviolent
movement Khudai
Khidmatgar,
Utmanzai, NW
Frontier, India

29

1968 - UN Security
Council unanimously
resolves mandatory
sanctions against
Rhodesia

30

1900 - Gerald
Gardiner, pacifist
Lord Chancellor,
born, Britain

31

1970 - Death of
Clare Sheridan,
pacifist sculptor,
Britain

June

War will cease when men refuse to fight. What are YOU going to do about it?

Peace Pledge Union poster (1938). For displaying it, six PPU officers were convicted of incitement to disaffection under Emergency Powers Regulations, 6 June 1940. They were bound over to "keep the peace" — the main object of the PPU and the poster.

MON

1

1660 - Mary Dyer hanged for nonviolent resistance to suppression of Quakers, Boston, Massachusetts, N America

TUE

2

1981 - Resumption of Pacific nuclear tests announced, France

WED

3

1950 - Committee for Legal Recognition of Conscientious Objection demands release of 13 imprisoned COs, Paris, France

INT'L DAY FOR CHILDREN AS
VICTIMS OF WAR

THU

4

1920 - Treaty of
Trianon signed,
settling WWI
between Allies and
Hungary, Versailles,
France

FRI

5

1950 - Racial
segregation on buses
ruled
unconstitutional,
Montgomery,
Alabama, USA

SAT

6

1940 - Six members
of Peace Pledge
Union bound over
for displaying "War
will cease when men
refuse to fight"
poster, Britain

SUN

7

1981 - Israel bombs
nuclear reactor,
Osirak, Iraq

JUNE

In 1965 the UN General Assembly adopted the Declaration on the Promotion among Youth of the Ideals of Peace, Mutual Respect and Understanding between Peoples, stressing the importance of youth in today's world.

Basic Facts about the United Nations, UN, 1998

MON

8

1980 - Computer sends out second false war alert in a week, USA

TUE

9

2019 - Thousands march, starting months of protests against erosion of rights by Chinese government, Hong Kong

WED

10

1970 - Parliament establishes school of peace and conflict theory for conscientious objectors, Norway

11

1970 - Evacuation of
US military base,
Libya

12

1840 - First World
Anti-Slavery
Convention signed,
London

13

1995 - To worldwide
condemnation,
France announces
new series of
nuclear tests in
Pacific

14

2000 - Leaders sign
agreement to work
towards unification,
N & S Korea

I wanted to demonstrate that there is something more powerful than what comes out of the barrel of a gun. Also, I wished to show them that I was neither pro-army nor pro-rioter but pro-people.

Will Warren, "Doing Something Constructive" [in Northern Ireland], *Peace News*, 12 October 1979

MON

15

1990 - 67 members of Rainforest Action Group arrested in timberyard occupation, Melbourne, Australia

TUE

16

1980 - Death of Will Warren, Quaker nonviolent activist, Britain

WED

17

1980 - Government announces cruise missile bases at Greenham Common & Molesworth, Britain

THU

18

2000 - Agreement to
cease hostilities
signed by Ethiopia &
Eritrea

FRI

19

2000 - 208 Christian
villagers massacred
by Muslim Laskar
Jihad, Duma, Spice
Islands, Indonesia

SOLSTICE

SAT

20

2019 - Appeal Court
rules government
ignored international
humanitarian law in
licensing arms sales
to Saudi Arabia,
London, Britain

SUN

21

1920 - Supreme
Allied Council pro-
poses that 42 annual
reparations pay-
ments be made to
Belgium, France and
Britain by Germany

JUNE

I dream of giving birth to a child who will ask, "Mother, what is war?"
Eve Merriam

MON

22

1980 - 20,000 in Labour Party march against cruise and Trident missiles, Britain

TUE

23

1995 - Widows and mothers rally for peace, Grozny, Chechnya

WED

24

1859 - Battle leading to founding of Red Cross fought between Savoy and Austria, Solferino, Savoy

25

1950 - War started
by N Korean
advance into S Korea

INT'L DAY FOR VICTIMS OF
TORTURE

26

1950 - National day
of protest against
Group Areas Act,
S Africa

27

1950 - UN Security
Council agrees
military assistance to
S Korea

28

1970 - US troops
withdraw from
Cambodia

He's fighting for Democracy, he's fighting for the Reds,
He says it's for the peace of all.
He's the one who must decide who's to live and who's to die,
And he never sees the writing on the wall.

Buffy Sainte Marie, *Universal Soldier*, 1963

MON

29

1895 - 7000
Doukhobors burn
huge mass of
weapons,
Transcaucasia,
Russian Empire

TUE

30

1930 - Last Allied
troops leave
occupied Rhineland,
Germany

WED

CANADA DAY
(HOL CAN)

I

1970 - Women
against Daddy
Warbucks destroy
files of 8 draft
boards, New York,
USA

THU
2

1970 - "Tiger cages"
for political
prisoners exposed,
S Vietnam

(HOL US)

FRI
3

1980 - 4 stoned to
death for sexual
"offences", Iran

INDEPENDENCE DAY (US)

SAT
4

1979 - First sit-in
against nuclear waste
transport, Sharpness,
Britain

○

SUN
5

1970 - 10-minute
march for amnesty
for conscientious
objectors & other
political prisoners,
Madrid, Spain

It is crucial that we begin to understand peace to mean not only an end to war, but an end to all the ways we do violence to ourselves, each other, the animals, the earth.

Pam McAllister, *Reweaving the Web of Life*

MON

6

1970 - Government
announces
resumption of arms
sales to S Africa,
Britain

TUE

7

2005 - 52 killed in 4
suicide bombing
attacks on public
transport, London,
Britain

WED

8

1980 - Nuclear
waste train stopped
by protesters,
Sharpness,
Gloucestershire,
Britain

9

1940 - German
"protection"
accepted by Romania

10

1990 - UN evacuates
6000 refugees to
Italy from Albania

11

1920 - Plebiscite
votes to remain in
Germany,
E & W Prussia

◗
DAY OF COMMEMORATION (IRE)

12

1920 - Russia
recognises
independence of
Lithuania

The results of war are always identical, however good the intentions of the war makers, and however "collective" their actions: people are slaughtered and a passionate sense of wrong and desire for vengeance are created in the survivors — feelings which make yet further wars inevitable.

Aldous Huxley, Letter to Leonard Woolf

MON

13

1985 - International Live Aid concerts raise £50M for Ethiopian famine relief, Wembley, Britain & Philadelphia, USA

TUE

14

1935 - 7000 "Peace pledgers" rally in Albert Hall, London, Britain

WED

15

1980 - Replacement of Polaris by Trident nuclear missiles in mid-1980s announced by government, Britain

THU

16

1920 - 12-day Allies-Germany Conference on reparations ends with referral to a Commission, Spa, Belgium

FRI

17

1950 - UN Security Council sets up military command in Korea

SAT

18

1970 - Death of Theodore Kloppenburg, nonviolent resister to S African apartheid, Netherlands

SUN

19

1980 - Because of Soviet invasion of Afghanistan, teams from 30 states boycott Olympic Games, Moscow, USSR

All bellicosity is foolish, for in studying the disadvantage of one's enemy, one loses sight of one's own advantage.

Democritus of Abdera, 4th century BC, Fragment b 237

●

MON

20

1985 - State of emergency declared, severely eroding civil rights, S Africa

TUE

21

1938 - Raymond Marcano gaoled 2 years for refusing military reserve service, Lille, France

WED

22

1980 - Government lifts embargo on arms for Chile, Britain

23

1940 - To contribute
to cost of war,
purchase tax
imposed, Britain

24

1988 - 10,000 form
human chain for a
cleaner North Sea,
W Germany

25

1995 - 7 killed by
bomb on Metro,
Paris, France

26

1947 - Central
Intelligence Agency
established, USA

Everywhere today there is more arming than before 1914. Everywhere more trumpets blow, and more cymbals clash, than before the World War. Technology has placed steel in the second rank, and chemistry in the first rank, and the whole of industry has been converted into an arsenal.

Carl von Ossietzky, *Die Weltbühne*, Germany, 10 May 1932

MON

27

1985 - Military coup
d'état, Uganda

TUE

28

2005 - IRA
announces
immediate end to
paramilitary activities
in favour of
democratic process,
Ireland

WED

29

1920 - No More
War demonstrations
by disabled veterans,
Germany

30

1991 - START I
agreement on
strategic weapons
signed by USA &
USSR, Moscow, USSR

31

2007 - 38-year use
of army for domestic
security ended,
N Ireland

1

1920 - Gandhi begins
movement of
non-co-operation,
India

2

1990 - Iraq invades
Kuwait

AUGUST

Be what you want to become. Thus, if you want to have free elections, begin by freely electing someone. If you want to have free speech, speak freely. If you want a trade union, found a trade union.
Solidarnosc, Poland, 1980

MON

○
(HOL SCOT/IRE)

3

1970 - First underwater firing of Poseidon missile, *USS James Madison*

TUE

4

1940 - Italian army invades British Somaliland

WED

5

1950 - Concerned about slow progress to European unity, 150 youths from several countries remove French/German border posts

HIROSHIMA DAY

THU

6

1945 - Atomic bomb
dropped on
Hiroshima, Japan

FRI

7

1970 - Cease-fire on
Suez Canal

SAT

8

1945 - USSR
declares war on
Japan

NAGASAKI DAY

SUN

9

1990 - UN Security
Council denounces
Iraq's annexation of
Kuwait

AUGUST

War is not to be thought of as dying for what you believe in, but as killing for what you believe in.
Stuart Morris, *Conscripting Christianity*, 1937

MON

10

1920 - Treaty settling WWI between Allies and Turkey signed, Sèvres, France

TUE

11

1920 - Russia recognises independence of Latvia

WED

12

1930 - Turkey invades Iran

THU
13
1890 - Stuart Morris, pacifist activist, born, Britain

FRI
14
1980 - Strike begins at Lenin Shipyard - later leads to Solidarnosc - Gdansk, Poland

SAT
15
1945 - End of WW2 Japanese front

SUN
16
1945 - Treaty demarcating new frontier signed by Poland and USSR

AUGUST

They shall beat their swords into ploughshares and their spears into pruning hooks; nation shall not lift up sword against nation, neither shall they learn war any more.

Isaiah, II:4 (Authorised Version) — Text for the sculpture outside UN Building, New York City, USA

MON
17
1985 - 54 killed by car bomb in east Beirut, Lebanon

TUE
18
1990 - UN Security Council demands freeing of prisoners by Iraq

WED
19
1970 - Minuteman III, first MIRV missile, deployed, USA

MUHARRAM
(ISLAMIC NEW YEAR 1442)

THU

20

1980 - Members of
5th International
Nonviolent March
for Demilitarisation
arrested and then
released, Bucharest,
Romania

FRI

21

1950 - UN moves to
permanent HQ in
New York City, USA

INT'L DAY FOR VICTIMS OF
VIOLENCE BASED ON RELIGION
OR BELIEF

SAT

22

1910 - Japan formally
annexes Korea

SUN

23

1940 - All-night air
raid on London
begins the German
"Blitz"

AUGUST

If we could be friends by just getting to know each other better, then what are our countries really arguing about? Nothing could be more important than not having a war if a war would kill everything.

Samantha Smith, aged 10, USA, in a letter to President Yuri Andropov, USSR, 1982, on a return from a visit to the Soviet Union at his invitation, following earlier correspondence initiated by her. She died in 1985 in an unconnected plane accident.

WEEK 35

MON

24

1945 - Death of
Alfred Salter, pacifist
parliamentarian,
Britain

TUE ◑

25

1990 - UN Security
Council declares
embargo against Iraq

WED

26

1985 - Death by
accident of Samantha
Smith, child peace
envoy, USA

THU

27

1985 - Military coup
d'état, Nigeria

FRI

28

1985 - 4 Blacks shot
dead on banned
march in support of
Nelson Mandela,
S Africa

SAT

29

1970 - 40,000
protest against
Vietnam War, Los
Angeles, California,
USA

SUN

30

1948 - Convention
on Protection of
Civilians in War
signed, Stockholm,
Sweden

Not peace at any price, but love at all costs.
Dick Sheppard, founder of the Peace Pledge Union

MON

31

1980 - Solidarnosc
founded, Lenin
Shipyard, Gdansk,
Poland

TUE

1

1920 - Carl von
Ossietzky founds
Nie Wieder Krieg
group, Berlin,
Germany

WED

○

2

1880 - Dick
Sheppard, pacifist
priest and founder of
Peace Pledge Union,
born, Britain

THU

3

1960 - Nuclear
disarmament march
to London leaves
Edinburgh, Scotland

FRI

4

1878 - Ruth Fry,
recorder of pacifism
in action, born,
Britain

SAT

5

2000 - Picnic cele-
brates 19-year strug-
gle to convert from
cruise missile base
to common land,
Greenham Common,
Berkshire, Britain

SUN

6

1920 - Russian
military offensive
against Poland

SEPTEMBER

If only the natural human instinct were given freedom to grow, undistorted by the harsh and unjust social organisation which divides the interest of humankind, we should have no foreign riots, no reprisals, no War, none of the grinding competition which produces degrading poverty even in time of peace

Sylvia Pankhurst, *The Worker's Dreadnought*, 11 August 1917

WEEK 37

MON

LABOUR DAY
(HOL CAN/US)

7

1960 - Death of
Sylvia Pankhurst,
antimilitarist
feminist, Ethiopia

TUE

8

1998 - World
Conference on
Family Violence
opens, Delhi, India

WED

9

1990 - Gulf War
Resisters paint No
War slogans at Air
Show, Farnborough,
Britain

THU

10

1970 - Charter of
Non-Alignment
agreed by non-
aligned states,
Lusaka, Zambia

FRI

11

1966 - 2 arrested for
leafletting open day,
military barracks,
Sutton Coldfield,
Britain

SAT

12

1990 - Allied-
German peace treaty
signed - penultimate
step before legal end
of WW2 - Moscow,
USSR

SUN

13

1977 - Special sitting
of UN General
Assembly as North-
South Conference,
New York, USA

SEPTEMBER

If we justify war it is because all peoples always justify the traits of which they find themselves possessed.

Ruth Benedict

MON

14

1930 - 107 Nazi candidates elected to Reichstag (parliament), Germany

TUE

15

1920 - 30 killed, 300 injured by bomb explosion, Wall Street, New York, USA

WED

16

1976 - 7 secondary school pupils "disappeared" for demonstrating against suppression of exams, Buenos Aires, Argentina

17

1980 - After civil
disobedience
campaign, govern-
ment concedes
Welsh language
television channel for
Wales, Britain

ROSH HASHANAH
(JEWISH NEW YEAR 5781)

18

1970 - Vietnam
Moratorium rallies
countrywide,
Australia

19

1970 - Syrian army
intervenes in Jordan

INT'L DAY OF PRAYER FOR
PEACE

20

2000 - Jury acquits
28 of criminally
destroying genetically
modified maize,
Norwich, Britain

SEPTEMBER

Our sons shall not be taken from us to unlearn all that we have been able to teach them of charity, mercy and patience. We women of one country will be too tender of those of another country to allow our sons to be trained to kill them.

Julia Ward Howe, Boston, Massachusetts, USA, 1870

MON

UN INT'L DAY OF PEACE

21

1980 - Dedication of
Peace Pagoda, Milton
Keynes, Britain

TUE

EQUINOX

22

1970 - Resumption
of arms exports to
Greece by USA

WED

23

1880 - First,
eponymous, boycott
over rent charges,
Co Mayo, Ireland

1960 - Nuclear
disarmament march
from Edinburgh
arrives London,
Britain

1970 - Civil war
ends, Jordan

INT'L DAY FOR TOTAL
ELIMINATION OF NUCLEAR
WEAPONS

1985 - Contract to
sell 132 military
aircraft to Saudi
Arabia signed by UK

1940 - Axis, 10-year
military and
economic alliance,
signed by Germany,
Italy and Japan

SEPT-OCT

Pat Pottle: Would you press the button you know is going to annihilate millions of people?
Air Commodore Magill: If the circumstances demanded it, I would.

Exchange, 14 February 1962, between Pat Pottle (defending himself), and Air Commodore Magill, Air Ministry Director of Operations (prosecution witness), trial of Wethersfield Six, Old Bailey, London

MON

28

2000 - Ariel Sharon visits site of Temple/ Dome of the Rock, sparking bloody intifada, Jerusalem, Israel/Palestine

TUE

29

1980 - 200,000 demonstrate against nuclear weapons, New York, USA

WED

30

1970 - 1400 draft cards burned in Vietnam War protest, Puerto Rico

1

1980 - Labour Party conference votes for unilateral nuclear disarmament, Blackpool, Britain

INT'L DAY OF NONVIOLENCE

2

2000 - Death of Pat Pottle, activist and printer of peace, Wales

3

1960 - Labour Party conference votes for British unilateral nuclear disarmament, Scarborough, Britain

4

1940 - Adolf Hitler & Benito Mussolini meet, Brenner Pass, Austria/Italy

All we are saying is
Give peace a chance.
John Lennon, 1969

MON

5

1960 - Radar
malfunction falsely
indicates massive
Soviet attack, Thule,
Greenland

TUE

6

2000 - "People
power" forces
Slobodan Milosevic
to accept electoral
defeat, Yugoslavia

WED

7

2000 - Rally against
Star Wars, Wall
Street, New York,
USA

THU
8
1988 - Nuclear
weapons plant
closed because of
contamination,
Rocky Flats, USA

FRI
9
1940 - John Lennon,
peaceful musician,
born, Liverpool,
Britain

SAT
10
1930 - Harold Pinter,
antimilitarist
playwright, born,
Britain

SUN
11
1940 - Campaign of
individual satyagraha
begins, India

OCTOBER

WEEK OF PRAYER FOR WORLD PEACE 11–18 OCTOBER

The week leading towards UN Day was established in 1974 as an opportunity for people of all faiths to focus on peace throughout the world.
Contact: Week of Prayer for World Peace;
www.weekofprayerforworldpeace.com

MON

12

1920 - Treaty signed between Poland and Russia, Tartu, Estonia

THANKSGIVING (CAN)
COLUMBUS DAY OBSERVED (US)
(HOL CAN/US)

TUE

13

2006 - Inquest rules reporter unlawfully killed in March 2003 by US troops at Shatt al Basra Bridge in Iraq, Britain

WED

14

1985 - Mass demonstration against nuclear power, Bonn, W Germany

15

1969 - Nuclear-
armed plane in air
collision with tanker
aircraft, killing 8,
Glen Bean, Kentucky,
USA

16

1940 - "Day of
National Mourning"
for loss of freedom
by conscription, USA

17

1910 - Death of Julia
Ward Howe, feminist
pacifist, Oak Glen,
Rhode Island, USA

18

1976 - Treaty to end
civil war, Rivadh,
Lebanon

OCTOBER

ONE WORLD WEEK 18–25 OCTOBER

Based on UN Day, One World Week is intended to encourage
people to link with international issues through taking up
overseas concerns in church, school, trade union etc.
Contact: One World Week, 35-39 London Street, Reading,
Berkshire, RG1 4PS, Britain; tel +44-118-938- 4933;
www.oneworldweek.org

MON
19

1720 - John
Woolman, Quaker
aboilitionist & war
tax resister, born,
New Jersey,
N America

TUE
20

1990 - Rallies against
Gulf War in 22
cities, USA

WED
21

1960 - Navy
launches its first
nuclear submarine,
Britain

THU

22

1960 - Inaugural meeting of Committee of 100, Britain

◐

FRI

23

1918 - US President Wilson's 14 Points accepted by Germany

UNITED NATIONS DAY

SAT

24

1945 - Formal establishment of United Nations Organisation

BST ENDS

SUN

25

1960 - Committee of 100 publicly launched, Britain

OCT-NOV

INTERNATIONAL DISARMAMENT WEEK 24–30 OCTOBER

Called for in the Final Document of of the Tenth UN Special Session on Disarmament in 1978, Disarmament Week is a time for pressing governments and arms manufacturers of the urgent need for disarmament of all kinds of weapons.
Contact your nearest national UNA.

MON

26

1980 - 50,000 march for nuclear disarmament, London, Britain

TUE

27

1920 - League of Nations HQ moved from Paris, France, to Geneva, Switzerland

WED

28

1970 - Retention of 4000 troops in Far East announced by government, Britain

29

1939 - Death of
Aarne Selinheimo,
founder of War
Resisters'
Movement, Finland

30

1910 - Death of
Henry Dunant,
founder of Red
Cross, Heiden,
Switzerland

31

1950 - United
Nations Children's
Fund (UNICEF)
established

1

1960 - British
government
announces
permission for US
Polaris submarines at
Holy Loch, Scotland

NOVEMBER

I would no more teach children military training than teach them arson, robbery or assassination.

Eugene Victor Debs

MON

2

1920 - Eugene Victor Debs, imprisoned as anti-war socialist activist, receives million votes in Presidential election, USA

TUE

3

1918 - Sailors mutiny against war, Kiel, Germany

WED

4

1950 - European Convention for Protection of Rights & Fundamental Freedoms signed, Rome, Italy

5

1978 - Voters agree
to leave
Zwentendorf nuclear
reactor unfuelled,
Austria

6

1950 - China allies
with North in war in
Korea

7

1910 - Death of Leo
Tolstoy, pacifist
author, Astapovo,
Russia

◐
REMEMBRANCE SUNDAY (UK)

8

1987 - 11 killed by
IRA bomb,
Remembrance
Sunday service,
Enniskillen, Northern
Ireland

NOVEMBER

In killing by order of your commander you are a murderer as much as a thief kills a rich man to rob him. He is tempted by money and you by the desire not to be punished, or to receive a reward.

Leo Tolstoy

MON

9

1955 - Withdrawal
from UN General
Assembly by S Africa

TUE

WORLD SCIENCE DAY FOR
PEACE & DEVELOPMENT

10

1995 - Ken
Saro-Wiwa & 8
other environmental
activists hanged,
Ogoniland, Nigeria

WED

MARTINMAS
REMEMBRANCE DAY (CAN)
VETERANS' DAY (US)
(HOL CAN/US)

11

1880 - Death of
Lucretia Mott,
feminist Quaker
abolitionist, USA

THU
12
1970 - Australian
government begins
withdrawal of troops
from Vietnam

FRI
13
1869 - Helene
Stocker, co-founder
of WRI, born,
Germany

SAT
14
1990 - Peace treaty
ending Poland-
Germany war (begun
1 Sep 1939) signed

SUN
15
1920 - First
Assembly of League
of Nations opens,
Geneva, Switzerland

NOVEMBER

Hugh of Avalon (c 1135–1200), Bishop of Lincoln from 1186, was the first recorded person to resist war taxes. He also spoke out against draconian laws regarding use of royal forests and, at the risk of his life, defended Jews against a riotous mob.

MON

16

1980 - 2000 in first women's action against militarism at Pentagon, Washington DC, USA

TUE

17

1200 - Death of St Hugh of Avalon, Bishop of Lincoln, resister of taxes to pay for Richard I's French wars, Britain

WED

18

1950 - French foreign minister supports establishment of European Defence Community and European Army, at Council of Europe

1990 - Treaty on
Conventional Forces
in Europe signed,
Paris, France

UNIVERSAL CHILDREN'S DAY

1940 - Agreement
on pooling of
technical knowledge
of weaponry by UK
& USA

1970 - USA resumes
bombing of
N Vietnam

1960 -
Demonstrator
arrested for swim-
ming onto nuclear
submarine during
launch, Groton,
Connecticut, USA

NOVEMBER

No one has a right to sit down and feel hopeless. There is too much work to do.

Dorothy Day

MON

23

1860 - Karl Hjalmar Branting, Nobel Peace laureate, born, Sweden

TUE

24

1915 - Henry Ford announces chartering of peace ship Oscar II for diplomatic mission to Europe, New York City, USA

WED

INT'L DAY FOR ELIMINATION OF VIOLENCE AGAINST WOMEN

25

1925 - 12 gaoled for incitement to mutiny, London, Britain

THANKSGIVING
(HOL US)

26

1945 - "Save Europe
from Starvation"
rally, London, Britain

27

1970 - Death of
Trevor Hatton, peace
activist, Britain

28

1990 -
Demonstration in
support of CO
Ronald Jean Baptiste,
McGuire USAF base,
New Jersey, USA

29

1980 - Death of
Dorothy Day,
co-founder of
Catholic Worker
movement, USA

NOV-DEC

Nonviolence is really tough. You don't practise nonviolence by attending conferences — you practise it on the picket lines.

Cesar Chavez

○

MON

30

1950 - Fellowship of
Reconciliation
section founded,
India

TUE   PRISONERS FOR PEACE DAY

1

1830 - Peace Society
founded, Geneva,
Switzerland

WED

2

1990 - Army kills 14
civilians, Santiago
Atitlan, Guatemala

1980 - 3 nuns and
lay missionary killed
by paramilitaries,
El Salvador

1970 - Cesar Chavez
gaoled 20 days for
refusing to call off
United Farmworkers
lettuce boycott,
California, USA

1980 - UN General
Assembly adopts
Charter of
University for Peace,
Costa Rica

1979 - Report of
Brandt Commission
on North-South
issues published

DECEMBER

Peace is a spirit, and not an intellectual abstraction; it is life, not a theory.
Elihu Burritt, 1846

MON

7

1970 - Treaty recognising Oder-Neisse line as frontier signed by West Germany & Poland

TUE

8

1810 - Elihu Burritt, pacifist activist, born, Connecticut, USA

WED

9

1995 - 40-state conference agrees plan to rebuild Bosnia

THU

10

1910 - International
Peace Bureau
awarded Nobel
Peace Prize, Oslo,
Norway

FRI

11

1937 - Withdrawal
from League of
Nations by Italy

SAT

12

1920 - Martial law
imposed, Cork,
Ireland, UK

SUN

13

1560 - Maximilien,
Duc de Sully, author
of first modern plan
for permanent
peace, born, Rosny,
France

DECEMBER

I am drawn more to this cause [elimination of war by international law and organisation] than to any other.

Andrew Carnegie, 1907

●

MON

14

1910 - Carnegie
Endowment for
International Peace,
founded,
Washington DC,
USA

TUE

15

1920 - Second
conference on
German WW1
reparations opens,
Brussels, Belgium

WED

16

1920 - Permanent
Court of
International Justice
created, The Hague,
Netherlands

1970 - Sea-bed
adopted as common
heritage of
humankind by UN

1990 - UN Treaty on
Migrant Rights
signed

1940 - Phil Ochs,
peace singer, born

1990 - Reservist
Yolanda Huet-
Vaughan refuses
orders for Gulf War,
Kansas, USA

DECEMBER

At first I thought I was fighting to save rubber trees. Then I thought I was fighting to save the Amazon. Now I realise I am fighting for humanity.

Chico Mendes

◑
SOLSTICE

MON

21

1890 - First formal observation of Peace Sunday (Sunday before Christmas), Britain

TUE

22

1920 - Second conference on German WWI reparations adjourns, Brussels, Belgium

WED

23

1920 - In attempted peaceful settlement, partition of Ireland, with 2 internal parliaments, legislated, London, Britain

24

1990 - Gulf Peace
Team sets up camp,
Judayyidat Ar'ar, Iraq

CHRISTMAS DAY
(HOL UK/IRE/CAN/US)

25

1960 - Mass march
of students for
nuclear
disarmament,
Ottawa, Canada

ST STEPHEN'S DAY
(HOL UK/IRE/CAN)

26

1988 - Funeral of
Chico Mendes,
murdered for his
struggle against
destruction of rain
forests, Brazil

27

1815 - Peace Society
founded, USA

The only important thing is to know that if one works well in a potato field the potatoes will grow. If one works among men they will grow — that is reality. The rest is smoke. It is important to know that words do not move mountains. Work, exacting work, moves mountains.

Danilo Dolci

MON

HOLY INNOCENTS' DAY

28

1915 - Government
decides in principle
to introduce military
conscription, Britain

TUE

29

1890 - Massacre by
army of 300 Sioux
children, women &
men, Wounded
Knee, S Dakota,
USA

WED

○

30

1997 - Death of
Danilo Dolci,
nonviolent social
revolutionary, Italy

NEW YEAR'S EVE

31

1915 - Fellowship of
Reconciliation
section founded,
USA

NEW YEAR'S DAY
(HOL UK/IRE/CAN/US)
WORLD DAY OF PEACE

1

2021 - Suggested
dates (and
quotations) for
future diaries
welcome anytime

(HOL SCOT)

2

3

Forward Planner 2021

	January		February		March	
Mon			1	5	1	9
Tue			2		2	
Wed			3		3	
Thu			4		4	
Fri	1		5		5	
Sat	2		6		6	
Sun	3		7		7	
Mon	4	1	8	6	8	10
Tue	5		9		9	
Wed	6		10		10	
Thu	7		11		11	
Fri	8		12		12	
Sat	9		13		13	
Sun	10		14		14	
Mon	11	2	15	7	15	11
Tue	12		16		16	
Wed	13		17		17	
Thu	14		18		18	
Fri	15		19		19	
Sat	16		20		20	
Sun	17		21		21	
Mon	18	3	22	8	22	12
Tue	19		23		23	
Wed	20		24		24	
Thu	21		25		25	
Fri	22		26		26	
Sat	23		27		27	
Sun	24		28		28	
Mon	25	4			29	13
Tue	26				30	
Wed	27				31	
Thu	28					
Fri	29					
Sat	30					
Sun	31					

Forward Planner 2021

	April		May		June	
Mon						
Tue					1	
Wed					2	
Thu	1				3	
Fri	2				4	
Sat	3		1		5	
Sun	4	Easter	2		6	
Mon	5	14	3	18	7	23
Tue	6		4		8	
Wed	7		5		9	
Thu	8		6		10	
Fri	9		7		11	
Sat	10		8		12	
Sun	11		9		13	
Mon	12	15	10	19	14	24
Tue	13		11		15	
Wed	14		12		16	
Thu	15		13		17	
Fri	16		14		18	
Sat	17		15		19	
Sun	18		16		20	
Mon	19	16	17	20	21	25
Tue	20		18		22	
Wed	21		19		23	
Thu	22		20		24	
Fri	23		21		25	
Sat	24		22		26	
Sun	25		23		27	
Mon	26	17	24	21	28	26
Tue	27		25		29	
Wed	28		26		30	
Thu	29		27			
Fri	30		28			
Sat			29			
Sun			30			
Mon			31	22		

	July		August		September	
Mon						
Tue						
Wed					1	
Thu	1				2	
Fri	2				3	
Sat	3				4	
Sun	4		1		5	
Mon	5	27	2	31	6	36
Tue	6		3		7	
Wed	7		4		8	
Thu	8		5		9	
Fri	9		6		10	
Sat	10		7		11	
Sun	11		8		12	
Mon	12	28	9	32	13	37
Tue	13		10		14	
Wed	14		11		15	
Thu	15		12		16	
Fri	16		13		17	
Sat	17		14		18	
Sun	18		15		19	
Mon	19	29	16	33	20	38
Tue	20		17		21	
Wed	21		18		22	
Thu	22		19		23	
Fri	23		20		24	
Sat	24		21		25	
Sun	25		22		26	
Mon	26	30	23	34	27	39
Tue	27		24		28	
Wed	28		25		29	
Thu	29		26		30	
Fri	30		27			
Sat	31		28			
Sun			29			
Mon			30	35		
Tue			31			

Forward Planner 2021

	October		November		December	
Mon			1	44		
Tue			2			
Wed			3		1	
Thu			4		2	
Fri	1		5		3	
Sat	2		6		4	
Sun	3		7		5	
Mon	4	40	8	45	6	49
Tue	5		9		7	
Wed	6		10		8	
Thu	7		11		9	
Fri	8		12		10	
Sat	9		13		11	
Sun	10		14		12	
Mon	11	41	15	46	13	50
Tue	12		16		14	
Wed	13		17		15	
Thu	14		18		16	
Fri	15		19		17	
Sat	16		20		18	
Sun	17		21		19	
Mon	18	42	22	47	20	51
Tue	19		23		21	
Wed	20		24		22	
Thu	21		25		23	
Fri	22		26		24	
Sat	23		27		25	
Sun	24		28		26	
Mon	25	43	29	48	27	52
Tue	26		30		28	
Wed	27				29	
Thu	28				30	
Fri	29				31	
Sat	30					
Sun	31					

Calendar 2019

JANUARY

MON	7 14 21 28
TUE	1 8 15 22 29
WED	2 9 16 23 30
THU	3 10 17 24 31
FRI	4 11 18 25
SAT	5 12 19 26
SUN	6 13 20 27

FEBRUARY

MON	4 11 18 25
TUE	5 12 19 26
WED	6 13 20 27
THU	7 14 21 28
FRI	1 8 15 22
SAT	2 9 16 23
SUN	3 10 17 24

MARCH

MON	4 11 18 25
TUE	5 12 19 26
WED	6 13 20 27
THU	7 14 21 28
FRI	1 8 15 22 29
SAT	2 9 16 23 30
SUN	3 10 17 24 31

APRIL

MON	1 8 15 22 29
TUE	2 9 16 23 30
WED	3 10 17 24
THU	4 11 18 25
FRI	5 12 19 26
SAT	6 13 20 27
SUN	7 14 21 28

MAY

MON	6 13 20 27
TUE	7 14 21 28
WED	1 8 15 22 29
THU	2 9 16 23 30
FRI	3 10 17 24 31
SAT	4 11 18 25
SUN	5 12 19 26

JUNE

MON	3 10 17 24
TUE	4 11 18 25
WED	5 12 19 26
THU	6 13 20 27
FRI	7 14 21 28
SAT	1 8 15 22 29
SUN	2 9 16 23 30

JULY

MON	1 8 15 22 29
TUE	2 9 16 23 30
WED	3 10 17 24 31
THU	4 11 18 25
FRI	5 12 19 26
SAT	6 13 20 27
SUN	7 14 21 28

AUGUST

MON	5 12 19 26
TUE	6 13 20 27
WED	7 14 21 28
THU	1 8 15 22 29
FRI	2 9 16 23 30
SAT	3 10 17 24 31
SUN	4 11 18 25

SEPTEMBER

MON	2 9 16 23 30
TUE	3 10 17 24
WED	4 11 18 25
THU	5 12 19 26
FRI	6 13 20 27
SAT	7 14 21 28
SUN	1 8 15 22 29

OCTOBER

MON	7 14 21 28
TUE	1 8 15 22 29
WED	2 9 16 23 30
THU	3 10 17 24 31
FRI	4 11 18 25
SAT	5 12 19 26
SUN	6 13 20 27

NOVEMBER

MON	4 11 18 25
TUE	5 12 19 26
WED	6 13 20 27
THU	7 14 21 28
FRI	1 8 15 22 29
SAT	2 9 16 23 30
SUN	3 10 17 24

DECEMBER

MON	2 9 16 23 30
TUE	3 10 17 24 31
WED	4 11 18 25
THU	5 12 19 26
FRI	6 13 20 27
SAT	7 14 21 28
SUN	1 8 15 22 29

Calendar 2020

JANUARY

MON	6	13	20	27
TUE	7	14	21	28
WED	1	8	15	22	29
THU	2	9	16	23	30
FRI	3	10	17	24	31
SAT	4	11	18	25
SUN	5	12	19	26

FEBRUARY

MON	3	10	17	24
TUE	4	11	18	25
WED	5	12	19	26
THU	6	13	20	27
FRI	7	14	21	28
SAT	1	8	15	22	29
SUN	2	9	16	23

MARCH

MON	2	9	16	23	30
TUE	3	10	17	24	31
WED	4	11	18	25
THU	5	12	19	26
FRI	6	13	20	27
SAT	7	14	21	28
SUN	1	8	15	22	29

APRIL

MON	6	13	20	27
TUE	7	14	21	28
WED	1	8	15	22	29
THU	2	9	16	23	30
FRI	3	10	17	24
SAT	4	11	18	25
SUN	5	12	19	26

MAY

MON	4	11	18	25
TUE	5	12	19	26
WED	6	13	20	27
THU	7	14	21	28
FRI	1	8	15	22	29
SAT	2	9	16	23	30
SUN	3	10	17	24	31

JUNE

MON	1	8	15	22	29
TUE	2	9	16	23	30
WED	3	10	17	24
THU	4	11	18	25
FRI	5	12	19	26
SAT	6	13	20	27
SUN	7	14	21	28

JULY

MON	6	13	20	27
TUE	7	14	21	28
WED	1	8	15	22	29
THU	2	9	16	23	30
FRI	3	10	17	24	31
SAT	4	11	18	25
SUN	5	12	19	26

AUGUST

MON	3	10	17	24	31
TUE	4	11	18	25
WED	5	12	19	26
THU	6	13	20	27
FRI	7	14	21	28
SAT	1	8	15	22	29
SUN	2	9	16	23	30

SEPTEMBER

MON	7	14	21	28
TUE	1	8	15	22	29
WED	2	9	16	23	30
THU	3	10	17	24
FRI	4	11	18	25
SAT	5	12	19	26
SUN	6	13	20	27

OCTOBER

MON	5	12	19	26
TUE	6	13	20	27
WED	7	14	21	28
THU	1	8	15	22	29
FRI	2	9	16	23	30
SAT	3	10	17	24	31
SUN	4	11	18	25

NOVEMBER

MON	2	9	16	23	30
TUE	3	10	17	24
WED	4	11	18	25
THU	5	12	19	26
FRI	6	13	20	27
SAT	7	14	21	28
SUN	1	8	15	22	29

DECEMBER

MON	7	14	21	28
TUE	1	8	15	22	29
WED	2	9	16	23	30
THU	3	10	17	24	31
FRI	4	11	18	25
SAT	5	12	19	26
SUN	6	13	20	27

Calendar 2021

JANUARY

MON	4	11	18	25	
TUE	5	12	19	26	
WED	6	13	20	27	
THU	7	14	21	28	
FRI	1	8	15	22	29
SAT	2	9	16	23	30
SUN	3	10	17	24	31

FEBRUARY

MON	1	8	15	22
TUE	2	9	16	23
WED	3	10	17	24
THU	4	11	18	25
FRI	5	12	19	26
SAT	6	13	20	27
SUN	7	14	21	28

MARCH

MON	1	8	15	22	29
TUE	2	9	16	23	30
WED	3	10	17	24	31
THU	4	11	18	25	
FRI	5	12	19	26	
SAT	6	13	20	27	
SUN	7	14	21	28	

APRIL

MON	5	12	19	26	
TUE	6	13	20	27	
WED	7	14	21	28	
THU	1	8	15	22	29
FRI	2	9	16	23	30
SAT	3	10	17	24	
SUN	4	11	18	25	

MAY

MON	3	10	17	24	31
TUE	4	11	18	25	
WED	5	12	19	26	
THU	6	13	20	27	
FRI	7	14	21	28	
SAT	1	8	15	22	29
SUN	2	9	16	23	30

JUNE

MON	7	14	21	28
TUE	1	8	15	22	29
WED	2	9	16	23	30
THU	3	10	17	24
FRI	4	11	18	25
SAT	5	12	19	26
SUN	6	13	20	27

JULY

MON	5	12	19	26	
TUE	6	13	20	27	
WED	7	14	21	28	
THU	1	8	15	22	29
FRI	2	9	16	23	30
SAT	3	10	17	24	31
SUN	4	11	18	25	

AUGUST

MON	2	9	16	23	30
TUE	3	10	17	24	31
WED	4	11	18	25	
THU	5	12	19	26	
FRI	6	13	20	27	
SAT	7	14	21	28	
SUN	1	8	15	22	29

SEPTEMBER

MON	6	13	20	27
TUE	7	14	21	28
WED	1	8	15	22	29
THU	2	9	16	23	30
FRI	3	10	17	24
SAT	4	11	18	25
SUN	5	12	19	26

OCTOBER

MON	4	11	18	25	
TUE	5	12	19	26	
WED	6	13	20	27	
THU	7	14	21	28	
FRI	1	8	15	22	29
SAT	2	9	16	23	30
SUN	3	10	17	24	31

NOVEMBER

MON	1	8	15	22	29
TUE	2	9	16	23	30
WED	3	10	17	24	
THU	4	11	18	25	
FRI	5	12	19	26	
SAT	6	13	20	27	
SUN	7	14	21	28	

DECEMBER

MON	6	13	20	27	
TUE	7	14	21	28	
WED	1	8	15	22	29
THU	2	9	16	23	30
FRI	3	10	17	24	31
SAT	4	11	18	25	
SUN	5	12	19	26	

HOUSMANS
World Peace Directory
● 2020 ●

This comprehensive and up-to-date Directory is provided for the *Peace Diary* by the **Housmans Peace Resource Project**, and edited by Albert Beale. **To make the best use of it, please read the next two pages.**

There is a difficult balance to be struck between the usefulness, for many people, of the information in this format, and the fact that the full World Peace Database — from which this Directory is derived — is available on-line at **www.housmans.info/wpd**. Your feedback about this is encouraged.

Groups omitted from this printed version tend to be the more localised or specialised groups — and those which are least efficient at responding to communications from the database editor! The complete on-line information is searchable, and it is also possible to obtain your own copy of the full database.

To keep the database up to date, organisations are contacted regularly by post, and also (where possible) by e-mail. But we rely on other input as well: if your group changes any of its contact details, please send the information without waiting to be asked. There is never a wrong time to send information.

Some information, such as changes in telephone numbering systems, is often available in the country concerned long before it can be obtained elsewhere — so please help by sending any such information you know of.

This Directory is copyright © Housmans Peace Resource Project, 2019. Even where non-profit organisations are allowed to re-use sections of the Directory at nominal charge, *permission must be obtained first*.

Disclaimer: Organisations listed are not necessarily responsible for their inclusion, nor for the way they are described, nor for the terminology used to describe their country.

All correspondence about the Directory should be sent to: **Housmans Peace Resource Project, 5 Caledonian Road, London N1, UK (tel +44-20-7278 4474; fax +44-20-7278 0444; e-mail worldpeace@gn.apc.org)**. Information is preferred in writing.

Directory Introduction

This is the 67th Peace Directory to be published with the Housmans Peace Diary. It is intended to help people find contact points for issues which interest them, and also to be a day-to-day reference resource for activists.

What's in the Directory?

The 2020 Directory lists over 1400 national and international organisations, covering the breadth of the peace movement – with the emphasis on grassroots, non-governmental groups – as well as major bodies in related fields such as environmental and human rights campaigning.

This year, around one-third of the groups listed have either had their information amended since last year's Directory, or are newly included this year.

How to find things in the Directory

Check both the national and international listings if necessary. If you can't find exactly what you want, try a less specialised organisation which might include what you're looking for. (And see the previous page for the availability of further information.)

International organisations are listed alphabetically. The national listings are in alphabetical order of English-language country name; the organisations are then arranged alphabetically within each country. Organisations' names (and addresses) are generally in the language of the country concerned.

Whilst aware of political sensitivities, we use commonly accepted postal and administrative divisions of the world to decide what is or isn't a "country". This doesn't mean we support or oppose countries' divisions or mergers – we just want the Directory to be easy to use.

In the national listings we don't repeat the country name at the end of each address, so you will need to add it.

How the entries are set out

The organisation's name is in **bold print**; or, if the name is that of a magazine, in ***bold italics***. Any common abbreviation is shown [in square brackets], in **bold** or ***bold italics*** as appropriate. Most organisations then have codes (in round brackets) giving an indication of their politics and activities (**see Note 1**). The address is shown next. Then we give (in brackets) any telephone number (**see Note 2**), fax number (**see Note 3**), electronic mail address (**see Note 4**), and web site address (**see Note 4**). Magazines published by the organisation are then shown in *italics*. Where the listing is itself a publication, details of frequency etc may be given next (**see Note 5**). There may be brief additional information where necessary.

The **Notes**, including our standard abbreviations, are given opposite.

Notes

1. Codes used to explain something about the listed organisation are as follows. The codes for international bodies in the left-hand column are used to show an official link to tbe body (or to one of its national affiliates in the country concerned). If these are not sufficient, the general codes on the right are used.

AI	Amnesty International	**AL**	Alternativist / Anarchist
FE	Friends of the Earth International	**AT**	Arms Trade / Conversion
FR	International Fellowship of Reconciliation	**CD**	Citizen Diplomacy / People-to-People
GP	Greenpeace International	**CR**	Conflict Resolution / Mediation
IB	International Peace Bureau	**DA**	Disarmament / Arms Control
IP	International Physicians for the Prevention of Nuclear War	**EL**	Environmental / Ecological
		HR	Equality / Minority & Human Rights
PC	Pax Christi International	**ND**	Nuclear Disarmament
SC	Service Civil International	**PA**	Anti-Militarist / Pacifist
SE	Servas International	**PO**	Positive Action / Lifestyle
SF	Society of Friends (Quakers)	**RA**	Radical Action / Direct Action
UN	World Federation of United Nations Associations	**RE**	Research into Peace, Conflict / Peace Education
WL	Women's International League for Peace and Freedom	**RP**	Religious Peace Group
		SD	Social Defence / Civilian-Based Defence
WP	World Peace Council	**TR**	War Tax Resistance / Peace Tax Campaigning
WR	War Resisters' International	**TW**	Development / Liberation / Third World
		WC	International Workcamps
		WF	World Federalists / World Citizens

2. Telephone numbers are given in standard international format: +[country code]-[area code]-[local number]. The "+" indicates the international access code used in the country you're phoning from. The area code (if there is one) is given without any national trunk prefix digit(s) that are used in the country concerned – for calls *within* the country you must add them if they exist. Exceptionally, a few countries without area codes still require an extra digit (generally 0) at the start of their national number for internal calls; the main culprits are Belgium, France, Switzerland, South Africa and Thailand. Note that for calls between neighbouring countries there are often non-standard codes outside the normal system.

3. The telephone number of a facsimile (telefax) machine is given without repeating codes which are the same as in the preceding ordinary telephone number; "fax" alone means the fax number is identical to the phone number. Because many groups share a fax machine, always start your message by saying clearly which person and organisation it is meant for.

4. The e-mail and web site addresses are given in standard internet format. (The e-mail address is the one with the "@" in it.) The "http://" which, by definition, starts every web address is **not** repeated each time here.

5. Abbreviations used in connection with publications are:

dly	daily	**x yrly**	x per year	**ea**	each
wkly	weekly	**annl**	annual	**pa**	per annum
ftly	fortnightly	**irreg**	irregular	**ftm**	free to members
mthly	monthly	**occl**	occasional	**nfp**	no fixed price / donation

Abolition 2000 International Secretariat (ND EL), c/o International Peace Bureau, Marienstr 19-20, 10117 Berlin, Germany (+49-30-1208 4549) (www.abolition2000.org). Global network to eliminate nuclear weapons.

Alliance Against Genocide (HR), c/o Genocide Watch, 1405 Cola Drive, McLean, VA 22101, USA (+1-202-643 1405) (communications@genocidewatch.org) (www.genocidewatch.com). Formerly Alliance Against Genocide.

Alternatives to Violence Project International (CR), PO Box 164, Purchase, NY 10577, USA (avp.international). International network of national AVP organisations. AVP groups organise training to aid creative responses to potentially violent situations.

Amnesty International – International Secretariat [AI] (HR RE), Peter Benenson House, 1 Easton St, London WC1X 0DW, Britain (+44-20-7413 5500) (fax 7956 1157) (contactus@amnesty.org) (www.amnesty.org). *Newsletter, Annual Report.* East Asia office (Hong Kong) +852-3963 7100; Southern Africa office (Johannesburg) +27-11-283 6000; Middle East and North Africa office (Beirut) +961-1-748751.

Architects & Planners for Justice in Palestine [APJP] (HR), c/o 100 Whitchurch Lane, Edgware, Middx HA8 6QN, Britain (info@apjp.org) (apjp.org).

Asian Human Rights Commission [AHRC] (HR), Unit 1 & 2 – 12/F, Hopeful Factory Centre, 10-16 Wo Shing St, Fotan, NT, Hong Kong (+852-2698 6339) (fax 2698 6367) (communications@ahrc.asia) (www.humanrights.asia). Engage in daily interventions as well as institutional issues.

Association of World Citizens [AWC] (WF CD RE), PO Box 1206, Novato, CA 94948-1206, USA (+1-415-893 1369) (suezipp@worldcitizen.org) (www.worldcitizensunited.org).

Association pour la Prévention de la Torture / Association for the Prevention of Torture [APT] (HR), BP 137, 1211 Genève 19, Switzerland (+41-22 919 2170) (fax 22 919 2180) (apt@apt.ch) (www.apt.ch). Works to improve legal frameworks and detention monitoring, to prevent torture and other ill-treatment.

Bahá'í International Community – Office of Public Information (RP), PO Box 155, 3100101 Haifa, Israel (+972-4-835 8194) (fax 835 3312) (opi@bwc.org) (www.bahai.org).

One Country. Magazine office: Suite 120, 866 UN Plaza, New York, NY 10017, USA.

Bellona Foundation (EL), Vulkan 11, 0178 Oslo, Norway (+47-2323 4600) (fax 2238 3862) (info@bellona.no) (bellona.org). Other international office in Brussels. Offices also in Russia (Murmansk and St Petersburg).

Carta de la Paz / Letter of Peace (RE), C/Modolell 41, 08021 Barcelona, Spain (+34-93 414 5936) (fax) (secretaria@cartadelapaz.org) (www.letterofpeace.org). *Information Paper.* Petition to UN. South America office, Chile: +56-2-274 7151. Central America and Caribbean, Dominican Republic: +1809-508 6879. North America, Mexico: +52-66-2213 9827. Central Europe, Switzerland: +41-22-860 2304.

Center for Global Nonkilling [CGNK] (RE PA), 3653 Tantalus Dr, Honolulu, HI 96822-5033, USA (+1-808-536 7442) (info@nonkilling.org) (nonkilling.org). To promote change towards the measurable goal of a killing-free world.

Centre for Humanitarian Dialogue [HD Centre] (CR RE), 114 Rue de Lausanne, 1202 Genève, Switzerland (+41-22 908 1130) (fax 22 908 1140) (info@hdcentre.org) (www.hdcentre.org). Independent confidential mediation. Works with political and civil leaders to establish dialogue.

Child Rights International Network [CRIN] (HR), Cottage 2, Old Paradise Yard, 20 Carlisle Lane, London SE1 7LG, Britain (info@crin.org) (home.crin.org). Supports UN Convention on rights of children. Formerly Child Rights Information Network. Work includes opposing mutilation of children.

Church and Peace (SF FR PC), Mittelstr 4, 34474 Diemlstadt-Wethen, Germany (+49-5694-990 5506) (fax 1532) (IntlOffice@church-and-peace.org) (www.church-and-peace.org). *Theology and Peace / Théologie et Paix / Theologie und Frieden.* European ecumenical network.

Climate Action Network International [CAN] (EL), Khaldeh, Dakdouk Bldg – 3rd floor, Mount Lebanon, Lebanon (+961-1-447192) (fax 448649) (administration@climatenet-work.org) (www.climatenetwork.org). Network of 1300 organisations in 120 countries.

Co-ordinating Committee for International Voluntary Service [CCIVS] (SC TW WC EL HR), UNESCO House, 1 rue Miollis, 75732 Paris Cedex 15, France (+33-14568 4936) (fax 14568 4934) (secretariat@ccivs.org) (www.ccivs.org).

Coalition for the International Criminal Court – UN Office [CICC] (HR), c/o WFM, 708 Third Ave – Suite 1715, New York, NY 10017, USA (+1-212-687 2863) (fax 599

1332) (cicc@coalitionfortheicc.org)
(www.coalitionfortheicc.org). Also ICC office,
Den Haag (+31-70-311 1080)
(cicc-hague@coalitionfortheicc.org).

Coordination Internationale pour une Culture de Non-violence et de Paix (RE PO DA), 148 rue du Faubourg Saint Denis, 75010 Paris, France (+33-14036 0660) (secretariat@nvpnetwork.net) (www.nvpnetwork.net).
International Network for a Culture of Nonviolence and Peace.

Ecumenical Accompaniment Programme in Palestine and Israel [EAPPI] (RP HR CD CR SF), c/o World Council of Churches (Public Witness section), PO Box 2100, 1211 Genève 2, Switzerland (+41-22 791 6108) (fax 22 791 6122) (eappi@wcc-coe.org) (www.eappi.org).
Accompanying Palestinians and Israelis in non-violent actions; advocacy to end occupation. Also: PO Box 741, Jerusalem 91000 (+972-2-626 2458).

European Bureau for Conscientious Objection [EBCO] (WR SC), 35 Rue Van Elewyck, 1050 Bruxelles, Belgium (+32-2 648 5220) (ebco@ebco-beoc.org) (www.ebco-beoc.org).

European Institute of Peace [EIP] (RE), Rue des deux Églises 25, 1000 Bruxelles, Belgium (+32-2 430 7360) (info@eip.org) (www.eip.org). Independent, "augmenting EU's peace agenda".

European Network Against Arms Trade [ENAAT] (AT), Anna Spenglerstr 71, 1054 NH Amsterdam, Netherlands (+31-20-616 4684) (info@stopwapenhandel.org) (www.enaat.org).

Fédération Internationale de l'Action des Chrétiens pour l'Abolition de la Torture [FIACAT] (HR), 27 rue de Maubeuge, 75009 Paris, France (+33-14280 0160) (fax 14280 2089) (fiacat@fiacat.org) (www.fiacat.org).

Fédération Internationale des Ligues des Droits de l'Homme [FIDH] (HR), 17 Passage de la Main d'Or, 75011 Paris, France (+33-14355 2518) (fax 14355 1880) (contact@fidh.org) (www.fidh.org). International Federation of Human Rights Leagues. At EU: +32-2 609 4423. At UN: +1-646-395 7103. At ICC: +31-70-356 0259.

Friends of the Earth International [FoEI] (EL), PO Box 19199, 1000 GD Amsterdam, Netherlands (+31-20-622 1369) (fax 639 2181) (www.foei.org). Europe office in Brussels (+32-2 893 1000) (www.foeeurope.org).

Friends World Committee for Consultation [FWCC] (SF), 173 Euston Rd, London NW1, Britain (+44-20-7663 1199) (world@friendsworldoffice.org) (fwccworld.org). Also 4 regional offices.

Africa: PO Box 41946, Nairobi, Kenya; Americas: 1506 Race St, Philadelphia, PA 19102, USA; Asia & West Pacific: PO Box 6063, O'Connor, ACT 2602, Australia; Europe & Middle East: PO Box 1157, Histon CB24 9XQ, Cambs, Britain.

Gesellschaft für Bedrohte Völker – International (HR TW), Postfach 2024, 37010 Göttingen, Germany (+49-551-499060) (fax 58028) (info@gfbv.de) (www.gfbv.de). *Pogrom*. Society for Threatened Peoples. Campaigns against genocide and ethnocide.

Global Action to Prevent War (RE ND DA HR), 866 UN Plaza – Suite 4050, New York, NY 10017, USA (+1-212-818 1815) (fax 818 1857) (coordinator@globalactionpw.org) (www.globalactionpw.org).
Transnational civil society and academic network. Legacy of World Order Models Project in 1990s. Aims for "integrated approach to enhancing security and ending war-related violence".

Global Alliance for Ministries and Infrastructures of Peace [GAMIP] (DA), Chemin de la Caracole 58, 1294 Genthod, Genève, Switzerland (+41-22 535 7370) (www.gamip.org).
Formerly Global Alliance for Ministries and Departments of Peace.

Global Anabaptist Peace Network (RP), c/o Mennonite World Conference, 50 Kent Ave – Suite 206, Kitchener, ON, N2G 3R1, Canada (+1-519-571 0060) (fax 226-647 4224) (Kitchener@mwc-cmm.org).

Global Campaign Against US/NATO Military Bases (ND CD), c/o Peace and Neutrality Alliance, 17 Castle St, Dalkey, Co Dublin, Ireland, Republic of (contact@noUSNATObases.org) (nousnatobases.org). Worldwide network.

Global Campaign on Military Spending – Co-ordination Office [GCOMS] (DA AT), c/o Centre Delàs d'Estudis per la Pau, c/ Erasme de Janer 8 – entresol – despatx 9, 08001 Barcelona, Spain (+34-93-441 1947) (coordination.gcoms@ipb.org) (demilitarize.org).
Organise Global Day of Action on Military Spending. A project of the International Peace Bureau; main IPB office in Berlin (+49-30-1208 4549).

Global Ecumenical Network for the Abolition of Military Chaplaincies (RP), c/o IDK, Postfach 280312, 13443 Berlin, Germany (global-network@ militaerseelsorge-abschaffen.de) (www.globnetabolishmilitarychaplaincy. webnode.com). Opposes co-option of churches by military, financial links between arms industry and churches, and churches' acceptance of warfare.

INTERNATIONAL ORGANISATIONS

Global Initiative to End All Corporal Punishment of Children [HR], The Foundry, 17 Oval Way, London SE11, Britain (+44-20-7713 0569) (info@endcorporalpunishment.org) (www.endcorporalpunishment.org).

Global Network Against Weapons and Nuclear Power in Space (PA EL RA), PO Box 652, Brunswick, ME 04011, USA (+1-207-607 4255) (globalnet@mindspring.com) (www.space4peace.org).

Global Partnership for the Prevention of Armed Conflict [GPPAC] (RE CR), Laan van Meerdervoort 70, 2517 AN Den Haag, Netherlands (+31-70-311 0970) (info@gppac.net) (www.gppac.net).

Green Cross International [GCI] (EL TW DA CR HR), 9-11 rue de Varembé, 1202 Genève, Switzerland (+41-22 789 1662) (fax 22 789 1695) (gcinternational@gci.ch) (www.gcint.org).
Focuses on interface between security and sustainability, by working on conflicts arising from environmental degradation and on environmental consequences of warfare.

Greenpeace International (EL), Ottho Heldringstr 5, 1066 AZ Amsterdam, Netherlands (+31-20-718 2000) (fax 718 2002) (info.int@greenpeace.org) (www.greenpeace.org/international).

Housmans Peace Resource Project [HPRP] (CD RE), 5 Caledonian Rd, London N1, Britain (+44-20-7278 4474) (fax 7278 0444) (worldpeace@gn.apc.org) (www.housmans.info).
Housmans World Peace Database & Directory.

Human Rights in China [HRIC] (HR), 110 Wall St, New York, NY 10005, USA (+1-212-239 4495) (hrichina@hrichina.org) (www.hrichina.org). Hong Kong Office (+852-2710 8021) (hrichk@hrichina.org).

Human Rights Watch [HRW] (HR), Empire State Building – 34th Floor, 350 5th Ave, New York, NY 10118-3299, USA (+1-212-290 4700) (fax 736 1300) (www.hrw.org). EU liaison office in Brussels (+32-2 732 2009) (fax 2 732 0471). Offices also in: Britain, Canada, France, Germany, Netherlands, South Africa.

Institute for Economics and Peace (RE), 205 Pacific Hwy, St Leonards, Sydney, NSW 2065, Australia (+61-2-9901 8500) (info@economicsandpeace.org) (economic-sandpeace.org). Office also in USA (+1-646-963 2160).

International Action Network on Small Arms [IANSA] (AT DA), 777 United Nations Plaza – 3E, Nww York, NY 10017, USA (communication@iansa.org) (www.iansa.org).

International Association of Lawyers Against Nuclear Arms [IALANA] (IB ND AT DA), Marienstr 19/20, 10117 Berlin, Germany (+49-30-2065 4857) (fax 2065 3837) (office@ialana.info) (www.ialana.info). UN office: c/o LCNP, +1-212-818 1861; Pacific office: +64-9-524 8403.

International Association of Lawyers Against Nuclear Arms – UN Office [IALANA] (IB ND AT DA), c/o LCNP, 220 E 49th St – Suite 1B, New York, NY 10017-1527, USA (+1-212-818 1861) (fax 818 1857) (johnburroughs@lcnp.org) (www.ialana.info). Main office, Germany (+49-30-2065 4857).
Pacific office +64-9-524 8403.

International Campaign for Boycott, Disinvestment and Sanctions Against Israel (HR RA), c/o PACBI, PO Box 1701, Ramallah, West Bank, Palestine (bdsmovement.net).

International Campaign to Abolish Nuclear Weapons [ICAN] (ND), 150 Route de Ferney, 1211 Genève 2, Switzerland (+41-22 788 2063) (info@icanw.org) (www.icanw.org). Launched by IPPNW and others in 2007. Works towards a nuclear weapons convention. Asia Pacific office, Australia (+61-3-9023 1958).

International Campaign to Ban Landmines – Cluster Munitions Coalition [ICBL – CMC] (AT), 2 Chemin Eugène-Rigot, 1202 Genève, Switzerland (+41-22 920 0325) (fax 22 920 0115) (icbl@icbl.org) (www.icblcmc.org).
Also www.icbl.org, www.stopclustermunitions.org.

International Coalition to Ban Uranium Weapons [ICBUW] (AT DA), Marienstr 19-20, 10117 Berlin, Germany (+49-30-2065 4857) (info@icbuw.eu) (www.icbuw.eu).

International Committee for Robot Arms Control [ICRAC] (AT DA), c/o Noel Sharkey, Department of Computer Science, University of Sheffield, Western Bank, Sheffield 10, Yorks, Britain (www.icrac.net).
For peaceful use of robotics. Campaigns for regulation of robot weapons.

International Council of Voluntary Agencies / Conseil International des Agences Bénévoles [ICVA] (HR TW), 26-28 ave Giuseppe Motta, 1202 Genève, Switzerland (+41-22 950 9600) (secretariat@icvanetwork.org) (www.icvanetwork.org).
Global network of humanitarian NGOs and human rights groups "promoting principled and effective humanitarian action".

International Fellowship of Reconciliation [IFOR] (RP IB), Postbus 1528, 3500 BM Utrecht, Netherlands (+31-30-303 9930) (office@ifor.org) (www.ifor.org).

International Friendship League [IFL] (CD), PO Box 217, Ross-on-Wye HR9 9FD, Britain (+44-1989-566745) (info@iflworld.org) (iflworld.org). *Courier.*

International Humanist and Ethical Union [IHEU] (HR PO), 39 Moreland St, London EC1, Britain (+44-20-7490 8468) (office-iheu@iheu.org) (www.iheu.org). *International Humanist News.* In USA: +1-518-632 1040.

International Institute for Peace through Tourism / Institut International pour la Paix par le Tourisme [IIPT] (CD), 685 Cottage Club Rd – Unit 13, Stowe, VT 05672, USA (+1-802-253 8671) (fax 253 2645) (ljd@iipt.org) (www.iipt.org). Committed to making travel and tourism a global peace industry; believe that every traveller is potentially an ambassador for peace.

International Network of Engineers and Scientists for Global Responsibility [INES] (DA ND), Marienstr 19-20, 10117 Berlin, Germany (+49-30-3199 6686) (fax 3199 6689) (office@inesglobal.net) (www.inesglobal.net).

International Network of Museums for Peace [INMP] (IB RE), c/o Kyoto Museum for World Peace, 56-1 Toji-in Kitamachi, Kita, Kyoto 603-8577, Japan (inmpoffice@gmail.com) (tinyurl.com/INMPMuseumsForPeace). Worldwide network of peace museums, gardens, and other peace-related sites, centres and institutions, which share the desire to build a culture of peace.

International Peace Bureau [IPB] (AT TW RE ND TR), Marienstr 19-20, 10117 Berlin, Germany (+49-30-1208 4549) (info@ipb-office.berlin) (www.ipb.org). *IPB News.* Main programme: disarmament for development. Work includes Global Campaign on Military Spending. Most broadly-based international peace networking body. Also office in Geneva; and GCOMS co-ordination office in Barcelona.

International Peace Initiative for Syria (CR PA RE), c/o Study Centre for Peace and Conflict Resolution, 7461 Stadtschlaining, Burg, Austria (info@peaceinsyria.org) (www.peaceinsyria.org). Opposes all military solutions. Stresses importance of a ceasefire and de-escalation, and of priority involvement of unarmed civil society in negotiations. Works with World Social Forum.

International Peace Institute [IPI] (RE DA CR), 777 United Nations Plaza, New York, NY 10017-3521, USA (+1-212-687 4300) (fax 983 8246) (ipi@ipinst.org) (www.ipinst.org).

Supports multilateral disarmament negotiations. Independent think-tank – "promoting the prevention and settlement of conflict". Offices also in Austria and Bahrain. Originally called International Peace Academy.

International Peace Institute – Middle East Regional Office [IPI] (RE DA CR), 51-52 Harbour House, Bahrain Financial Harbour, Manama, Bahrain (+973-1721 1344) (www.ipinst.org). Main office in USA. Independent think-tank – "promoting the prevention and settlement of conflict".

International Peace Institute – Vienna Office [IPI] (RE DA CR), Freyung 3, 1010 Wien, Austria (+43-1-533 8881) (www.ipinst.org). Main office in USA. Independent think-tank – "promoting the prevention and settlement of conflict".

International Peace Research Association [IPRA] (RE), c/o Risk and Conflict Network, Dept of Media & Communication Design, Northumbria University, Newcastle-upon-Tyne NE1 8ST, Britain (+44-191-227 3567) (www.iprapeace.org).

International Physicians for the Prevention of Nuclear War [IPPNW] (ND RE TW), 339 Pleasant St – Third floor, Malden, MA 02148, USA (+1-617-440 1733) (ippnwbos@ippnw.org) (ippnw.org).

International Secretariat of Nuclear-Free Local Authorities (ND EL), c/o Nuclear-Free Local Authorities Secretariat, Manchester City Council, Town Hall, Manchester M60 3NY, Britain (+44-161-234 3244) (fax 234 3379) (s.morris4@manchester.gov.uk) (www.nuclearpolicy.info).

International Tibet Network (HR), c/o Tibet Society UK, 2 Baltic Place, London N1 5AQ, Britain (mail@tibetnetwork.org) (www.tibet-network.org). Formerly International Tibet Support Network. Links 180 groups around the world. Local Tibet support groups can also be found via www.tibet.org.

Interpeace (CR), 7-9 Chemin de Balexert, 1219 Châtelaine, Genève, Switzerland (+41-22 917 8593) (fax 22 917 8039) (info@interpeace.org) (www.interpeace.org). Set up by UN; now independent peacebuilding group. Supports societies to build lasting peace. Regional offices: Nairobi, Abidjan, Guatemala City, New York, Brussels.

Journal of Resistance Studies (RE RA PO), c/o Irene Publishing, Sparsnäs 1010, 66891 ED, Sweden (editor@resistance-journal.org) (resistance-journal.org).

Mayors for Peace (CD ND DA), c/o Hiroshima Peace Culture Foundation, 1-5 Nakajima-cho, Naka-ku, Hiroshima 730-0811, Japan (+81-82-242 7821) (fax 242 7452)

(mayorcon@pcf.city.hiroshima.jp)
(www.mayorsforpeace.org).
Mayors for Peace Newsletter.

Mediators Beyond Borders International
(CR), 1901 North Fort Myer Dr – Ste 405,
Arlington, VA 22209, USA
(+1-703-528 6552) (fax 528 5776)
(info@mediatorsbeyondborders.org)
(mediatorsbeyondborders org).
Office also in Netherlands.

Nansen Dialogue Network [NDN] (CR CD),
Bjørntjerne Bjørnsonsgt 2, 2609 Lillehammer,
Norway (+47-6126 5400) (fax 6126 5440)
(contact@nansen-dialogue.net)
(www.nansen-dialogue.net).

NATO Watch (DA ND RE). The Bothy, 29
Erradale, Gairloch IV21 2DS, Britain
(+44-1445 771086) (idavis@natowatch.org)
(natowatch.org). *Observatory.*
Collates information about NATO. Provides
regular briefings.

**No to War – No to NATO / Na i Ryfel! – Na i
NATO / Não à Guerra – Não à NATO** (RA
DA ND), c/o IALANA, Marienstr 19-20, 10117
Berlin, Germany (+41-30-2065 4857)
(fax 2065 3837) (info@no-to-nato.org)
(www.no-to-nato.org).
International network to delegitimise NATO.
Co-ordination of groups in many NATO
states; organises actions against NATO
events. Also c/o Arielle Denis, Mouvement de
la Paix, in France
(Arielle.Denis@mvtpaix.org).

Nonviolence International (IB PA), 4000
Albermarle St NW – Suite 401, Washington,
DC 20016, USA (+1-202-244 0951)
(info@nonviolenceinternational.net)
(nonviolenceinternational.net).
Links resource centres promoting use of nonviolent action. Has nonviolence promotion
centre at UN (+1-212-971 9777).

Nonviolent Peaceforce [NP] (CR HR), 13
chemin de Levant – Bat A, 01210 Ferney
Voltaire, France (+33-967 461948)
(headoffice@nonviolentpeaceforce.org)
(www.nonviolentpeaceforce.org). Offices in
Belgium, and in USA (+1-612-871 0005).

**Organisation for the Prohibition of
Chemical Weapons [OPCW]** (DA), Johan
de Wittlaan 32, 2517 JR Den Haag,
Netherlands (+31-70-416 3300)
(fax 360 3535) (public.affairs@opcw.org)
(www.opcw.org).

Orthodox Peace Fellowship [OPF] (FR),
Kanisstr 5, 1811 GJ Alkmaar, Netherlands
(+31-72-515 4180)
(office@incommunion.org)
(incommunion.org). *In Communion.*

**Parliamentarians for Nuclear
Non-proliferation and Disarmament
[PNND]** (ND), c/o Prague Vision Institute for
Sustainable Security, Lipanská 4, 13000

Praha 3, Czech Republic (+420-773 638867)
(alyn@pnnd.org) (pnnd.org). Europe office,
Basel; UN office, New York. Also London
office.
Provides parliamentarians with information
on nuclear weapons policies; helps them
become engaged in nuclear non-proliferation
and disarmament.

Pax Christi International (RP IB CD RE CR),
Rue du Progrès 323, 1030 Bruxelles,
Belgium (+32-2 502 5550) (fax 2 502 4626)
(hello@paxchristi.net) (www.paxchristi.net).
Newsletter. Network of autonomous
organisations – Catholic.

**Peace Brigades International / Brigadas
Internacionales de Paz / Brigades de Paix
Internationales [PBI]** (HR CD CR RE),
Village Partenaire, Rue de Fernard Bernier
15, 1060 Bruxelles, Belgium
(+32 2 543 4443)
(admin@peacebrigades.org)
(www.peacebrigades.org).
Projects in Colombia, Guatemala, Mexico,
Honduras, Kenya, Indonesia.

**Peace Research Institute Oslo / Institutt for
Fredsforskning [PRIO]** (RE CR), PO Box
9229, Grønland, 0134 Oslo, Norway (+47-
2254 7700) (fax 2254 7701) (info@prio.no)
(www.prio.no). *Journal of Peace Research;
Security Dialogue.* Journals from: SAGE
Publications, 6 Bonhill St, London EC2,
Britain (+44-20-7374 0645).

**Peacebuilding Support Office of the United
Nations** (CR RE), UN Secretariat – 30th
Floor, New York, NY 10017, USA (+1-212-
963 9999) (www.un.org/en/peacebuilding).
Formerly United Nations Peacebuilding
Commission.

PEN International (HR), Unit A, Koops Mill
Mews, 162-164 Abbey St, London SE1 2AN,
Britain (+44-20-7405 0338)
(info@pen-international.org)
(www.pen-international.org).
Includes Writers in Prison Committee,
Writers for Peace Committee.

People to People International [PTPI] (CD),
2405 Grand Blvd – Suite 500, Kansas City,
MO 64108, USA (+1-816-531 4701) (fax 561
7502) (ptpi@ptpi.org) (www.ptpi.org).

Privacy International (HR), 62 Britton St,
London EC1, Britain (+44-20-3422 4321)
(info@privacyinternational.org)
(www.privacyinternational.org). For data
protection, and control of surveillance.

**Pugwash Conferences on Science and
World Affairs** (ND EL RE TW), 1211
Connecticut Ave NW – Suite 800,
Washington, DC 20036, USA (+1-202-478
3440) (pugwashdc@aol.com) (pugwash.org).
Offices also in Rome (+39-06-687 8376),
Geneva (+41-22 907 3667), London
(+44-20-7405 6661).

INTERNATIONAL ORGANISATIONS

Quaker Council for European Affairs [QCEA] (SF HR PA EL AT), Square Ambiorix 50, 1000 Brussel, Belgium (+32-2 230 4935) (fax 2 230 6370) (office@qcea.org) (www.qcea.org). *Around Europe.*

Quaker UN Office – Geneva [QUNO] (SF HR TW EL CR), 13 Av du Mervelet, 1209 Genève, Switzerland (+41-22 748 4800) (fax 22 748 4819) (quno@quno.ch) (www.quno.org). *Geneva Reporter.*

Red Antimilitarista de América Latina e Caribe [RAMALC] (WR), c/o ACOOC, Cr 19 – 33A – 26/1, Bogotá, Colombia (ramalc.org). *Rompiendo Filas.*

Registry of World Citizens [WCR] (WF IB WP RE), Les Nids, 49190 St Aubin de Luigné, France (abc@recim.org) (www.recim.org).

Religions for Peace (RP IB RE CR TW), 777 United Nations Plaza, New York, NY 10017, USA (+1-212-687 2163) (fax 983 0098) (info@rfp.org) (religionsforpeace.org). Formerly World Conference of Religions for Peace. Regional offices in Asia, Europe, Latin America, Africa.

School Day of Non-Violence and Peace / Día Escolar de la No-Violencia y la Paz [DENIP] (RE), Apdo Postal 77, 11510 Puerto Real, Spain (denip.pax@gmail.com) (denip.webcindario.com). (30 January, anniversary of Mahatma Gandhi's death).

Sea Shepherd (EL RA), PO Box 8628, Alexadria, VA 22306, USA (+1-818-736 8357) (fax -360-370 5651) (info@seashepherd.org) (seashepherd.org). Nature conservation on the high seas. Use direct action to confront those attacking the ecosystem.

Search for Common Ground – Brussels Office (RE CD CR), Rue Belliard 205 – bte 13, 1040 Bruxelles, Belgium (+32-2 736 7262) (fax 2 732 3033) (brussels@sfcg.org) (www.sfcg.org). Conflict transformation projects in 34 countries. Washington DC Office (+1-202-265 4300); West Africa Office, Freetown (+232-22-223479).

Sennacieca Asocio Tutmonda – Worker Esperantists [SAT] (CD PA EL HR), 67 Av Gambetta, 75020 Paris, France (+33-14797 7190) (kontakto@satesperanto.org) (www.satesperanto.org). *Sennaciulo.*

Servas International [SI] (CD PO), c/o Jonny Sågänger, Reimersholmsgatan 47 – plan 2, 11740 Stockholm, Sweden (helpdesk@servas.org) (www.servas.org). World hospitality network for peace and goodwill. Building understanding by facilitating personal contacts between people of different nationalities.

Service Civil International – International Office [SCI] (WC PA TW PO HR), Belgiëlei 37, 2018 Antwerpen, Belgium (+32-3 226 5727) (fax 3 232 0344) (info@sciint.org) (www.sciint.org).

Sikh Human Rights Group (HR CR), 89 South Rd, Southall UB1, Middlesex, Britain (shrg@shrg.net) (shrg.net).

Statewatch (HR CD), c/o MDR, 88 Fleet St, London EC4Y 1DH, Britain (+44-20-3691 5227) (office@statewatch.org) (www.statewatch.org). Covers Europe. Critical research in fields of state, justice, home affairs, accountability, etc.

Stockholm International Peace Research Institute [SIPRI] (RE), Signalistgatan 9, 16972 Solna, Sweden (+46-8-655 9700) (sipri@sipri.org) (www.sipri.org). *SIPRI Yearbook.*

Third World Network [TWN] (TW), 131 Jalan Macalister, 10400 Penang, Malaysia (+60-4-226 6728) (fax 226 4505) (twn@twnetwork.org) (www.twn.my). *Third World Resurgence*; *Third World Network Features.*
Latin America Secretariat: ITEM, Av 18 de Julio 2095/301, Montevideo 11200, Uruguay.
Africa Secretariat: 9 Olienu St, PO Box AN 19452, Accra-North, Ghana (fax +233-21-511188).
Also publishes *South-North Development Monitor (SUNS).*

Transnational Institute [TNI] (HR ND RE TW EL), PO Box 14656, 1001 LD Amsterdam, Netherlands (+31-20-662 6608) (fax 675 7176) (tni@tni.org) (www.tni.org). *Transnational Institute Series.*
Research in support of social movements.

UN Non-Governmental Liaison Service (New York Office) [UN-NGLS] (EL HR PO TW), Room DC1-1106, United Nations, New York, NY 10017, USA (+1-212-963 3125) (fax 963 8712) (info@un-ngls.org) (www.un-ngls.org).

UN Research Institute for Social Development [UNRISD] (HR TW EL), Palais des Nations, 1211 Genève 10, Switzerland (+41-22 917 3020) (fax 22 917 0650) (info.unrisd@un.org) (www.unrisd.org). *UNRISD News.*
Research on social dimensions of problems affecting development. Research programmes include: Social Policy and Development; Sustainable Development; Gender and Development.

Unfold Zero (ND), c/o Basel Peace Office, University of Basel, Petersgraben 27, 4051 Basel, Switzerland (www.unfoldzero.org). Network for nuclear weapons abolition. Focus on action through UN system. Joint project of various national and international disarmament campaigns.

INTERNATIONAL ORGANISATIONS

UNICEF, 3 United Nations Plaza, New York, NY 10017, USA (+1-212-326 7000) (fax 887 7465) (aaltamirano@unicef.org) (www.unicef.org).

United Nations Department for Disarmament Affairs (AT CR ND DA), UN Headquarters Bldg (Rm DN25-12), New York, NY 10017, USA (+1-212-963 1570) (fax 963 4066) (www.un.org/disarmament).

United Nations Institute for Disarmament Research [UNIDIR] (RE), Palais des Nations, 1211 Genève 10, Switzerland (+41-22 917 1141) (fax 22 917 0176) (unidir@unog.ch) (www.unidir.org).

Universala Esperanto-Asocio [UEA] (HR CD PO), Nieuwe Binnenweg 176, 3015 BJ Rotterdam, Netherlands (+31-10-436 1044) (fax 436 1751) (uea@co.uea.org). *Esperanto. Kontakto.*

War Resisters' International [WRI] (PA RA HR TR CR), 5 Caledonian Rd, London N1 9DX, Britain (+44-20-7278 4040) (fax 7278 0444) (info@wri-irg.org) (wri-irg.org). *The Broken Rifle; CO Update; War Profiteers News.* Network of organisations of nonviolent activists, pacifists, conscientious objectors, etc. Also, tel +44-20-3355 2364.

Women Living Under Muslim Laws – International Solidarity Network [WLUML] (HR CD), PO Box 28455, London N19 5JT, Britain (+44-20-7263 0285) (fax 7561 9882) (wluml@wluml.org) (www.wluml.org). Arica and Middle East office: PO Box 5330, Dakar Fann, Dakar, Senegal (grefels@gmail.com). Asia office: PO Box 5192, Lahore, Pakistan (sgah@sgah.org.pk). Includes Violence is Not our Culture campaign (www.violenceisnotourculture.org).

Women's International League for Peace and Freedom [WILPF] (PA HR AT ND), CP 28, 1 rue de Varembé, 1211 Genève 20, Switzerland (+41-22 919 7080) (fax 22 919 7081) (secretariat@wilpf.ch) (www.wilpf.org). WILPF UN Office: 777 UN Plaza – 6th Floor, New York, NY 10017, USA (+1-212-682 1265) (fax 286 8211). Projects of UN office include (www.peacewomen.org) and (www.reachingcriticalwill.org).

World Congress of Faiths (RP), 21 Maple St, London W1T 4BE, Britain (+44-1935-864055) (enquiries@worldfaiths.org) (www.worldfaiths.org).

World Federalist Movement – Institute for Global Policy [WFM-IGP] (WF HR RE TW), 708 3rd Ave – Suite 1715, New York, NY 10017, USA (+1-212-599 1320) (fax 599 1332) (info@wfm-igp.org) (www.wfm-igp.org). Also: Bezuidenhoutseweg 99A, 2594 AC Den Haag, Netherlands (+31-70-363 4484).

World Federation of United Nations Associations / Fédération Mondiale des Associations pour les NU [WFUNA/FMANU] (TW HR), Palais des Nations – Room E4-2A, 1211 Genève 10, Switzerland (+41-22 917 3239) (info@wfuna.org) (www.wfuna.org). Also: 1 United Nations Plaza – Rm 1177, New York, NY 10017, USA (+1-212-963 5610) (wfunany@wfuna.org).

World Future Council Foundation (WF EL), Dorotheenstr 15, 22301 Hamburg, Germany (+49-40-3070 91420) (fax 3070 91414) (info@worldfuturecouncil.org) (www.worldfuturecouncil.org). Promotes sustainable future. Other offices: UN (Geneva) (+41-22 555 0950); UK (+44-20-3356 2771) (info.uk@worldfuturecouncil.org); China (+86-10-6500 8172) (info.china@worldfuturecouncil.org).

World Information Service on Energy [WISE] (EL ND RA), Postbus 59636, 1040 LC Amsterdam, Netherlands (+31-20-612 6368) (info@wiseinternational.org) (www.wiseinternational.org). *WISE/NIRS Nuclear Monitor.* Grassroots-oriented anti-nuclear information. Works with NIRS in USA.

World Orchestra for Peace [WOP] (CD UN PO), c/o Charles Kaye, 26 Lyndale Ave, London NW2 2QA, Britain (+44-20-7317 8433) (ckconsult19@gmail.com) (www.worldorchestraforpeace.com). Also tel +44-7967-108974. Established 1995. Designated UNESCO Artist for Peace in 2010.

World Peace Council / Consejo Mondial de la Paz [WPC] (ND TW), Othonos St 10, 10557 Athinai, Greece (+30-210 3316 326) (fax 210 3251 576) (wpc@otenet.gr) (www.wpc-in.org).

World Rainforest Movement (EL HR), Avenida General María Paz 1615 – Of 3, 11400 Montevideo, Uruguay (+598-2-605 6943) (fax) (wrm@wrm.org.uy) (wrm.org.uy).

World Service Authority [WSA] (WF HR PA CD), 5 Thomas Circle NW – Suite 300, Washington, DC 20005, USA (+1-202-638 2662) (fax 638 0638) (info@worldservice.org) (www.worldservice.org). *World Citizen News.*

World Student Christian Federation – Inter-Regional Office [WSCF] (TW RP HR), Ecumenical Centre, BP 2251, 1211 Genève 2, Switzerland (+41-22 791 6358) (fax 22 791 6221) (wscf@wscf.ch) (www.wscfglobal.org). *Federation News; Student World.*

Youth for Exchange and Understanding [YEU] (CD), Ave du Suffrage Universel 49, 1030 Bruxelles, Belgium (+32-2 649 2048) (fax) (info@yeu-international.org) (www.yeu-international.org). Also Portugal office (+351-289-813074).

AFGHANISTAN

Revolutionary Association of the Women of Afghanistan [RAWA] (HR), see under Pakistan (www.rawa.org).

Women, Peace & Security Research Institute [RIWPS] (RE), Taimani, Street 8 - House 43, Kabul (+93-792 615421) (info@riwps-afghanistan.org) (www.riwps-afghanistan.org).

ALBANIA

Albanian Human Rights Group [AHRG] (HR), St Ibrahim Rugova - 2/39, Green Park, Tiranë (+355-42-225060) (el.ballauri@gmail.com) (www.ahrg-al.org).

Fondacioni Shqiptar Zgjidhja e Konflikteve dhe Pajtimi i Mosmarrëveshjeve [AFCR] (RE CR), Rr "Him Kolli" - Pall PF Trade - Nr 5, Tiranë (+355-4-226 4681) (fax 226 4837) (mediationalb@abcom.al) (www.mediationalb.org). *Pajtimi*.

Komiteti Shqiptar i Helsinkit / Albanian Helsinki Committee (HR), Rr Brigada VIII - Pll Tekno Projekt - Shk 2 - Ap 10, Tiranë (+355-4-223 3671) (fax) (office@ahc.org.al) (www.ahc.org.al).

ANDORRA

Partit Verds d'Andorra (EL), Apartat de Correus 2136, Andorra la Vella AD500 (+376-363797) (andorraverds@gmail.com) (www.verds.ad). Green Party.

ANGOLA

Search for Common Ground in Angola (CR CD), 15 rua D2 - Capolo II, Kilamba-Kiaxi, Luanda (angola@sfcg.org) (www.sfcg.org).

ARGENTINA

Fundación Servicio Paz y Justicia [SER-PAJ] (FR IB HR), Piedras 730, 1070 Buenos Aires (+54-11-4361 5745) (secinstitucional@serpaj.org.ar) (serpaj.org.ar).

Greenpeace Argentina (GP), Zabala 3873, 1427 Buenos Aires (+54-11-4551 8811) (fax) (activismo@infogreenpeace.org.ar) (www.greenpeace.org/argentina).

ARMENIA

Civil Society Institute [CSI] (HR), 43 Aygestan 11th St, Yerevan 0025 (+374-10-574317) (csi@csi.am) (www.csi.am).

AUSTRALIA

Act for Peace [AFP] (RP RE TW DA), c/o National Council of Churches in Australia, Locked Bag Q199, Sydney, NSW 1230 (+61-2-8259 0800) (www.actforpeace.org.au).

Alternatives to Violence Project (CR), c/o AVP(NSW), PO Box 161, Lane Cove, NSW 1595 (+61-2-9449 8415) (avpaus@avp.org.au) (www.avp.org.au).

Amnesty International Australia (AI), Locked Bag 23, Broadway, NSW 2007 (+61-2-8396 7600) (fax 9217 7663) (supporter@amnesty.org.au) (www.amnesty.org.au).

Anabaptist Association of Australia and New Zealand (RP), 190 Magpie Hollow Rd, South Bowenfels, NSW 2790 (+61-2-6351 2896) (aaanz.info@gmail.com) (www.anabaptist.asn.au).

Anglican Pacifist Fellowship - Australia [APF] (RP), c/o Philip Huggins, 5 Docker St, Richmond, Vic 2121 (phuggins@melbourne.anglican.com.au).

Anti-Nuclear Alliance of Western Australia [ANAWA] (ND EL), 5 King William St, Bayswater, WA 6053 (+61-8-9272 4252) (admin@anawa.org.au) (www.anawa.org.au).

Australia East Timor Friendship Assocaiation - South Australia [AEFTA-SA] (HR), PO Box 240, Goodwood, SA 5034 (+61-8-8344 3511) (www.aetfa.org.au).

Australia West Papua Association (HR), PO Box 105, Bunbury, WA 6231 (ash@freewestpapua.org) (www.freewestpapuaperth.org).

Australian Anti-Bases Campaign Coalition [AABCC] (IB WP AT ND RA), PO Box A899, Sydney South, NSW 1235 (+61-4-1829 0663) (denis@anti-bases.org) (www.anti-bases.org).

Burma Campaign Australia (HR), c/o 4 Goulburn St - Level 1 - Suite 110, Sydney, NSW 2000 (+61-2-9264 7694) (admin@aucampaignforburma.org) (www.aucampaignforburma.org).

Centre for Peace Studies (RE EL SD), University of New England, Armidale, NSW 2351 (+61-2-6773 2442) (fax 6773 3350) (hware@une.edu.au) (www.une.edu.au/study/peace-studies). Organise annual Nonviolence Film Festival.

Christian Peacemaker Teams Australasia [CPTA] (RP RA CR), PO Box 738, Mona Vale, NSW 1660 (+61-2-9997 4632) (doug.hynd@netspeed.com.au). An initiative of various church groups.

Coalition for Justice & Peace in Palestine [CJPP] (HR), PO Box 144, Glebe, NSW 2037 (cjpp@coalitionforpalestine.org) (www.coalitionforpalestine.org).

Conflict Resolution Network [CRN] (CR UN RE), PO Box 1016, Chatswood, NSW 2057 (+61-2-9419 8500) (crn@crnhq.org) (www.crnhq.org).

Ecumenical Accompaniment Programme in Palestine and Israel - Australia (RP HR), c/o National Council of Churches in Australia, Locked Bag Q199, Sydney, NSW 1230 (+61-2-8259 0800) (www.ncca.org.au/eappi).

AUSTRALIA

Footprints for Peace (ND EL), PO Box 632, Fremantle South, WA 6162 (marcus@footprintsforpeace.org) (www.footprintsforpeace.net).

Friends of the Earth (FE RA PO), PO Box 222, Fitzroy, Vic 3065 (+61-3-9419 8700) (fax 9416 2081) (foe@foe.org.au) (www.foe.org.au).

Graham F Smith Peace Foundation (CR EL HR RE), c/o Oxfam Building, Level 2, 5-7 Hutt St, Adelaide, SA 5000 (+61-8-8240 7680) (contact@artspeacefoundation.org) (www.artspeacefoundation.org).

Greenpeace Australia Pacific (GP), 33 Mountain St, Ultimo, NSW 2007 (+61-2-9281 6100) (fax 9280 0380) (support.au@greenpeace.org) (www.greenpeace.org.au).

Greens (WA) (EL HR DA), PO Box 3022, East Perth, WA 6892 (+61-8-9221 8333) (fax 9221 8433) (office@wa.greens.org.au) (www.wa.greens.org.au). *Green Issue.*

Independent and Peaceful Australia Network [IPAN] (PA DA), PO Box 573, Coorparoo, Qld 4151 (+61-431-597256) (ipan.australia@gmail.com) (pan.org.au). Opposes overseas military bases.

Institute for Social Ecology (EL AL RA), PO Box 5208, West End, Brisbane, Qld 4101 (+61-4-2179 4776).

International Volunteers for Peace [IVP] (SC), 56 Clinton St, Goulburn, NSW 2580 (+61-2-4821 3350) (admin@ivp.org.au) (www.ivp.org.au).

Medical Association for Prevention of War [MAPW] (IP), PO Box 1379, Carlton, Vic 3053 (+61-3-9023 1958) (mapw@mapw.org.au) (www.mapw.org.au).

Nonlethal Security for Peace Campaign (DA RE WF), PO Box 724, Avalon Beach, NSW 2107 (info@tamingwar.com) (www.nonlethalsecurityforpeace.com).

Pace e Bene Australia [PeBA] (PA RP), 5/63 Roslyn St, Brighton, Vic 3186 (+61-3-9592 5247) (d.hess@ozemail.com.au). For nonviolence and cultural transformation.

Pax Christi (PC IB), PO Box 31, Carlton South, Vic 3053 (+61-3-9893 4946) (mscjust@smartchat.net.au) (www.paxchristi.org.au). *Disarming Times.* Also NSW (+61-2-9550 3845).

People for Nuclear Disarmament (NSW) [PND] (ND RE), 499 Elizabeth St, Surry Hills, Sydney, NSW 2010 (+61-2-9319 4296) (johnhallam2001@yahoo.com.au). *Peace Action.*

People for Nuclear Disarmament - Western Australia [PND] (IB ND), 5 King William St, Bayswater, WA 6053 (+61-8-9272 4252) (jovall@iinet.net.au).

People's Charter to Create a Nonviolent World (PA TW EL), PO Box 68, Daylesford, Vic 3460 (flametree@riseup.net) (thepeoplesnonviolencecharter.wordpress.com).

Quaker Service Australia (SF TW), Unit 14, 43-53 Bridge Rd, Stanmore, NSW 2048 (+61-2-8054 0400) (administration@qsa.org.au) (www.qsa.org.au). *QSA Newsletter.*

Religions for Peace Australia (RP), 71 Wellington St, Flemington, Vic 3031 (+61-4-3999 5761) (wcrpaust@iinet.net.au) (religionsforpeaceaustralia.org.au).

Reprieve Australia (HR), PO Box 4296, Melbourne, VIC 3001 (+61-3-9670 4108) (contact@reprieve.org.au) (www.reprieve.org.au). Campaigns against death penalty.

SafeGround (DA), PO Box 2143, Morphettville, SA 5043 (info@safeground.org.au) (safeground.org.au). Work to reduce impact of explosive remnants of war.

Schweik Action Wollongong (SD), PO Box U129, Wollongong, NSW 2500 (+61-2-4228 7860) (fax 4221 5341) (brian_martin@uow.edu.au) (www.bmartin.cc/others/SAW.html).

Servas Australia (SE), c/o Pam Webster, 2 Warili Rd, Frenchs Forest, 2076 (+61-2-9451 9669) (secretary@servas.org.au) (www.servas.org.au).

Society of Friends (SF), PO Box 556, Kenmore, Qld 4069 (ymsecretary@quakers.org.au) (www.quakers.org.au).

Tasmanian Quaker Peace & Justice Committee [TQPJC] (SF PA), PO Box 388, North Hobart, Tas 7002 (+61-400-925385).

Universal Peace Federation - Australia [UPF] (RP), PO Box 642, Burwood, NSW 1805 (oceaniahq@gmail.com) (www.upf.org).

Vision of Humanity (RE), PO Box 42, St Leonards, NSW 1590 (+61-2-9901 8500) (info@visionofhumanity.org) (www.visionofhumanity.org).

War Resisters' League [WRL] (WR AL HR), PO Box 451, North Hobart, Tas 7002 (+61-3-6278 2380) (pdpjones@mpx.com.au).

Women's International League for Peace and Freedom [WILPF] (WL ND), PO Box 934, Dickson, ACT 2602 (wilpf.australia@wilpf.org.au) (wilpf.org.au). *Peace & Freedom.*

World Citizens Association (Australia) [WCAA] (WF), PO Box 6318, University of New South Wales, Sydney, NSW 1466 (C.Hamer@unsw.edu.au) (www.worldcitizens.org.au). *The Bulletin.*

AUSTRIA

Amnesty International Österreich (AI), Möringgasse 10, 1150 Wien (+43-1-78008) (fax 780 0844) (office@amnesty.at) (www.amnesty.at).

Arbeitsgemeinschaft für
Wehrdienstverweigerung und
Gewaltfreiheit [ARGE WDV] (WR),
Schotteng 3A/1/4/59, 1010 Wien
(+43-1-535 9109) (fax 532 7416)
(argewdv@verweigert.at)
(www.verweigert.at).

Bürgermeister für den Frieden in
Deutschland und Österreich (CD ND DA),
see under Germany.

Begegnungszentrum für Aktive
Gewaltlosigkeit / Centre for Encounter and
Active Nonviolence [BFAG] (WR TW EL),
Wolfgangerstr 26, 4820 Bad Ischl
(+43-6132-24590)
(info@begegnungszentrum.at)
(www.begegnungszentrum.at).
Rundbrief.

Die Grünen (EL AL PO), Rooseveltplatz 4-5,
1090 Wien (+43-1-2363 9980) (fax 526 9110)
(bundesbuero@gruene.at) (www.gruene.at).
Green Party.

Franz Jägerstätter House (PC), St Radegund
31, 5121 Ostermiething (+43-6278-8219)
(pfarre.stradegund@dioezese-linz.at)

Internationaler Versöhnungsbund [IVB]
(FR), Lederergasse 23/III/27, 1080 Wien
(+43-1-408 5332) (fax)
(office@versoehnungsbund.at)
(www.versoehnungsbund.at).

IPPNW Österreich [OMEGA] (IP),
Schulgasse 40/17, 1180 Wien
(+43-2988-6236) (office@ippnw.at)
(www.ippnw.at).

Konfliktkultur (CR PO), Breitenfeldergasse
2/14, 1080 Wien (+43-699-1944 1313)
(office@konfliktkultur.at)
(www.konfliktkultur.at).

Österreichische Gesellschaft für
Aussenpolitik und die Vereinten Nationen
[OEGAVN] (UN), Reitschulgasse 2/2,
Hofburg/Stallburg, 1010 Wien
(+43-1-535 4627) (office@oegavn.org)
(www.una-austria.at).

Österreichisches Netzwerk für Frieden und
Gewaltfreiheit (RE), c/o IVB, Lederergasse
23/III/27, 1080 Wien
(www.friedensnetzwerk.at).

Österreichisches Studienzentrum für
Frieden und Konfliktlösung [ÖSFK/ASPR]
(HR PA RE CR), Rochusplatz 1, 7461
Stadtschlaining, Burg (+43-3355-2498) (fax
2662) (aspr@aspr.ac.at) (www.aspr.ac.at).
Study Centre for Peace and Conflict
Resolution.

Pax Christi Österreich [PXÖ] (PC),
Kapuzinerstr 84, 4020 Linz
(+43-732-7610 3254) (office@paxchristi.at)
(www.paxchristi.at). *Pax.*

Peace Museum Vienna (RE), Blutgasse 3/1,
1010 Wien
(office@peacemuseumvienna.com)
(www.peacemuseumvienna.com).
Includes Windows for Peace project in city
streets.

AZERBAIJAN

Azerbaycan Insan Huquqlarini Mudafie
Merkezi / Human Rights Centre of
Azerbaijan [AIHMM/HRCA] (HR), PO Box
31, Baku 1000 (+994-12-492 1369) (fax)
(eldar.hrca@gmail.com)
(penitentiary.ucoz.ru).
Human Rights in Azerbaijan.

BANGLADESH

Bangladesh Interreligious Council for
Peace and Justice [BICPAJ] (FR IB PC CR
EL), 14/20 Iqbal Rd, Mohammadpur, Dhaka
1207 (+880-2-914 1410) (fax 812 2010)
(bicpaj@bijoy.net) (www.bicpaj.org).

Bangladesh Peace Council [BDC] (WP), Flat
3A1 - House No 8, Road No 6 - Block C,
Banani, Dhaka 1213 (+88-2-882 7007)
(dr.maguassem@gmail.com)
(www.bd-pc.org).

Manush Manusher Jonnyo (HR EL CD PO
TW), Nahar Peace Garden, 202/1 Tutpara
Main Rd, Khulna Metro 9100
(fax +880-41-725071)
(manusmanusherjonnyo@gmail.com).
Ideas for a Better Bangladesh.

Service Civil International [SCI] (SC), 57/15
East Razabazar, Panathath West, Dhaka
1215 (+880-2-935 3993)
(scibangladesh@gmail.com)
(scibangladesh.org).

BARBADOS

Barbados Inter-Religious Organisation
[BIRO] (RP), c/o Roman Catholic Diocese of
Bridgetown, PO Box 1223, Bridgetown
(vincentblackett@hotmail.com).
Affiliated to Religions for Peace International.

BELARUS

Alternativnaya Grazhdanskaya Sluzhba /
Campaign for Alternative Civilian Service
in Belarus [AGS] (HR PA), Bakinskaya Str
8-44, 220007 Minsk (+375-25-999 4699)
(ags.belarus@gmail.com)
(ags.by).

Belrad Institute of Radiation Safety (EL), 2
Marusinsky - pereulok 27, Minsk 220053
(+375-17-289 0383) (fax 289 1354)
(belrad@nsys.by) (www.belrad-institute.org).

Byeloruskiy Khelcynskiy Komitet /
Belarusian Helsinki Committee [BHC]
(HR), Karl Liebknecht St 68 - off 1201,
220036 Minsk (+375-17-222 4800)
(fax 222 4801) (office@belhelcom.org)
(www.belhelcom.org).

Green Cross Belarus (EL TW DA CR),
Oktiabrsky St 16 - Building 3, 220030 Minsk
(+375-17-210 0062) (fax 227 1146)
(gcb@greencross.by) (www.greencross.by).

BELGIUM

Abolition 2000 Belgium (ND), c/o
Vredesactie, Patriottenstr 27, 2600 Berchem
(+32-3-281 6839) (lene@vredesactie.be)
(www.abolition2000.be).

BELGIUM

ACAT – Belgique Francophone (HR), Quai aux Foins 53, 1000 Bruxelles (+32-2 223 0159) (fax) (a.cat.belgique@gmail.com) (www.acat-belgique-francophone.be). *ACAT-info.*

ACAT België-Vlaanderen (HR), Zevenkerken 4, 8200 Sint-Andries (+32-50 406132) (info@acat-belgie-vlaanderen.org) (www.acat-belgie-vlaanderen.org).

Agir pour la Paix (WR), 35 rue van Elewyck, Ixelles, 1050 Bruxelles (+32-2 648 5220) (info@agirpourlapaix.be) (agirpourlapaix.be).

Amis de la Terre / Friends of the Earth Belgium (Wallonia and Brussels) [AT] (FE PO), Rue Nanon 98, 5000 Namur (+32-81 390639) (fax 81 390638) (contact@amisdelaterre.be) (www.amisdelaterre.be). *Saluterreliens.*

Amnesty International Belgique Francophone [AIBF] (AI), Rue Berckmans 9, 1060 Bruxelles (+32-2 538 8177) (fax 2 537 3729) (aibf@aibf.be) (www.amnesty.be). *Libertés!.*

Amnesty International Vlaanderen (AI), Kerkstr 156, 2060 Antwerpen (+32-3 271 1616) (fax 3 235 7812) (amnesty@aivl.be) (www.aivl.be).

Artsen Voor Vrede [AVV] (IP), Karel Van de Woesti St 18, 9300 Aalst. *Gezondheidszorg en Vredesvraagstukken.*

Association Médicale pour la Prévention de la Guerre Nucléaire [AMPGN] (IP), 51 Ave Wolvendael, 1180 Bruxelles (de.salle.philippe@skynet.be) (ampgn-belgium.be).

Brigades de Paix Internationales [BPI/PBI] (HR CR CD RE), 23 rue Lt F Wampach, 1200 Bruxelles (+32-473 873136) (info@pbi-belgium.be) (www.pbibelgium.be).

Climaxi – Friends of the Earth (Flanders & Brussels) (FE ND HR), Maria-Hendrikaplein 5, 9000 Gent (+32-9 242 8752) (fax 9 242 8751) (famke@climaxi.org) (www.climaxi.org).

Comité de Surveillance OTAN [CSO] (ND PA RE), rue des Cultivateurs 62, 1040 Bruxelles (+32-2 511 6310) (fax) (info@csotan.org) (www.csotan.org). *Alerte OTAN.* They keep an eye on NATO.

Commission Justice et Paix – Belgique francophone (RP), Rue Maurice Liétart 31/6, 1150 Bruxelles (+32-2 738 0801) (fax 2 738 0800) (info@justicepaix.be) (www.justicepaix.be).

Flemish War and Peace Museum (RE), Ijzertoren, Ijzerdijk 49, 8600 Diksmuide (+32-51 500286) (info@aanceijzer.be) (www.museumaandeijzer.be).

Greenpeace (GP), Haachtsesteenweg 159, 1030 Brussel (+32-2 274 0200) (fax 2 274 0230) (info.be@greenpeace.org) (www.greenpeace.org/belgium).

Groupe Interconfessionnel de la Réconciliation / Kinshasa [GIR] (FR), Route de Longchamp 26, 1348 Louvain-la-Neuve (buangajos@hotmail.com).

I Stop the Arms Trade (AT RA PA), c/o Vredesactie, Patriottenstr 27, 2600 Berchem (+32-3 281 6839) (ikstopwapenhandel@vredesactie.be) (istopthearmstrade.eu). Non-violent direct action against EU arms trade.

Intal Globalize Solidarity (WP TW), 53 Chausée de Haecht, 1210 Bruxelles (+32-2 209 2350) (fax 2 209 2351) (info@intal.be) (www.intal.be).

Pax Christi Vlaanderen [PCV] (PC RE CD ND CR), Italiëlei 98A, 2000 Antwerpen (+32-3 225 1000) (paxchristi@paxchristi.be) (www.paxchristi.be). *Koerier.*

Pax Christi Wallonie-Bruxelles [PCWB] (PC), Rue Maurice Liétart 31/1, 1150 Bruxelles (+32-2 738 0804) (fax 2 738 0800) (info@paxchristiwb.be) (www.paxchristiwb.be). *Signes des Temps.*

Register van Wereldburgers / Registry of World Citizens [RW] (WF PA TW), Vredestr 65, 2540 Hove (+32-3 455 7763) (verstraeten.jean@belgacom.net) (www.recim.org/cdm). *Overleven door Wereldrecht / Survival by World Law.*

Religions for Peace – Belgium (RP), Av de la Reine 7, 1030 Bruxelles (frndali@wcrp.be).

Say No (PA), A Beernaerstr 28a, 1170 Brussel (+32-497 934716) (info@desertie.be) (www.sayno.be). Anti-militarist choral project.

Servas – Belgium & Luxembourg (SE), c/o Rita Dessauvage, Kloosterweg 30, 1652 Beersel-Alsemberg (belgium@servas.org) (belgium.servas.org).

Sortir de la Violence [SDV] (FR CR RE), Blvd du Souverain 199, 1160 Bruxelles (+32-2 679 0644) (info@sortirdelaviolence.org) (www.sortirdelaviolence.org).

VIA (SC WC), Belgiëlei 37, 2018 Antwerpen (+32-3 707 1614) (via@viavzw.be) (www.viavzw.be).

Vlaams Vredesinstituut / Flemish Peace Institute (RE), Leuvenseweg 86, 1000 Brussel (+32-2 552 4591) (fax 2 552 4408) (vredesinstituut@vlaamsparlement.be) (www.vlaamsvredesinstituut.eu). Also www.flemishpeaceinstitute.eu.

Vredesactie (WR AT ND), Patriottenstr 27, 2600 Berchem, Antwerpen (+32-3 281 6839) (info@vredesactie.be) (www.vredesactie.be). *Vredesactie.*

Vrouwen in 't Zwart / Femmes en Noir / Women in Black [WiB] (PA DA HR), c/o Ria Convents, Vismarkt 8, 3000 Leuven (+32-16 291314) (marianne.vandegoorberg@telnet.be) (snellings.telenet.be/womeninblackleuven).

BERMUDA

Amnesty International Bermuda (AI), PO Box HM 2136, Hamilton HM JX (+1441-296 3249) (director@amnestybermuda.org).

BHUTAN

People's Forum for Human Rights (HR), see under Nepal.

BOSNIA-HERZEGOVINA

Centar za ivotnu Sredinu [CZZS] (FE), Miša Stupara 5, 78000 Banja Luka (+387-5143 3140) (fax 5143 3141) (info@czzs.org) (czzs.org).

Centar za Nenasilnu Akciju / Centre for Nonviolent Action [CNA] (CD CR PA RE), Kranjceviceva 33, 71000 Sarajevo (+387-3326 0876) (fax 3326 0875) (cna.sarajevo@nenasilje.org) (www.nenasilje.org). See also in Serbia.

Nansen Dialogue Centre Sarajevo [NDC Sarajevo] (CR), Hakije Kulenovica 10, 71000 Sarajevo (+387-33-556846) (fax 556845) (ndcsarajevo@nansen-dialogue.net) (www.ndcsarajevo.net).

WhyNjet / Why Not (WR), Demala Bijedica 309, 71000 Sarajevo (+387-33-618461) (info@zastone.ba) (www.zastone.ba). Formerly Kampanja za Prigovor Savjesti u BiH.

BOTSWANA

Society of Friends (Quakers) (SF), c/o Shelagh Willet, Box 20166, Gaborone (+267-394 7147) (willet.shelagh@botsnet.bw).

BRAZIL

ACAT Brasil (HR), Praça Clovis Bevilaqua 351 – sala 701, 01018-001 São Paulo – SP (+55-11-3101 6084) (fax) (acatbrasil.international@gmail.com). Affiliated to FIACAT.

Associação das Nações Unidas – Brasil [ANUBRA] (UN), Av Brigadeiro Faria Lima 1485 – North Tower – 19th Floor, 01452-002 São Paulo – SP (+55-11-3094 7984) (fax) (unab@unab.org.br) (www.unab.org.br).

Centro Brasileiro de Solidariedade aos Povos e Luta pela Paz [CEBRAPAZ] (WP CD SD ND), Rua Marconi 34 – Conj 51, República, 01047-000 São Paulo – SP (+55-11-3223 3469) (cebrapaz@cebrapaz.org.br) (cebrapaz.org.br).

Commissão Pastoral da Terra [CPT] (PC), Edificio Dom Abel – 1º andar, Rua 19 – Nº 35, 74030-090 Centro Goiânia, Goiás (+55-62-4008 6466) (fax 4008 6405) (cpt@cptnacional.org.br) (www.cptnacional.org.br).

Green Cross Brazil (EL TW DA HR), Centro Empresarial Brasilia – SRTVS – Q 701 – Bloco A – Salas 311 e 31, 70340-907 Brasilia (+55-61-3226 4613) (greencrossbrazil.gcb@gmail.com) (gcint.org.br).

Serviço de Paz [SERPAZ] (RE DA CR), Rua 1º de Março 776 – sala 4 – Centro, 93010-210 São Leopoldo – RS (+55-51-3592 6106) (fax 2111 1411) (serpaz@serpaz.org.br) (www.serpaz.org.br).

Serviço Voluntário Internacional [SVI-Brasil] (SC), Rua Ribeiro Junqueira 161 – Sl 3, Mangabeiras, Belo Horizonte – MG (+55-11-99439 1794) (pedro@svibrasil.org) (www.svibrasil.org).

BRITAIN

38 Degrees (EL HR TW), Room 134, 40 Bowling Green Lane, London EC1 (+44-20-7970 6023) (emailtheteam@38degrees.org.uk) (www.38degrees.org.uk). Organises internet lobbying on progressive issues.

Abolition 2000 UK (ND), 162 Holloway Rd, London N7 8DQ (mail@abolition2000uk.org) (www.abolition2000uk.org).

Acronym Institute for Disarmament Diplomacy (RE), Werks Central, 15-17 Middle St, Brighton BN1, Sussex (+44-1273 737219) (info@acronym.org.uk) (acronym.org.uk).

Action on Armed Violence (AT DA TW HR), 405 Mile End Rd, Bow, London E3 (info@aoav.org.uk) (aoav.org.uk).

Ahmadiyya Muslim Community (RP HR), c/o Baitul Futuh Mosque, 181 London Rd, Morden, Surrey SM4 (+44-333-240 0490) (enquiries@ahmadiyya.org.uk) (Ahmadiyya.org.uk). Anti-violence and pro freedom of thought group.

Aldermaston Women's Peace Camp(aign) [AWPC] (WR ND RA), c/o 8 Millar House, Merchants Rd, Bristol BS8 4HA (info@aldermaston.net) (www.aldermaston.net). Monthly Aldermaston peace camps; and other actions.

Alternatives to Violence Project – Britain [AVP Britain] (CR PO), 28 Charles Sq, London N1 6HT (+44-20-7324 4755) (info@avpbritain.org.uk) (www.avpbritain.org.uk).

Amnesty International – UK Section [AIUK] (AI), Human Rights Action Centre, 17-25 New Inn Yard, London EC2A 3EA (+44-20-7033 1500) (fax 7033 1503) (info@amnesty.org.uk) (www.amnesty.org.uk).

Anabaptist Network (RP), PO Box 68073, London N22 9HS (admin@anabaptistnetwork.com) (www.anabaptistnetwork.com).

Anglican Pacifist Fellowship [APF] (WR IB RP), Peace House, 19 Paradise St, Oxford OX1 1LD (enquiries@anglicanpeacemaker.org.uk) (www.anglicanpeacemaker.org.uk). *The Anglican Peacemaker.*

For explanation of codes and abbreviations, see introduction

Article 36 (DA), 19 Barnardo Road, Exeter EX2 4ND (info@article36.org) (www.article36.org). Working to change law relating to weapons.

At Ease (HR), Bunhill Fields Meeting House, Quaker Court, Banner St, London EC1Y 8QQ (+44-20-7490 5223) (info@atease.org.uk) (www.atease.org.uk). Advice, counselling for military personnel.

Baby Milk Action (TW PO EL), 4 Brooklands Ave, Cambridge CB2 8BB (+44-1223-464420) (info@babymilkaction.org) (www.babymilkaction.org). *EMA Update.*

Balkans Peace Park Project – UK Committee [B3P] (CD EL), c/o Rylstone Lodge, Rylstone, Skipton BD23 6LH, N Yorks (+44-1756-730231) (A.T.I.Young@bradford.ac.uk) (www.balkanspeacepark.org)

Baptist Peace Fellowship [BPF] (FR), c/o 21 Kingshill, Cirencester GL7 1DE, Gloucestershire (bobgardiner@yahoo.co.uk) (www.baptist-peace.org.uk). *BPF Newsletter.*

Before You Sign Up, 11 Manor Rd, Stratford-upon-Avon, Warwickshire CV37 (info@beforeyousignup.info) (www.beforeyousignup.info). For people thinking of joining the armed forces.

Bertrand Russell Peace Foundation [BRPF] (RE PA ND), Unit 5, Churchill Business Park – Private Road No 2, Colwick, Nottingham NG4 2HF (+44-115-970 8318) (fax 942 0433) (elfeuro@compuserve.com) (www.russfound.org). *The Spokesman.*

Bloomsbury Ad Hoc Committee [BADHOC] (EL RA PA), c/o 26 Museum Chambers, Little Russell St, London WC1A 0NN (badhoc@activist.com).

Boycott Israel Network [BIN] (HR TW), c/o PSC, Box BM PSA, London WC1N 3XX (info@boycottisraelnetwork.net) (www.boycottisraelnetwork.net). Expansion of the Boycott Israeli Goods Campaign.

Bradford University Department of Peace Studies (RE CR TW), Bradford BD7 1DP, West Yorks (+44-1274-235235) (fax 235240) (www.brad.ac.uk/acad/peace/).

Brighton Peace & Environment Centre [BPEC] (RE EL), 39-41 Surrey St, Brighton BN1, Sussex (+44-1273-766610) (info@bpec.org) (www.bpec.org).

British American Security Information Council [BASIC] (RE AT ND), 3 Whitehall Court, London SW1 (+44-20-7766 3461) (basicuk@basicint.org) (www.basicint.org). *BASIC Reports.*

Building Bridges for Peace (CR), c/o 2 Crossways, Cott Lane, Dartington, Totnes TQ9 6HE, Devon (info@buildingbridgesforpeace.org) (www.buildingbridgesforpeace.org). Conflict transformation through empathy.

Campaign Against Arms Trade [CAAT] (WR AT IB RA), Unit 4, 5-7 Wells Terrace, London N4 3JU (+44-20-7281 0297) (enquiries@caat.org.uk) (www.caat.org.uk). *CAAT News.*

Campaign against Climate Change [CCC] (EL RA), Top Floor, 5 Caledonian Rd, London N1 9DX (+44-20-7833 9311) (info@campaigncc.org) (www.campaigncc.org).

Campaign Against Criminalising Communities [CAMPACC] (HR), c/o 44 Ainger Rd, London NW3 (+44-20-7586 5892) (estella24@tiscali.co.uk) (www.campacc.org.uk).

Campaign for Better Transport [CBT] (EL), 70 Cowcross St, London EC1M 6EJ (+44-20-3746 2225) (info@bettertransport.org.uk) (www.bettertransport.org.uk).

Campaign for Earth Federation / World Federalist Party (WF), c/o Ian Hackett, 1 Kenilworth Rd, London W5 5PB (worldfederalistparty@gmail.com) (www.federalunion.org.uk).

Campaign for Freedom of Information [CFI] (HR), Free Word Centre, 60 Farringdon Rd, London EC1 (+44-20-7324 2519) (admin@cfoi.org.uk) (www.cfoi.org.uk).

Campaign for Homosexual Equality [CHE] (HR), c/o London Friend, 86 Caledonian Rd, London N1 9DN (+44-7941-914340) (info@c-h-e.org.uk) (www.c-h-e.org.uk).

Campaign for Human Rights in the Philippines [CHRP UK] (HR), c/o Kanlungan Filipino Consortium, Unit 1, Fountayne Business Centre, Broad Lane, London N15 (info@chrp.org.uk) (www.chrp.org.uk).

Campaign for Human Rights in Turkey (HR), c/o Turkish & Kurdish Community Centre, Former Library, Howard Rd, London N16 8PU (+44-20-7275 8440) (fax 7275 7245).

Campaign for Nuclear Disarmament [CND] (IB ND RA RE), 162 Holloway Rd, London N7 8DQ (+44-20-7700 2393) (enquiries@cnduk.org) (www.cnduk.org). *Campaign!.*

Campaign for Nuclear Disarmament Cymru / Yr Ymgyrch dros Ddiarfogi Niwclear [CND Cymru] (ND RA AT DA), c/o 72 Heol Gwyn, Yr Alltwen, Pontardawe SA8 3AN (+44-1792-830330) (heddwch@cndcymru.org) (www.cndcymru.org). *Heddwch.*

Campaign for Press and Broadcasting Freedom [CPBF] (HR), 2nd floor, 23 Orford Rd, Walthamstow, London E17 9NL (freepress@cpbf.org.uk) (www.cpbf.org.uk). *Free Press.*

Campaign for the Accountability of American Bases [CAAB] (ND PA RA), 59 Swarcliffe Rd, Harrogate HG1, Yorks

(+44-1423-884076)
(mail@caab.corner.org.uk)
(www.caab.org.uk).

Campaign Opposing Police Surveillance [COPS] (HR), 5 Caledonian Rd, London N1 9DX (info@campaignopposingpolicesurveillance.com) (campaignopposingpolicesurveillance.com).

Campaign to Protect Rural England (EL PO), 5-11 Lavington St, London SE1 0NZ (+44-20-7981 2800) (fax 7981 2899) (info@cpre.org.uk) (www.cpre.org.uk). Campaigns include opposing fracking.

Centre for Alternative Technology / Canolfan y Dechnoleg Amgen [CAT] (EL PO AL), Machynlleth, Powys SY20 9AZ (+44-1654-705950) (fax 702782) (info@cat.org.uk) (www.cat.org.uk). *Clean Slate.*

Centre for International Peacebuilding (CR RE TW EL), The White House, 46 High St, Buntingford, Herts SG9 9AH (+44-1763-272662) (eirwenharbottle@gmail.com).

Centre for Trust, Peace and Social Relations [CTPSR] (RE), 5 Innovation Village, Coventry University Technology Park, Cheetah Rd, Coventry CV1 2TT (+44-24-7765 1182) (info.ctpsr@coventry.ac.uk) (www.coventry.ac.uk).

Centre of Religion, Reconciliation and Peace (RE RP), University of Winchester, Sparkford Rd, Winchester SO22, Hampshire (+44-1962-841515) (fax 842280) (www.winchester.ac.uk).

Chernobyl Children's Project (UK) (PO EL CD), Kinder House, Fitzalan St, Glossop SK13, Derbyshire (+44-1457-863534) (ccprojectuk@gmail.com) (www.chernobyl-children.org.uk).

Children of Peace (CR HR), 1st Floor, The Roller Mill, Mill Lane, Uckfield TN22 5AA, Sussex (+44-1825-768074) (info@childrenofpeace.org.uk) (www.childrenofpeace.org.uk). Charity working in Israel, Palestine, Jordan.

Christian Aid (TW), 35-41 Lower Marsh, London SE1 (+44-20-7620 4444) (fax 7620 0719) (info@christian-aid.org) (www.christianaid.org).

Christian Campaign for Nuclear Disarmament [CCND] (ND RP), 162 Holloway Rd, London N7 8DQ (+44-20-7700 4200) (christians@cnduk.org) (www.christiancnd.org.uk). *Ploughshare.*

Christian International Peace Service [CHIPS] (RP CR PO RE), 17 Hopton House, Loughborough Estate, London SW9 7SP (+44-20-7078 7439) (info@chipspeace.org) (www.chipspeace.org).

Church & Peace (RP CR RE), 39 Postwood Green, Hertford Heath SG13 7QJ (+44-1992-416442) (IntlOffice@church-and-peace.org) (www.church-and-peace.org).

City to Sea (EL PO), Unit D, Albion Dockside Studios, Hanover Place, Bristol BS1 6UT (info@citytosea.org.uk) (www.citytosea.org.uk). Campaign to stop plastic pollution at source.

Climate Outreach (EL), The Old Music Hall, 106-108 Cowley Rd, Oxford OX4 1JE (+44-1865-403334) (info@climateoutreach.org) (climateoutreach.org). Formerly Climate Outreach and Information Network.

Close Capenhurst Campaign (EL), c/o News From Nowhere, 96 Bold St, Liverpool L1 (closecapenhurst@gmail.com) (close-capenhurst.org.uk). Opposes uranium enrichment plant in Cheshire.

Co-operation Ireland (GB) (CD), Windy Ridge, Courtlands Hill, Pangbourne RG8, Berkshire (+44-118-976 7790) (fax) (murphy992@btinternet.com) (www.cooperationireland.org).

Coal Action Network (EL RA), Steade Rd, Sheffield S7 (info@coalaction.org.uk) (www.coalaction.org.uk).

Commonweal Collection (RE AL PA EL), c/o J B Priestley Library, Bradford University, Bradford BD7 1DP, Yorks (+44-1274-233404) (commonweal@riseup.net) (bradford.ac.uk/library/libraries-and-collections/). Peace library.

Community for Reconciliation [CfR] (RP), Barnes Close, Chadwich, Malthouse Lane, Bromsgrove, Worcs B61 0RA (+44-1562-710231) (fax 710278) (cfrenquiry@aol.com) (www.cfrbarnesclose.co.uk). *Newslink.*

Conciliation Resources (CR), Burghley Yard, 106 Burghley Rd, London NW5 1AL (+44-20-7359 7728) (fax 7359 4081) (cr@c-r.org) (www.c-r.org).

Concord Media (PA EL TW), 22 Hines Rd, Ipswich IP3 9BG, Suffolk (+44-1473-726012) (sales@concordmedia.org.uk) (www.concordmedia.org.uk).

Conflict and Environment Observatory [CEOBS] (DA EL RE), Bridge 5 Mill, 22a Beswick St, Ancoats, Manchester M4 (ceobs.org). Previously Toxic Remnants of War Project.

Conflict Research Society [CRS] (RE), c/o Hugh Miall, 45 Ethelbert Rd, Canterbury CT1 3NF, Kent (conflictresearchsociety@kent.ac.uk) (www.conflictresearchsociety.org).

Conscience – Taxes for Peace not War (TR WR HR), 108 Wenlock Studios, 50-52 Wharf Rd, London N1 7EU (+44-20-3515 9132) (info@conscienceonline.org.uk) (www.conscienceonline.org.uk). *Conscience Update.*

Conway Hall Ethical Society (HR RE), Conway Hall, Red Lion Sq, London WC1 4RL (+44-20-7405 1818) (admin@conwayhall.org.uk) (www.conwayhall.org.uk). *Ethical Record.* Formerly South Place Ethical Society.

Cord (TW CR), Floor 9, Eaton House, 1 Eaton Rd, Coventry CV1 2FJ (+44-24-7708 7777) (info@cord.org.uk) (www.cord.org.uk). International peacebuilding charity.

Corporate Occupation (HR RA TW), c/o Corporate Watch, 84b Whitechapel High St, London E1 7QX (tom@shoalcollective.org) (www.corporateoccupation.org). Opposes occupation of Palestine.

Corporate Watch (EL RA AL), c/o Freedom Press, Angel Alley, 84b Whitechapel High St, London E1 7QX (+44-20-7426 0005) (contact@corporatewatch.org) (www.corporatewatch.org). *News Update.*

Cuba Solidarity Campaign (TW WC), c/o UNITE, 33-37 Moreland St, London EC1V 8BB (+44-20-7490 5715) (office@cuba-solidarity.org.uk) (www.cuba-solidarity.org.uk). *Cuba Si.*

Cumbrians Opposed to a Radioactive Environment [CORE] (EL), Dry Hall, Broughton Mills, Broughton-in-Furness, Cumbria LA20 (+44-1229-716523) (fax) (martin@corecumbria.co.uk) (www.corecumbria.co.uk).

Cymdeithas y Cymod / FoR Wales (FR PA CR), c/o 42 St Patrick's Drive, Pen-y-Bont ar Ogwr / Bridgend, CF31 1RP (cymdeithasycymod@gmail.com) (www.cymdeithasycymod.org.uk).

Cymru dros Heddwch / Wales for Peace (RE DA), c/o Welsh Centre for International Affairs, Temple of Peace, Cathays Park, Cardiff CF10 (+44-29-2082 1051) (janeharries@wcia.org.uk) (www.walesforpeace.org).

Cynghrair Wrth-Niwclear Cymru / Welsh Anti-Nuclear Alliance [CWNC/WANA] (EL), PO Box 90, Llandrindod Wells, Powys LD1 9BP (info@wana.wales) (www.wana.wales).

Darvell Bruderhof (RP PA PO), Brightling Rd, Robertsbridge, Sussex TN32 5DR (+44-1580-883330) (darvell@bruderhof.com) (www.bruderhof.com). Anabaptist community.

Defend the Right to Protest [DTRTP] (HR), BM DTRTP, London WC1N 3XX (info@defendtherighttoprotest.org) (www.defendtherighttoprotest.org).

Drone Campaign Network (DA), c/o Peace House, 19 Paradise St, Oxford OX1 (DroneCampaignNetwork@riseup.net) (www.dronecampaignnetwork.org.uk). Network of organisations and academics.

Drone Wars UK (DA HR), c/o FoR, 19 Paradise St, Oxford OX1 (chris@dronewars.net) (www.dronewars.net). Opposes growing British use of armed drones.

East London Against the Arms Fair [ELAAF] (AT), c/o Garden Cafe, 7 Cundy Rd, Custom House, London E16 (elaaf@hotmail.co.uk) (elaaf.org).

Opposing regular massive arms fair in Docklands.

Economic Issues Programme of the Society of Friends (SF HR EL), QPSW, Friends House, 175 Euston Rd, London NW1 2BJ (+44-20-7663 1000) (suzannei@quaker.org.uk) (www.quaker.org.uk/economic-juctice). *Earth & Economy newsletter.*

Ecumenical Accompaniment Programme in Palestine and Israel – British and Irish Group [EAPPI] (RP HR SF SD), c/o QPSW, Friends House, 173 Euston Rd, London NW1 2BJ (+44-20-7663 1144) (eappi@quaker.org.uk) (www.quaker.org.uk/eappi).

Edinburgh Peace and Justice Centre (CR ND PA RE HR), 5 Upper Bow, Edinburgh EH1 2JN (+44-131-629 1058) (contact@peaceandjustice.org.uk) (peaceandjustice.org.uk). *Peace and Justice News.*
Promotes nonviolence, conflict resolution.

Egypt Solidarity Initiative (HR), c/o MENA Solidarity Network, Unit 193, 15-17 Caledonian Rd, London N1 (campaign@egyptsolidarityinitiative.net) (egyptsolidarityinitiative.org).

Ekklesia (RP RE), 235 Shaftesbury Ave, London WC2 (+44-20-7836 3930) (info@ekklesia.co.uk) (www.ekklesia.co.uk).

End Violence Against Women Coalition (HR), 17-25 New Inn Yard, London EC2 (+44-20-7033 1559) (admin@evaw.org.uk) (www.endviolenceagainstwomen.org.uk).

Environmental Investigation Agency [EIA] (EL), 62/63 Upper St, London N1 (+44-20-7354 7960) (ukinfo@eia-international.org) (www.eia-international.org). Also in USA.

Environmental Network for Central America [ENCA] (EL HR), c/o Janet Bye, 5 St Edmund's Place, Ipswich IP1 (+44-20-8769 0492) (enca.info@gmail.com) (www.enca.org.uk). *ENCA.*
Works with affected communities.

Equity and Peace (CR), c/o 9 The Arcade, Belsay, Northumberland NE20 (+44-1661-881894) (www.equityandpeace.com).

Esperanto-Asocio de Britio [EAB] (PO HR), Esperanto House, Station Rd, Barlaston, Stoke-on-Trent, Staffs ST12 9DE (+44-1782-372141) (eab@esperanto.org.uk) (www.esperanto.org.uk)
EAB Update; La Brita Esperantisto.

Ethical Consumer Research Association (EL PO AL), Unit 21, 41 Old Birley St, Manchester M15 (+44-161-226 2929) (fax 226 6277) (enquiries@ethicalconsumer.org) (www.ethicalconsumer.org). *Ethical Consumer.*

EuroPal Forum (HR), 21 Chalton St, London NW1 1JD (+44-20-3289 6057) (admin@europalforum.org.uk) (europalforum.org.uk).
Mobilises in support of Palestinian rights.

Extinction Rebellion (EL RA PO), The Exchange, Brick Row, Stroud GL5 1DF, Glos (extinctionrebellion@risingup.org.uk) (www.ExtinctionRebellion.org.uk). Actions for climate and economic justice.

Faith & Resistance Network (RP RA), c/o QPSW, Friends House, 175 Euston Rd, London NW1 (faithandresistanceblog.wordpress.com).

Faslane Peace Camp (ND RA AL), Shandon, Helensburgh, Dunbartonshire, G84 8NT (+44-1436-820901) (faslane30@gmail.com) (faslanepeacecamp.wordpress.com).

Fellowship of Reconciliation [FoR] (FR WR), Peace House, 19 Paradise St, Oxford OX1 1LD (+44-1865-250781) (office@for.org.uk) (www.for.org.uk). *Peacelinks.* Covers England and Scotland.

Fitnah – Movement for Women's Liberation (HR), BM Box 1919, London WC1N 3XX (fitnah.movement@gmail.com) (www.fitnah.org). *Fitnah.* Opposes misogynist cultural and religious customs.

Fly Kites Not Drones (CD HR PA PO), c/o VCNV-UK, 31 Carisbrooke Rd, St Leonards-on-Sea TN38, Sussex (kitesnotdrones@gmail.com) (www.flykitesnotdrones.org). Non-violence project for young people.

ForcesWatch (PA HR RE), 5 Caledonian Rd, London N1 (+44-20-7837 2822) (office@forceswatch.net) (www.forceswatch.net).

Free Tibet Campaign (HR TW EL), 28 Charles Sq, London N1 6HT (+44-20-7324 4605) (fax 7324 4606) (mail@freetibet.org) (www.freetibet.org). *Free Tibet.*

Freedom from Torture (HR), 111 Isledon Rd, London N7 (+44-20-7697 7777) (fax 7697 7799) (www.freedomfromtorture.org). *Survivor.* Supports survivors of torture.

Friends of Lebanon (FOL) (CR RE SD), Unit 35, 61 Praed St, London W2 1NS (+44-1923-606385) (mail@friendsoflebanon.org) (www.friendsoflebanon.org).

Friends of the Earth – England, Wales and Northern Ireland [FOE] (FE PO), The Printworks, 1st Floor, 139 Clapham Rd, London SW9 0HP (+44-20-7490 1555) (fax 7490 0881) (info@foe.co.uk) (friendsoftheearth.uk).

Friends of the Earth Cymru / Cyfeillion y Ddaear Cymru (FE), 33 The Balcony, Castle Arcade, Cardiff CF10 1BY (+44-29-2022 9577) (cymru@foe.co.uk) (www.foecymru.co.uk).

Friends of the Earth Scotland (FE), Thorn House, 5 Rose St, Edinburgh EH2 2PR (+44-131-243 2700) (fax 243 2725) (info@foe.scot) (www.foe.scot).

Gandhi Foundation (HR RE PO), Kingsley Hall, Powis Rd, Bromley-by-Bow, London E3 3HJ (contact@gandhifoundation.org) (www.gandhifoundation.org). *The Gandhi Way.*

Gender Action for Peace and Security UK [GAPS] (HR RE AT CR), c/o Women for Women International UK, 32-36 Loman St, London SE1 0EH (+44-20-7922 7836) (info@gaps-uk.org) (gaps-uk.org). Network of organisations and individual experts.

Global Justice Now (TW HR), 66 Offley Rd, London SW9 0LS (+44-20-7820 4900) (offleyroad@globaljustice.org.uk) (www.globaljustice.org.uk). *Ninety Nine.* Formerly World Development Movement.

Global Witness (EL HR TW CR), Lloyds Chambers, 1 Portsoken St, London E1 (+44-20-7492 5820) (fax 7492 5821) (mail@globalwitness.org) (www.globalwitness.org). Also in USA.

GM Watch (EL), c/o 26 Pottergate, Norwich NR2 1DX, Norfolk (+44-1603-624021) (fax 766552) (ngin@gmwatch.org) (www.gmwatch.org). Analyses and counters GM industry propaganda.

GM-Free Cymru (EL), c/o Dyffryn Dwarch, Abermawr, nr Mathry, Pembrokeshire SA62 (gm@caerhys.co.uk) (www.gmfreecymru.org).

GM-free Scotland (EL), c/o 35 Hamilton Drive, Glasgow G12 (gmfreescotland@yahoo.co.uk) (gmfreescotland.blogspot.co.uk).

Greater Manchester & District CND [GM&DCND] (ND), Bridge 5 Mill, 22a Beswick St, Ancoats, Manchester M4 7HR (+44-161-273 8283) (gmdcnd@gn.apc.org) (gmdcnd.com). *Nuclear Alert.*

Green Christian [GC] (EL PO), 97 Plumpton Ave, Hornchurch RM12 6BB, Essex (info@greenchristian.org.uk) (www.greenchristian.org.uk). *Green Christian.*

Green CND (ND), c/o CND, 162 Holloway Rd, London N7 (+44-20-7700 2393).

Green Party of England and Wales (EL ND HR RA), The Biscuit Factory – A Block (201), 100 Clements Rd, London SE16 4DG (+44-20-3691 9400) (office@greenparty.org.uk) (www.greenparty.org.uk). *Green World.*

Greener UK (EL), c/o Green Alliance, 4th Floor, Victoria Charity Centre, 11 Belgrave Rd, London SW1V 1RB (amount@green-alliance.org.uk) (greeneruk.org). Tracking environmental implications of BREXIT.

GreenNet (TW HR PO), The Green House, 244-254 Cambridge Heath Rd, London E2 9DA (+44-330-335 4011) (info@gn.apc.org) (www.gn.apc.org).

Greenpeace UK (GP), Canonbury Villas, London N1 2PN (+44-20-7835 8100) (info.uk@greenpeace.org) (www.greenpeace.org.uk). *Connect.*

Gun Control Network (AT RE PO EL), PO Box 11495, London N3 2FE (gcn-uk@btconnect.com) (www.gun-control-network.org).

Housmans Bookshop (WR EL AL HR), 5 Caledonian Rd, Kings Cross, London N1 9DX (+44-20-7837 4473) (fax 7278 0444) (shop@housmans.com) (www.housmans.com). *Peace Diary & World Peace Directory.* Peace/political books, magazines, cards, etc.

Human Rights Watch – London Office (HR), First Floor, Audrey House, 16-20 Ely Place, London EC1 (+44-20-7618 4700) (londonoutreach@hrw.org) (www.hrw.org/london).

Humanists UK (HR PO), 39 Moreland St, London EC1V 8BB (+44-20-7324 3060) (fax 7324 3061) (info@humanists.uk) (humanism.org.uk). Formerly British Humanist Association.

Humanity United for Universal Demilitarisation [HUFUD] (PA PO DA), 14a Lakeside Rd, London W14 0DU (info.hufud@gmail.com) (www.hufud.org). For universal abolition of militarism and weapons.

Index on Censorship (HR RA TW), 292 Vauxhall Bridge Rd, London SW1V 1AE (+44-20-7963 7262) (david@indexoncensorship.org) (www.indexoncensorship.org). *Index on Censorship.*

Inter Faith Network for the UK (RP CR CD), 2 Grosvenor Gardens, London SW1W 0DH (+44-20-7730 0410) (fax 7730 0414) (ifnet@interfaith.org.uk) (www.interfaith.org.uk).

International Alert [IA] (RE CR HR CD), 346 Clapham Rd, London SW9 (+44-20-7627 6800) (fax 7627 6900) (general@international-alert.org) (www.international-alert.org).

International Association for Religious Freedom – British Chapter (HR), c/o Essex Hall, 1 Essex St, London WC2R 3HY (Pejman_Khojasteh@btinternet.com) (www.iarf.net). *IARF World.*

International Campaign to Abolish Nuclear Weapons – UK [ICAN-UK] (ND), c/o MEDACT, 28 Charles Sq, London N1 6HT (infouk@icanw.org) (www.icanw.org/unitedkingdom).

International Friendship League – UK (CD), PO Box 578, Northampton NN5 4WY (www.ifl.org.uk).

International Service [UNAIS] (TW UN), Second Floor, Rougier House, 5 Rougier St, York YO1 6HZ (+44-1904-647799) (fax 652353) (contact@internationalservice.org.uk) (www.internationalservice.org.uk).

International Voluntary Service [IVS] (SC), Thorn House, 5 Rose St, Edinburgh EH2 2PR (+44-131-243 2745) (fax 243 2747) (info@ivsgb.org) (ivsgb.org). *Interactions.*

Iona Community (FR PA HR), 21 Carlton Court, Glasgow G5 9JP (+44-141-429 7281) (admin@iona.org.uk) (www.iona.org.uk). *The Coracle.* (On Iona: +44-1681-700404).

Israeli Committee Against House Demolitions UK [ICAHD UK] (HR RA), BM ICAHD UK, London WC1N 3XX (+44-20-3740 2208) (info@icahduk.org) (www.icahduk.org). Opposes Israeli occupation of Palestinian land.

JD Bernal Peace Library (RE), c/o Marx Memorial Library, 37a Clerkenwell Green, London EC1R 0DU (+44-20-7253 1485) (archives@mml.xyz) (www.marx-memorial-library.org). *Theory and Struggle.*

Jews for Justice for Palestinians [JJP] (HR), 20-22 Wenlock Rd, London N1 7GU (jjfpexecutive@gmail.com) (jjfp.com).

Jubilee Debt Campaign (TW), The Grayston Centre, 28 Charles Sq, London N1 6HT (+44-20-7324 4722) (info@jubileedebt.org.uk) (jubileedebt.org.uk). *Drop It!.*

Jubilee Scotland (TW), 41 George IV Bridge, Edinburgh EH1 1EL (+44-131-225 4321) (mail@jubileescotland.org.uk) (www.jubileescotland.org.uk). Successor to Jubilee 2000 Scottish Coalition.

Justice & Peace Scotland / Ceartas agus Sith (RP), 65 Bath St, Glasgow G2 2BX (+44-141-333 0238) (office@justiceandpeacescotland.org.uk) (justiceandpeacescotland.org.uk).

Justice, Peace and Integrity of Creation project of the Columban Fathers [JPIC] (RP), St Joseph's, Waford Way, Hendon, London NW4 4TY (+44-20-8202 2555) (fax 8202 5775) (jpicssc@btconnect.com) (www.columbans.co.uk). *Vocation for Justice.*

Khulisa – Breaking the cycle of violence (CD CR PO), Wells House (Unit 7), 5-7 Wells Terrace, London N4 (+44-20-7561 3727) (info@khulisa.co.uk) (www.khulisa.co.uk). Modelled on programmes in South Africa.

Kick Nuclear (EL RA), c/o CND, 162 Holloway Rd, London N7 8DQ (+44-20-7700 2393) (kicknuclearlondon@gmail.com) (kicknuclear.com). Opposes UK's addiction to nuclear power.

Labour CND (ND), c/o 480 Lymingon Rd, Highcliffe, Christchurch BH23 5HG (+44-1425-279307) (info@labourcnd.org.uk) (www.labourcnd.org.uk).

Land Justice Network (HR EL RA), c/o The Land Magazine, Monkton Wyld Court, Charmouth, Bridport, Dorset DT6 (landjusticeuk@gmail.com) (www.landjustice.uk). Network challenging use and ownership of land.

Liberation (HR TW DA CR), 77 St John St, Clerkenwell, London EC1M 4NN (+44-20-7324 2498) (info@liberationorg.co.uk) (www.liberationorg.co.uk). *Liberation.*

Liberty – The National Council for Civil Liberties (HR), Liberty House, 26-30 Strutton Ground, London SW1P 2HR (+44-20-7403 3888) (fax 7799 5306) (www.libertyhumanrights.org.uk).

Living Streets (EL HR PO), 4th Floor, Universal House, 83-94 Wentworth St, London E1 7SA (+44-20-7377 4900) (info@livingstreets.org.uk) (www.livingstreets.org.uk).

Local Futures / ISEC [ISEC-UK] (EL), PO Box 239, Totnes TQ9 9DP (+44-1392-581175) (info@localfutures.org) (www.localfutures.org).

London Catholic Worker [LCW] (RP RA PA AL), 49 Mattison Rd, London N4 (+44-20-8348 8212) (londoncatholicworker@yahoo.co.uk) (www.londoncatholicworker.org). *London Catholic Worker.*

London Mining Network [LMN] (HR EL), Finfuture, 225-229 Seven Sisters Rd, London N4 (contact@londonminingnetwork.org) (www.londonminingnetwork.org).

London Region CND [LRCND] (ND), Mordechai Vanunu House, 162 Holloway Rd, London N7 8DQ (+44-20-7607 2302) (www.londoncnd.org). *Peaceline.*

Low-Impact Living Initiative [LILI] (PO EL), Redfield Community, Winslow MK18, Bucks (+44-1296-714184) (fax) (lili@lowimpact.org) (www.lowimpact.org).

Low-Level Radiation Campaign [LLRC] (EL), Times Building, South Crescent, Llandrindod Wells, Powys LD1 5DH (+44-1597-824771) (lowradcampaign@gmail.com) (www.llrc.org).

MEDACT (IP IB EL), The Grayston Centre, 28 Charles Sq, London N1 6HT (+44-20-7324 4739) (fax 7324 4734) (office@medact.org) (www.medact.org). *Communiqué.*

Medical Aid for Palestinians [MAP] (HR), 33a Islington Park St, London N1 1QB (+44-20-7226 4114) (fax 7226 0880) (info@map.org.uk) (www.map.org.uk). *Witness.*

Merseyside CND (ND), 151 Dale St, Liverpool L2 2AH (+44-151-229 5282) (mcnd@care4free.net) (www.mcnd.org.uk).

Methodist Peace Fellowship [MPF] (FR PA), c/o Marie Dove, 17 Fangdale Court, Bridlington, Yorks YO16 (+44-1262-679612) (marie.dove@gmail.com) (mpf.org.uk). *Peace in the 21st Century.*

Milton Keynes Peace & Justice Network (ND HR DA), 300 Saxon Gate West, Central Milton Keynes, Bucks MK9 2ES (office@mkpeaceandjustice.org.uk) (www.mkpeaceandjustice.org.uk). *MK Network News.*

Mines Advisory Group [MAG] (DA TW PO), Suite 3A, South Central, 11 Peter St, Manchester M2 5QR (+44-161-236 4311) (fax 236 6244) (info@maginternational.org) (www.maginternational.org).

Movement for Compassionate Living [MCL] (PO EL), 105 Cyfyng Rd, Ystalyfera, Swansea SA9 2BT (+44-1639-841223) (mcl.vegany@googlemail.com) (www.MCLveganway.org.uk).

Movement for the Abolition of War [MAW] (IB), c/o 11 Venetia Rd, London N4 1EJ (+44-20-3397 3019) (info@abolishwar.org.uk) (www.abolishwar.org.uk). *Abolish War.*

Musicians for Peace and Disarmament [MPD] (IB ND DA), c/o Tony Lamb, 37 Bolton Gdns, Teddington TW11 9AX (info.mpdconcerts@gmail.com) (www.mpdconcerts.org). *Newsletter.*

National Federation of Atheist, Humanist and Secularist Student Societies [AHS] (HR), 39 Moreland St, London EC1 (communications@ahsstudents.org.uk) (ahsstudents.org.uk).

National Justice & Peace Network [NJPN] (RP), 39 Eccleston Sq, London SW1V 1BX (+44-20-7901 4864) (fax 7901 4821) (admin@justice-and-peace.org.uk) (www.justice-and-peace.org.uk). *Justice and Peace.*

National Secular Society [NSS] (HR), 25 Red Lion Sq, London WC1R 4RL (+44-20-7404 3126) (enquiries@secularism.org.uk) (www.secularism.org.uk).

Network for Peace [NfP] (DA ND PA), 5 Caledonian Rd, London N1 9DX (mail@networkforpeace.org.uk) (www.networkforpeace.org.uk).

Network of Christian Peace Organisations [NCPO] (RP), c/o FOR, Peace House, 19 Paradise St, Oxford OX1 1LD (+44-1865-250781) (enquiries@ncpo.org.uk) (ncpo.org.uk).

New Economics Foundation [NEF] (EL CD PO), 10 Salamanca Place, London SE1 7HB (+44-20-7820 6300) (info@neweconomics.org) (www.neweconomics.org).

New Economy Organisers Network [NEON] (EL HR PO), 10 Salamanca Place, London SE1 7HB (hello@neweconomyorganisers.org) (neweconomyorganisers.org). Network of organisers.

New Israel Fund UK (HR), Unit 2, Bedford Mews, London N2 9DF (+44-20-7724 2266) (fax 7724 2299) (info@uknif.org) (uknif.org). Supports progressive civil society in Israel.

Nicaragua Solidarity Campaign [NSC] (HR TW WC), 86 Durham Rd, London N7 7DT (+44-20-7561 4836) (nsc@nicaraguasc.org.uk) (www.nicaraguasc.org.uk). *Nicaragua Now.*

Nipponzan Myohoji (RP), Peace Pagoda, Willen, Milton Keynes MK15 0BA, Bucks (+44-1908-663652) (fax). Also in London: -44-20-7228 9620.

BRITAIN

No 2 Nuclear Power (EL), c/o Pete Roche, Friends of the Earth Scotland, Thorn House, 5 Rose Street, Edinburgh EH2 (rochepete8@aol.com) (www.no2nuclearpower.org.uk). Provides nuclear website and nuclear information.

No Sweat (HR RA TW), 5 Caledonian Rd, London N1 (admin@nosweat.org.uk) (www.nosweat.org.uk). Against sweatshops; for workers' and TU rights.

NO2ID (HR), Box 412, 19-21 Crawford St, London W1H 1PJ (+44-20-7340 6077) (office@no2id.net) (www.no2id.net). *NO2ID Newsletter.* Opposes ID cards and the database state.

Non-Violent Resistance Network [NVRN] (RA ND PA), c/o David Polden, CND, 162 Holloway Rd, London N7 8DQ (+44-20-7700 2393) (davidtrpolden1@gmail.com). *Newsletter.*

Northern Friends Peace Board [NFPB] (SF), Victoria Hall, Knowsley St, Bolton BL1 2AS (+44-1204-382330) (nfpb@gn.apc.org) (nfpb.org.uk). *NFPB Update.*

Norwich Environment Resource Centre (EL PO), The Greenhouse, 42-46 Bethel St, Norwich NR2 1NR (+44-1603-631007) (www.GreenhouseTrust.co.uk).

Nuclear Awareness Group [NAG] (EL), 16 Back St, Winchester SO23 9SB, Hants (+44-1962-890160) (fax) (nuclearawarenessgroup.org.uk). *Newsletter.*

Nuclear Information Service [NIS] (RE ND), 35-39 London St, Reading RG1 4PS (+44-118-327 4935) (fax) (office@nuclearinfo.org) (nuclearinfo.org).

Nuclear Morality Flowchart Project (ND), c/o Martin Birdseye, 88 Fern Lane, Hounslow TW5 0HJ, Middlesex (+44-20-8571 1691) (info@nuclearmorality.com) (nuclearmorality.com). Helps people to think about ethical accountability.

Nuclear Trains Action Group [NTAG] (ND RA), c/o Mordechai Vanunu House, 162 Holloway Rd, London N7 8DR (+44-20-7700 2393) (www.nonucleartrains.org.uk). *Newletter.* Working Group of London Region CND.

Nuclear-Free Local Authorities Secretariat [NFLA] (ND EL), c/o Manchester City Council, Town Hall, Manchester M60 3NY (+44-161-234 3244) (fax 274 7379) (s.morris4@manchester.gov.uk) (www.nuclearpolicy.info).

Nukewatch UK (ND RA RE), c/o Edinburgh Peace & Justice Centre, 5 Upper Bow, Edinburgh EH1 2JN (+44-345 458 8365) (spotters@nukewatch.org.uk) (www.nukewatch.org.uk).

Oasis of Peace UK (CD CR HR), 192B Station Rd, Edgware HA8 7AR, Middx (+44-20-8952 4717) (office@oasisofpeace.org.uk) (www.oasisofpeaceuk.org). Formerly British Friends of NSWaS.

One World Week (HR TW EL), 35-39 London St, Reading RG1 4PS, Berks (+44-118-939 4933) (oww@oneworldweek.org) (www.oneworldweek.org).

OneVoice Movement – Europe (CD CR), Unit 4, Benwell Studios, 11-13 Benwell Rd, London N7 7BL (+44-20-8004 6431) (europe@OneVoiceMovement.org) (www.onevoicemovement.org). See also under Israel, Palestine, and USA.

Orthodox Peace Fellowship UK [OPF] (RP), c/o Seraphim Honeywell, "Birchenhoe", Crowfield, nr Brackley NN13 5TW, Northants (oxpeacefp@aol.com) (www.incommunion.org). *In Communion.*

Palestine Solidarity Campaign [PSC] (TW CR), Box BM PSA, London WC1N 3XX (+44-20-7700 6192) (fax 7700 5747) (info@palestinecampaign.org) (www.palestinecampaign.org).

Pax Christi (PC PA RE), Christian Peace Education Centre, St Joseph's, Watford Way, Hendon, London NW4 4TY (+44-20-8203 4884) (fax 8203 5234) (info@paxchristi.org.uk) (www.paxchristi.org.uk). *Justpeace.*

Peace Brigades International – UK Section [PBI UK] (PA RE HR CD), 1b Waterlow Rd, London N19 5NJ (+44-20-7281 5370) (fax) (admin@peacebrigades.org.uk) (peacebrigades.org).

Peace Education Network (RE), c/o Pax Christi, St Joseph's, Watford Way, London NW4 4TY (+44-20-8203 4884) (education@paxchristi.org.uk) (www.peace-education.org.uk).

Peace Hub – Quaker Peace and Justice Centre (SF PO CD), 41 Bull St, Birmingham B4 6AF (+44-121-238 2869) (office@peacehub.org.uk) (peacehub.org.uk).

Peace in Kurdistan (HR), 44 Ainger Rd, London NW3 3AT (+44-20-7586 5892) (estella24@tiscali.co.uk) (www.peaceinkurdistancampaign.com).

Peace Museum UK (RE PA CR), 10 Piece Hall Yard, off Hustlergate, Bradford BD1 1PJ (+44-1274-780241) (info@peacemuseum.org.uk) (www.peacemuseum.org.uk).

Peace News – for nonviolent revolution /PN] (WR HR AL RA ND), 5 Caledonian Rd, London N1 9DY (+44-20-7278 3344) (fax 7278 0444) (editorial@peacenews.info) (www.peacenews.info).

Peace One Day (CR PO RE), St George's House, 15 St George's Rd, Richmond, Surrey TW9 (+44-20-8334 9900) (fax 8948 0545) (info@peaceoneday.org) (www.peaceoneday.org).

Peace Party – Non-violence, Justice, Environment (PA HR EL), c/o John Morris, 39 Sheepfold Rd, Guildford GU2 9TT, Surrey (+44-1483-576400) (info@peaceparty.org.uk) (www.peaceparty.org.uk). *Peace*. Secular pacifist electoral movement.

Peace Pledge Union [PPU] (WR RE), 1 Peace Passage, Brecknock Rd, London N7 0BT (+44-20-7424 9444) (mail@ppu.org.uk) (www.ppu.org.uk). *Peace Matters*.

Peace Tax Seven (TR), c/o Woodlands, Ledge Hill, Market Lavington, Wilts SN10 (info@peacetaxseven.com) (www.peacetaxseven.com).

People & Planet (TW HR EL), The Old Music Hall, 106-108 Cowley Rd, Oxford OX4 1JE (+44-1865-403225) (people@peopleandplanet.org) (peopleandplanet.org). National student network.

People Against Rio Tinto and its Subsidiaries [PARTIZANS] (HR EL TW), 41A Thornhill Sq, London N1 1BE (+44-20-7700 6189) (fax) (partizans@gn.apc.org) (www.minesandcommunities.org).

Police Spies Out of Lives (HR), c/o 84b Whitechapel High St, London E1 7QX (cotact@policespiesoutoflives.org) (policespiesoutoflives.org). Supports women abused by undercover police.

Practical Action (PO TW), Schumacher Centre for Technology and Development, Bourton Hall, Bourton-on-Dunsmore, Rugby, Warwickshire CV23 9QZ (+44-1926-634400) (fax 634401) (enquiries@practicalaction.org.uk) (www.practicalaction.org).

Pugwash Conferences on Science and World Affairs (DA EL RE TW CR), Ground Floor Flat, 63A Great Russell St, London WC1B 3BJ (+44-20-7405 6661) (office@britishpugwash.org) (britishpugwash.org). *Pugwash Newsletter*. Part of international Pugwash network.

Quaker Concern for the Abolition of Torture [Q-CAT] (SF HR), c/o 38 The Mount, Heswall CH60 4RA, Wirral (+44-151-342 4425) (chasraws@onetel.com) (q-cat.org.uk).

Quaker Peace & Social Witness [QPSW] (SF DA PA), Friends House, 175 Euston Rd, London NW1 2BJ (+44-20-7663 1000) (qpsw@quaker.org.uk) (www.quaker.org.uk/qpsw).

Quaker Sustainability and Peace Programme (SF EL RE DA PA), QPSW, Friends House, 175 Euston Rd, London NW1 2BJ (+44-20-7663 1067) (fax 7663 1001) (survival@quaker.org.uk) (www.quaker.org.uk). Previously Peace and Disarmament Programme.

Radical Routes (AL PO), c/o Cornerstone Resource Centre, 16 Sholebroke Ave, Leeds LS7 3HB (+44-1603-767445) (enquiries@radicalroutes.org.uk) (www.radicalroutes.org.uk). Network of radical housing, worker & other co-ops.

Redress (HR), 87 Vauxhall Walk, London SE11 (+44-20-7793 1777) (fax 7793 1719) (info@redress.org) (www.redress.org). Seeks justice for torture survivors.

Religions for Peace UK [WCRP-UK] (RP RE), c/o 18 Little Acres, Ware SG12 9JW, Hertfordshire (+44-1920-465714) (fax) (secretary@religionsforpeace.org.uk) (www.religionsforpeace.org.uk).

Religious Society of Friends in Britain (Quakers) (SF), Friends House, Euston Rd, London NW1 2BJ (+44-20-7663 1000) (fax 7663 1001) (www.quaker.org.uk). *Quaker News; The Friend; Quaker Voices*.

Reprieve (HR), PO Box 72054, London EC3P 3BZ (+44-20-7553 8140) (info@reprieve.org.uk) (www.reprieve.org.uk).

Rethinking Security (RE DA EL), c/o Saferworld, The Grayston Centre, 28 Charles Sq, London N1 (celia@rethinkingsecurity.org.uk) (rethinkingsecurity.org.uk). Network of academics, activists, organisations.

Rising Tide UK [RTUK] (EL RA AL), c/o London Action Resource Centre, 62 Fieldgate St, Whitechapel, London E1 1ES (info@risingtide.org.uk) (www.risingtide.org.uk). Direct action for climate justice.

RoadPeace (EL RE HR), Shakespeare Business Centre, 245a Coldharbour Lane, London SW9 8RR (+44-20-7733 1603) (info@roadpeace.org) (roadpeace.org). Supports road traffic victims and families.

Saferworld (RE AT), The Grayston Centre, 28 Charles Sq, London N1 (+44-20-7324 4646) (fax 7324 4647) (general@saferworld.org.uk) (www.saferworld.org.uk). Helping people turn away from armed violence.

Scientists for Global Responsibility [SGR] (RE ND EL AT DA), Unit 2.8, Halton Mill, Mill Lane, Halton, Lancaster LA2 6ND, Lancashire (+44-1524-812073) (info@sgr.org.uk) (www.sgr.org.uk). *SGR Newsletter*.

Scotland's for Peace (ND RE AT), c/o 77 Southpark Ave, Glasgow G12 (+44-141-357 1529) (info@scotlanc4peace.org) (www.scotland4peace.org). Umbrella body.

Scottish Campaign for Nuclear Disarmament [SCND] (ND), 77 Southpark Ave, Glasgow G12 8LE (+44-141-357 1529) (scnd@banthebomb.org) (www.banthebomb.org). *Nuclear Free Scotland*.

Scottish Friends of Palestine (HR TW), 31 Tinto Rd, Glasgow G43 2AL (+44-141-637 8046) (info@scottish-friends-of-palestine.org) (www.scottishfriendsofpalestine.org).

Scrap Trident Coalition (ND PA RA), c/o Edinburgh Peace and Justice Centre, 5 Upper Bow, Edinburgh EH1 2JN (+44-131-629 1058) (scraptrident@gmail.com) (scraptrident.org). Network in Scotland.

BRITAIN

Sea Shepherd UK (EL RA), 27 Old Gloucester St, London WC1N 3AX (+44-300-111 0501) (admin@seashepherduk.org) (www.seashepherd.org.uk). Conserving nature on the high seas.

Seeds for Change (RA AL), Storey Institute, Meeting House Lane, Lancaster LA1 (+44-1524-509002) (contact@seedsforchange.org.uk) (www.seedsforchange.org.uk). Training for actions, campaigns, setting up co-ops.

Servas Britain (SE), c/o Nash Villa, Nash Lane, Marnhull, Sturminster Newton DT10, Dorset (info@servasbritain.net) (www.servasbritain.net).

Share The World's Resources [STWR] (TW EL), Office 128, 73 Holloway Rd, London N7 8JZ (+44-20-7609 3034) (info@sharing.org) (www.sharing.org). Sustainable economics to end global poverty.

Smash EDO (RA AT), c/o Unemployed Centre, 6 Tilbury Place, Brighton BN2 0GY, Sussex (smashedo@riseup.net) (smashedo.org).

Soil Association (EL PO TW), South Plaza, Marlborough St, Bristol BS1 (+44-117-314 5000) (fax 314 5001) (memb@soilassociation.org) (www.soilassociation.org). Scotland office: +44-131-666 2474.

South Cheshire & North Staffs CND [SCANS CND] (ND), Groundwork Enterprise Centre, Albany Works, Moorland Rd, Burslem, Stoke-on-Trent ST6 1EB, Staffs (+44-1782-829913) (scanscnd@ymail.com) (www.scanscnd.org). *Banner.*

Southdowns Peace Group (DA), c/o Vida, 22 Beaufort Rd, Bedhampton, Havant PO9 3HU (+44-23-9234 6696) (vida.henning@ntlworld.com).

Southern Region CND (ND), 3 Harpsichord Place, Oxford OX4 1BY (+44-1865-248357) (oxfordcnd@phonecoop.coop).

St Ethelburga's Centre for Reconciliation and Peace (CD CR RE RP), 78 Bishopsgate, London EC2N 4AG (+44-20-7496 1610) (fax 7638 1440) (enquiries@stethelburgas.org) (www.stethelburgas.org).

Stop Arming Israel (AT), c/o CAAT, Unit 4, 5-7 Wells Terrace, London N4 3JU (+44-20-7281 0297) (israel@caat.org.uk) (www.stoparmingisrael.org). Joint campaign of peace, solidarity, etc, groups.

Stop Climate Chaos Scotland [SCCS] (EL), 2nd Floor, Thorn House, 5 Rose St, Edinburgh EH2 2PR (+44-131-243 2701) (info@stopclimatechaosscotland.org) (www.stopclimatechaos.org/scotland). Development, environment, etc, groups' coalition.

Stop Hinkley (EL), 8 The Bartons, Yeabridge, South Petherton TA13 5LW, Somerset (+44-1749-860767) (admin@stophinkley.org) (www.stophinkley.org). Against nuclear power in south-west England.

Stop the War Coalition [STWC], 86 Durham Rd, London N7 (+44-20-7561 4830) (office@stopwar.org.uk) (www.stopwar.org.uk).

Student Christian Movement [SCM] (RP), Grays Court, 3 Nursery Rd, Edgbaston, Birmingham B15 3JX (+44-121-426 4918) (scm@movement.org.uk) (www.movement.org.uk).

Surfers Against Sewage [SAS] (EL), Unit 2, Wheal Kitty Workshops, St Agnes TR5 0RD, Cornwall (+44-1872-553001) (fax 552615) (info@sas.org.uk) (www.sas.org.uk). *Pipeline News.*

Syria Peace & Justice Group (CR CD AT DA), c/o LARC, 62 Fieldgate St, London E1 (syriapeaceandjustice@gmail.com) (syriapeaceandjustice.wordpress.com). Anti-militarist human rights campaign.

Syrian Human Rights Committee [SHRC] (HR), PO Box 123, Edgware HA8 0XF, Middlesex (fax +44-870-1377678) (walid@shrc.org) (www.shrc.org). Syrian human rights group in exile.

Tapol (HR AT TW RE), Durham Resource Centre, 86 Durham Rd, London N7 (+44-20-7561 7485) (info@tapol.org) (www.tapol.org).

The Brotherhood Church (WR AL EL), Stapleton, nr Pontefract, Yorkshire WF8 3DF (+44-1977-620381).

The Climate Coalition (EL), Romero House, 55 Westminster Bridge Rd, London SE1 7JB (+44-20-7870 2213) (admin@theclimatecoalition.org) (www.theclimatecoalition.org).

The Corner House (HR TW EL), Station Rd, Sturminster Newton, Dorset DT10 1BB (+44-1258-473795) (fax) (enquiries@thecornerhouse.org.uk) (www.thecornerhouse.org.uk). *Briefing Papers.*

The Forgiveness Project (CR PO), 10 Buckingham Palace Rd, London SW1W 0QP (+44-20-7821 0035) (fax) (info@theforgivenessproject.com) (www.theforgivenessproject.com).

"The Right to Refuse to Kill" Group [RRK] (PA HR), c/o PPU, 1 Peace Passage, London N7 0BT (+44-20-7247 3731) (edna.mathieson1@btinternet.com) (www.rrk.freeuk.com).

Tibet Foundation (HR), Hamilton House, Mabledon Place, London WC1H 9BB (+44-20-7930 6001) (info@tibet-foundation.org) (www.tibet-foundation.org).

Tibet Society (HR TW CR), 2 Baltic Place, London N1 5AQ (+44-20-7923 0021) (info@tibetsociety.com) (www.tibetsociety.com). Campaigns for Tibetan self-determination.

Tools for Self Reliance (TW PO WC), Ringwood Rd, Netley Marsh, Southampton SO40 7GY (+44-23-8086 9697) (fax 8086 8544) (info@tfsr.org) (www.tfsr.org). *Forging Links.*

Town and Country Planning Association [TCPA] (EL), 17 Carlton House Terr, London SW1Y 5AS (+44-20-7930 8903) (fax 7930 3280) (tcpa@tcpa.org.uk) (www.tcpa.org.uk). *Town & Country Planning.*

Trade Justice Movement (TW HR EL), 66 Offley Rd, London SW9 0LS (mail@tjm.org.uk) (www.tjm.org.uk).

Trident Ploughshares (WR ND RA), c/o Edinburgh Peace & Justice Centre, 5 Upper Bow, Edinburgh EH1 2JN (+44-345 458 8361) (tp2000@gn.apc.org) (tridentploughshares.org).

Turning the Tide (SF PO RA), Friends House, Euston Rd, London NW1 2BJ (+44-20-7663 1064) (fax 7663 1049) (stevew@quaker.org.uk) (www.turning-the-tide.org). *Making Waves.* Offers workshops, nonviolence training, etc.

Tyne & Wear CND (ND), 1 Rectory Ave, Gosforth, Newcastle-upon-Tyne NE3 1XS (+44-191-285 1290) (rhpg@btinternet.com)

UK Committee for UNICEF [UNICEF UK] (TW HR), UNICEF House, 30a Great Sutton St, London EC1 (+44-20-7490 2388) (fax 7250 1733) (www.unicef.org.uk).

UNA Exchange (UN WC PO), Temple of Peace, Cathays Park, Cardiff CF10 3AP (+44-29-2022 3088) (fax 2022 2540) (info@unaexchange.org) (www.unaexchange.org). *Opinions.*

UNA-UK Members for Civil Society Link with UN General Assembly [UNGA-Link UK] (UN), 11 Wilberforce House, 119 Worple Rd, London SW20 8ET (+44-20-8944 0574) (fax) (info@ungalink.org.uk) (www.ungalink.org.uk).

Unitarian and Free Christian Peace Fellowship [UPF] (RP), c/o Sue Woolley, 5 Martins Rd, Piddinston, Northampton NN7 2DN (+44-1604-870746) (www.unitariansocieties.org.uk/peace).

United Nations Association – UK [UNA-UK] (UN HR RE TW), 3 Whitehall Court, London SW1A 2EL (+44-20-7766 3454) (fax 7000 1381) (info@una.org.uk) (www.una.org.uk). *UNA-UK.*

United Reformed Church Peace Fellowship [URCPF] (RP), c/o Church and Society, United Reformed Church, 86 Tavistock Pl, London WC1H 9RT (+44-20-7916 8632) (fax 7916 2021) (church.society@urc.org.uk) (www.urc.org.uk/mission/peace-fellowship.html).

Uniting for Peace [UfP] (DA ND CD AT RE), 14 Cavell St, London E1 2HP (+44-20-7791 1717) (info@unitingforpeace.com) (unitingforpeace.com). *Uniting for Peace.* Also in Edinburgh (+44-131-446 9545).

Vegan Society (EL TW PO HR), Donald Watson House, 34-35 Ludgate Hill, Birmingham B3 1EH (+44-121-523 1730) (info@vegansociety.com) (www.vegansociety.com). *The Vegan.*

Vegetarian Society of the UK (EL TW PO), Parkdale, Dunham Rd, Altrincham, Cheshire (+44-161-925 2000) (fax 926 9182) (info@vegsoc.org) (www.vegsoc.org). *The Vegetarian.*

Veggies (PO EL), c/o Sumac Centre, 245 Gladstone St, Nottingham NG7 (+44-115-960 8254) (info@veggies.org.uk) (www.veggies.org.uk).

Veterans for Peace UK [VFP UK] (PA RA RE), 12 Dixon Rd, London SE25 6TZ (admin@vfpuk.org) (veteransforpeace.org.uk).

Voices for Creative Non-Violence UK [VCVN-UK] (PA CR), 31 Carisbrooke Rd, St Leonards-on-Sea TN38 0JN, Sussex (vcnvuk@gmail.com) (www.vcnv.org.uk).

Voluntary Service Overseas [VSO] (TW), 100 London Rd, Kingston-upon-Thames KT2, Surrey (+44-20-8780 7500) (enquiry@vsoint.org) (www.vsointernational.org).

Volunteer Action for Peace [VAP UK] (WC HR EL), 16 Overhill Rd, East Dulwich, London SE22 0PH (action@vap.org.uk) (www.vap.org.uk). Within UK, tel 0844-209 0927.

Volunteering Matters (PO CD), The Levy Centre, 18-24 Lower Clapton Rd, London E5 (+44-20-3780 5870) (information@volunteeringmatters.org.uk) (volunteeringmatters.org.uk). Formerly Community Service Volunteers.

War Child (RE PA PO), Studio 320, Highgate Studios, 53-79 Highgate Rd, London NW5 1TL (+44-20-7112 2555) (info@warchild.org.uk) (www.warchild.org.uk). Aid organisation for children in war zones.

War On Want [WOW] (TW), 44-48 Shepherdess Walk, London N1 7JP (+44-20-7324 5040) (fax 7324 5041) (support@waronwant.org) (www.waronwant.org)

Week of Prayer for World Peace (RP), c/o 126 Manor Green Rd, Epsom KT19 8LN, Surrey (+44-1628-530309) (j.jackson215@btinternet.com) (www.weekofprayerforworldpeace.com).

West Midlands CND [WMCND] (ND), 54 Allison St, Digbeth, Birmingham B5 5TH (+44-121-643 4617) (wmcndall@gmail.com) (www.wmcnd.org.uk).

West Midlands Quaker Peace Education Project [WMQPEP] (SF RE CR), 41 Bull St, Birmingham B4 6AF (+44-121-236 4796) (office@peacemakers.org.uk) (www.peacemakers.org.uk).

BRITAIN

Western Sahara Campaign UK (HR TW), Manora, Cwmystwyth, Aberystwyth SY23 4AF (+44-1974-282214) (coordinator@wsahara.org.uk) (www.wsahara.org.uk).

White Ribbon Campaign (PO), White Ribbon House, 1 New Rd, Mytholmroyd, Hebden Bridge HX7 5DZ (+44-1422-886545) (info@whiteribboncampaign.co.uk) (www.whiteribboncampaign.co.uk).

Women's International League for Peace and Freedom [UK WILPF] (WL), 52-54 Featherstone St, London EC1Y 8RT (+44-20-7250 1968) (ukwilpf.peace@gmail.com) (www.wilpf.org.uk). Also Scottish office (scottishwilpf@yahoo.co.uk).

Woodcraft Folk (PA EL PO RE TW), Units 9/10, 83 Crampton St, London SE17 (+44-20-7703 4173) (fax 7358 6370) (info@woodcraft.org.uk) (www.woodcraft.org.uk). *The Courier*. Co-operative children's and youth organisation.

Working Group on Conscientious Objection in the UK (HR), c/o ForcesWatch, 5 Caledonian Rd, London N1 (office@forceswatch.net). Network of pacifist and human rights groups.

World Future Council – UK Office (WF EL DA ND), 4th Floor, Rex House, 4-12 Regent St, London SW1Y 4PE (info.uk@worldfuturecouncil.org) (www.worldfuturecouncil.org). Promotes sustainable future.

World Harmony Orchestra (CD PO), 12d Princess Crescent, London N4 2HJ (www.worldharmonyorchestra.com). Raises funds for humanitarian causes.

World Peace Campaign, Hill House, Cookley, Kidderminster DY10 3UW, Worcs (+44-1562-851101) (fax 851824) (office@worldpeacecampaign.co.uk) (www.worldpeacecampaign.co.uk).

World Peace Prayer Society [WPPS] (RP PO EL RE), Allanton Sanctuary, Auldgirth, Dumfries DG2 0RY (+44-1387-740642) (allanton@worldpeace-uk.org) (www.worldpeace-uk.org). Promote the message "May peace prevail on earth".

Yorkshire CND (ND), The Deaf Centre, 25 Hallfield Rd, Bradford BD1 3RP, W Yorks (+44-1274-730795) (info@yorkshirecnd.org.uk) (www.yorkshirecnd.org.uk). *Action for Peace*.

Youth and Student CND [YSCND] (ND RA), 162 Holloway Rd, London N7 8DQ (+44-20-7700 2393) (yscnd@riseup.net) (www.yscnd.org).

BURMA

Peace Way Foundation (HR), see under Thailand.

CAMBODIA

Centre for Peace and Conflict Studies (RE), PO Box 93066, Siem Reap City (info@centrepeace.asia) (www.centrepeaceconflictstudies.org).

CANADA

Action by Christians Against Torture / Action des Chrétiens pour l'Abolition de la torture [ACAT-Canada] (HR), 2715 chemin de la Côte-Ste-Catherine, Montréal, QC, H3T 1B6 (+1-514-890 6169) (fax 890 6484) (info@acatcanada.org) (www.acatcanada.org).

Amnesty International Canadian Section – English Speaking (AI), 312 Laurier Ave E, Ottawa, ON, K1N 1H9 (+1-613-744 7667) (fax 746 2411) (members@amnesty.ca) (www.amnesty.ca). *The Activist*.

Amnistie Internationale – Section Canadienne Francophone (AI), 50 rue Ste-Catherine Ouest – bureau 500, Montréal, QC, H2X 3V4 (+1-514-766 9766) (fax 766 2088) (www.amnistie.ca). *Agir*.

Artistes pour la Paix (PA ND AT), CP 867 – Succursale C, Montréal, QC, H2L 4L6 (artistespourlapaix.org).

Baptist Peace Fellowship of North America – Bautistas por la Paz (RP), see under USA.

Canadian Centres for Teaching Peace (RE PO), 230 Belle Isle St, Shediac, NB, E4P 1G8 (+1-403-461 2469) (fax 309-407 6576) (stewartr@peace.ca) (www.peace.ca).

Canadian Coalition for Nuclear Responsibility / Regroupement pour la Surveillance du Nucléaire [CCNR] (ND EL CD), 53 Dufferin Rd, Hampstead, QC, H3X 2X8 (+1-514-489 5118) (ccnr@web.ca) (www.ccnr.org).

Canadian Peace Congress (WP), 125 Brandon Ave, Toronto, ON, M6H 2E2 (info@CanadianPeaceCongress.ca) (www.canadianpeacecongress.ca).

Canadian School of Peacebuilding (RE CR), Canadian Mennonite University, 500 Shaftesbury Blvd, Winnipeg, Manitoba, R3P 2N2 (+1-204-487 3300) (fax 837 7415) (csop@cmu.ca) (csop.cmu.ca).

Canadian Secular Alliance [CSA] (HR), 802 – 195 St Patrick St, Toronto, ON, M5T 2Y8 (+1-416-402 8856) (info@secularalliance.ca) (secularalliance.ca).

Centre de Ressources sur la Non-violence [CRNV] (WR EL), 75 Rue du Square Sir George Étienne Carter, Montréal, QC, H4C 3A1 (+1-514-504 5012) (crnv@nonviolence.ca) (nonviolence.ca).

Civilian Peace Service Canada (CD PO), 2106-1025 Richmond Rd, Ottowa, ON, K2B 8G8 (+1-613-721 9829) (gbreedyk@civilianpeaceservice.org) (civilianpeaceservice.ca).

Coalition for Gun Control, PO Box 90062, 1488 Queen St West, Toronto, ON, M6K 3K3 (+1-416-604 0209) (coalitionforguncontrol@gmail.com) (guncontrol.ca). Also in Montreal (−1-514-528 2360).

Coalition to Oppose the Arms Trade [COAT] (AT), 191 James St, Ottawa, ON, K1R 5M6 (+1-613-231 3076) (overcoat@rogers.com) (coat.ncf.ca).

Collectif Échec À la Guerre (PA RE DA), 5055A rue Rivard, Montréal, QC, H2J 2N9 (+1-514-919 7249) (info@echecalaguerre.org) (echecalaguerre.org).

Edmonton Peace Council (WP), 392 Meadowview Drive, Fort Saskatchewan, Alberta T8L 0N9 (+1-587-873 9739) (canadianpeace@gmail.com). *Alberta Peace News.*

Friends of the Earth / Les Ami(e)s de la Terre [FoE] (FE), 260 St Patrick St – Suite 300, Ottawa, ON, K1N 5K5 (+1-613-241 0085) (fax 241 7998) (foe@intranet.ca) (www.foecanada.org).

Greenpeace Canada (GP), 33 Cecil St, Toronto, ON, M5T 1N1 (+1-416-597 8408) (fax 597 8422) (supporter.ca@greenpeace.org) (www.greenpeace.ca).

Mennonite Central Committee Canada (RP HR EL), 134 Plaza Dr, Winnipeg, MB, R3T 5K9 (+1-204-261 6381) (fax 269 9875) (canada@mcccanada.ca) (www.mcccanada.ca).

Pace e Bene Canada (PA RP), 4058 Rivard, Montreal, Quebec, H2L 4H9 (veronow@sympatico.ca).

Peace Brigades International – Canada [PBI-Canada] (CR RE SD), 211 Bronson Ave – Suite 220, Ottawa, ON, K1R 6H5 (+1-613-237 6968) (info@pbicanada.org) (www.pbicanada.org).

Peace Magazine (PA AT CR), Box 248, Toronto P, Toronto, ON, M5S 2S7 (+1-416-789 2294) (office@peacemagazine.org) (www.peacemagazine.org). 4 yrly, Can$20 (Can$24 US, Can$35 elsewhere).

PeaceWorks, c/o MSCU Centre for Peace Advancement, CGUC, University of Waterloo, 140 Westmount Road North, Waterloo, ON, N2L 3G6 (+1-519-591 1365) (mail@peaceworks.tv) (peaceworks.tv). Youth movement.

Physicians for Global Survival (Canada) / Médecins pour la Survie Mondiale (Canada) [PGS] (IP IB), 30 Cleary Ave, Ottawa, ON, K2A 4A1 (+1-613-233 1982) (pgsadmin@web.ca) (pgs.ca).

Project Ploughshares (RE AT ND RP DA), 140 Westmount Rd North, Waterloo, ON, N2L 3G6 (+1-519-888 6541) (fax 888 0018) (plough@ploughshares.ca) (www.ploughshares.ca).

Religions for Peace – Canada / Religions pour la Paix – Canada (RP RE PA), 3333 Queen Mary Rd 490-1, Montréal, QC, H3Z 1A2 (pascale.fremond@videotron.ca).

Trudeau Centre for Peace, Conflict and Justice (RE), Monk School of Global Affairs, University of Toronto, 1 Devonshire Place, Toronto, ON, M5S 3K7 (+1-416-946 0326) (pcj.programme@utoronto.ca) (www.munkschool.utoronto.ca/trudeaucentre).

United Nations Association in Canada / Association canadienne pour les Nations-Unies [UNAC/ACNU] (UN EL RE HR CD), 400 – 30 Metcalfe St, Ottawa, ON, K1P 5L4 (+1-613-232 5751) (fax 563 2455) (info@unac.org) (unac.org).

USCC Doukhobors (RP CD PA), Box 760, Grand Forks, BC, V0H 1H0 (+1-250-442 8252) (fax 442 3433) (info@usccdoukhobors.org) (www.usccdoukhobors.org). *Iskra.* Union of Spiritual Communities of Christ.

Women's International League for Peace and Freedom [WILPF] (WL), PO Box 365, 916 West Broadway, Vancouver, BC, V5Z 1K7 (+1-604-224 1517) (judydavis@telus.net).

World Federalist Movement – Canada / Mouvement Fédéraliste Mondial (Canada) (WF), Suite 207, 110 – 323 Chapel St, Ottawa, ON, K1N 7Z2 (+1-613-232 0647) (wfcnat@web.ca) (www.worldfederalistscanada.org). *Mondial.*

CHAD

Tchad Non-Violence [TNV] (WR FR), BP 1266, N'Djamena (astnv@yahoo.fr).

CHILE

Comité Nacional pro Defensa de la Flora y Fauna [CODEFF] (FE), Ernesto Reyes 035, Providencia, Santiago (+56-2-777 2534) (administra@codeff.cl) (www.codeff.cl).

Grupo de Objeción de Conciencia "Ni Casco Ni Uniforme" (WR), Bremen 585, Ñuñoa, Santiago (+56-2-556 6066) (objetores@yahoo.com) (nicasconiuniforme.wordpress.com).

Grupo de Objeción de Conciencia – Rompiendo Filas (WR), Prat 289 – Oficina 2-A, Temuco (rompiendofilas@entodaspartes.org).

Servicio Paz y Justicia – Chile [SERPAJ] (FR), Orella Nº 1015, Valparaíso (+56-32-215 8239) (serpaj@serpajchile.cl) (serpajchile.cl).

CHINA

China Committee on Religion and Peace [CCRP] (RP), 23 Taipingqiao St, Xichen District, Beijing 100811 (+86-10-6619 1655) (fax 6619 1645) (ccrp1994@hotmail.com) (www.cppcc.gov.cn/ccrp).

For explanation of codes and abbreviations, see introduction

CHINA

Friends of Nature [FON] (EL), Rm 406, Building C, Huazhan Guoji Gongyu, 12 Yumin Road, Chaoyang District, Beijing 100029 (+86-10-6523 2040) (office@fonchina.org) (www.fon.org.cn).

Greenpeace China (GP), 3/F – Julong Office Building – Block 7, Julong Gardens, 68 Xinzhong St, Dongcheng District, Beijing 100027 (+86-10-6554 6931) (fax 6554 6932) (greenpeace.cn@greenpeace.org) (www.greenpeace.org/china). See also under Hong Kong for head office.

COLOMBIA

Acción Colectiva de Objetores y Objetoras de Conciencia [ACOOC] (WR), Cr 19 – No 33A – 26/1, Bogotá (+57-1-560 5058) (objecion@objetoresbogota.org) (objetoresbogota.org).

Liga Internacional de Mujeres pro Paz y Libertad [LIMPAL] (WL), Calle 44 – No 19-28 – Of 201, Bogotá (+57-1-285 0062) (limpal@limpalcolombia.org) (limpalcolombia.org).

CONGO, DEMOCRATIC REPUBLIC OF

Cercle des Jeunes Leaders pour la Paix / Circle of Young Leaders for Peace (RP), Av Kwango – No 7, Kintambo Magasin, Ngaliema, Dist Lukunga, Kinshasa (+243-81-514 0938) (jcsaki2000@yahoo.fr).

Groupe Interconfessionnel de la Réconciliation / Kinshasa [GIR] (FR), see under Belgium.

Life & Peace Institute (CR RP), Bukavu (for postal address see under Rwanda) (pieter.vanholder@life-peace.org).

Peace & Conflict Resolution Project (CR), for postal address see under Rwanda (+243-993-463279) (peacecrp@yahoo.com) (www.peaceconflictresolutionproject.webs.com). Based in Bukavu.

COSTA RICA

Centro de Estudios Para la Paz [CEPPA] (RE), Apdo 8-4820, 1000 San José (+506-2234 0524) (fax) (info@ceppacr.org) (www.ceppacr.org).

Monteverde Friends Meeting (SF), Monteverde 5655, Puntarenas (+506-2645 5530) (fax 2645 5302) (MonteverdeQuakers@gmail.com) (MonteverdeQuakers.org).

Religions for Peace – Costa Rica (RP), Apdo Postal 7288, 1000 San Jose (eduardoenrique_69@msn.com).

CROATIA

Centar za Žene Žrtve Rata / Centre for Women War Victims – ROSA [CŽŽR] (CR HR), Kralja Držislava 2, 10000 Zagreb (+385-1-455 1142) (fax 455 1128) (cenzena@zamir.net) (www.czzzr.hr). Feminist, anti-militarist.

Centar Za Mir, Nenasilje i Ljudska Prava – Osijek / Centre for Peace, Nonviolence and Human Rights (CR HR PC RE), Trg Augusta Šenoe 1, 31000 Osijek (+385-31-206886) (fax 206889) (centar-za-mir@centar-za-mir.hr) (www.centar-za-mir.hr).

Centar za Mirovne Studije / Centre for Peace Studies [CMS] (WR CR RE HR), Selska cesta 112a, 10000 Zagreb (+385-1-482 0094) (fax) (cms@cms.hr) (www.cms.hr).

Dalmatinski Komitet za Ljudska Prava [DK] (HR), Trumbucac 19, 21000 Split (+385-21-482805) (dkomit@cryptolab.net) (dalmatinskikomitet.com). Dalmatian Committee for Human Rights.

CUBA

Movimiento Cubano por la Paz y la Soberanía de los Pueblos (WP), Calle C No 670, e/ 27 y 29, Vedado, Habana (+53-7-831 9429) (secretariat@movpaz.cu) (www.movpaz.cu).

CYPRUS

Conciliation – Peace Economics Network (CR), PO Box 20209, Nicosia 1665 (costas@highwaycommunications.com).

Hands Across the Divide – Women Building Bridges in Cyprus (HR CD CR DA), Ellispontos 10, Dasoupolis 2015, Nicosia (handsacrossthedivide@gmail.com) (www.handsacrossthedivide.org). Supports feminist values and demilitaristion.

Oikologiki Kinisi Kyprou / Ecological Movement of Cyprus (EL), TK 28948, Nicosia 2084 (+357-2251 8787) (fax 2251 2710) (ecological_movement@cytanet.com.cy) (www.ecologicalmovement.org.cy). *Ecologiki Enimerosi.*

Philoi tis Gis (Kypros) / Friends of the Earth (Cyprus) [FOE] (FE), PO Box 53411, 361B St Andrews St, Lemesos 3035 (+357-2534 7042) (fax 2534 7043) (contact@foecyprus.org) (www.foecyprus.org).

CYPRUS (NORTHERN)

Hands Across the Divide – Women Building Bridges in Cyprus (HR CD CR DA), see under Cyprus (www.handsacrossthedivide.org). Supports feminist values and demilitaristion.

CZECH REPUBLIC

České Mírové Hnutí / Czech Peace Movement (WP), Josefa Houdka 123, 15531 Praha (mirovehnuti@email.cz) (www.mirovehnuti.cz).

Hnutí DUHA (FE RA), Údolní 33, 60200 Brno (+420-5 4521 4431) (fax 5 4521 4429) (info@hnutiduha.cz) (hnutiduha.cz). *Evergreen.*

Lékari za Bezpečný Život na Zemi /
Physicians for Global Security (IP), c/o
Vaclav Stukavec, Jižní 222, 46801
Jablonec nad Nisou 8 (+420-603 364224)
(stukav@volny.cz).

Nezávislé Sociálne Ekologické Hnutí /
**Independent Socio-Ecological Movement
[NESEHNUTÍ]** (WR EL HR AT), trída Kpt
Jaroše 18, 60200 Brno (+420-5 4324 5342)
(brno@nesehnuti.cz) (nesehnuti.cz).
Social Ecological Movement.

Památník Mohyla Míru / **Cairn of Peace
Memorial** (RE), K Mohyle Míru 200, 66458
Peace (+420-54 424 4724)
(www.muzeumbrnenska.cz).

DENMARK

Aldrig Mere Krig [AMK] (WR AT IB),
Nørremarksvej 4, 6880 Tarm
(+45-9737 3163) (info@aldridmerekrig.dk)
(aldridmerekrig.dk).
Ikkevold.

Amnesty International (AI), Gammeltorv 8 –
5 sal, 1457 København K (+45-3345 6565)
(amnesty@amnesty.dk) (www.amnesty.dk).

**Center for Konfliktlosning / Danish Centre
for Conflict Resolution** (CR RE), Dronning
Olgas Vej 30, 2000 Frederiksberg
(+45-3520 0550) (center@konfliktloesning.dk)
(www.konfliktloesning.dk).

Danske Laeger Mod Kernevåben [DLMK]
(IP), Langdalsvej 40, 8220 Brabrand, Aarhus
(+45-8626 4717) (povl.revsbech@gmail.com)
(www.danskelaegermodkernevaaben.dk).
Läkare mot Kärnvapen.

FN-Forbundet (UN WF), Tordenskjoldsgade
25 st th, 1055 København K (+45-3346 4690)
(fnforbundet@fnforbundet.dk)
(www.fnforbundet.dk).

Green Cross Denmark (EL TW DA HR), Abel
Cathrines Gade 3 – 1 sal, 1654 København V
(+45-2639 1555) (kbi@greencross.dk)
(greencross.dk).

**Klimabevaegelsen i Danmark / Climate
Movement Denmark** (EL), c/o Thomas
Meinart Larsen, JC Christensens Gade 2A –
3TV, 2300 København S
(sek@klimabevaegelsen.dk)
(www.klimabevaegeksen.dk).

**Kvindernes Internationale Liga for Fred og
Frihed [KILFF]** (WL RE), Vesterbrogade 10
– 2, 1620 København V (+45-3323 1097)
(wilpfdk@gmail.com) (kvindefredsliga.dk).

NOAH / Friends of the Earth Denmark (FE),
Nørrebrogade 39 – 1, 2200 København N
(+45-3536 1212) (fax 3536 1217)
(noah@noah.dk) (www.noah.dk).

**Plums Fond for Fred, Økologi og
Baeredygtighed / Plums Foundation for
Peace, Ecology and Sustainability** (DA HR
EL), Dronningensgade 14, 1420 København
K (+45-3295 4417)
(plumsfond@plumsfond.dk).
Previously Danish Peace Foundation /
Fredsfonden.

Servas Danmark (SE), c/o Jan Degrauwe,
Højbakkevej 32, 9440 Aabybro (+45-2048
5087) (info@servas.dk) (www.servas.dk).

EAST TIMOR

**Haburas Foundation / Friends of the Earth
Timor Leste** (FE), PO Box 390, Dili
(+670-331 0103)
(haburaslorosae@yahoo.com)
(www.haburasfoundation.org).

ECUADOR

**Servicio Paz y Justicia del Ecuador [SER-
PAJ]** (WR RP), Casilla 17-03-1567, Quito
(+593-22-257 1521) (fax)
(serpaj@ecuanex.org.ec)
(www.serpaj.org.ec).

EGYPT

**Arab Organisation for Human Rights
[AOHR]** (HR), 91 Merghani St, Heliopolis,
Cairo 11341 (+20-2-2418 1396) (fax 2418
5346) (alaa.shalaby@aohr.net)
(www.aohr.net).

**No to Compulsory Military Service
Movement** (WR), [post should be sent via
the WRI office in London] (+49-1763-141
5934) (NoMilService@gmail.com)
(www.nomilservice.com).

EL SALVADOR

**Centro Salvadoreño de Tecnologia
Apropiada [CESTA]** (FE), Apdo 3065, San
Salvador (+503-2213 1400) (fax 2220 6479)
(cesta@cesta-foe.org.sv)
(www.cesta-foe.org.sv).

ESTONIA

Eestimaa Rohelised / Estonian Green Party
(EL), Postkast 4740, 13503 Tallinn
(+372-502 6816) (info@erakond.ee)
(www.erakond.ee).

United Nations Association of Estonia (UN),
Veski 42, 50409 Tartu (+372-527 1051)
(una.estonia@gmail.com) (www.una.ee).

FINLAND

**Ålands Fredsinstitut / Åland Islands Peace
Institute** (RE HR CR), PB 85, 22101
Mariehamn, Åland (+358-18-15570)
(peace@peace.ax) (www.peace.ax).

Committee of 100 / Sadankomitea (WR IB
ND AT), Rauhanasema, Veturitori, 00520
Helsinki (sadankomitea@sadankomitea.fi)
(www.sadankomitea.fi).

Greenpeace Finland (GP), Iso Roobertinkatu
20-22 A (5 frs), 00120 Helsinki (+358-9-6229
2200) (fax 6229 2222)
(info.finland@greenpeace.org)
(www.greenpeace.fi).

**Laajan Turvallisuuden Verkosto / Wider
Security Network [WISE]** (CR DA),
Siltasaarenkatu 4 – 7th floor, 00530 Helsinki
(+358-44-972 4669) (info@widersecurity.fi)
(www.widersecurity.fi). Formerly Civil Society
Conflict Prevention Network.

FINLAND

Maan Ystävät / Friends of the Earth (FE), Mechelininkatu 36 B 1, 00260 Helsinki (+358-45-886 3958) (fax -2-237 1670) (toimisto@maanystavat.fi) (www.maanystavat.fi).

Peace Union of Finland / Suomen Rauhanliitto / Finlands Fredsförbundet (IB FR ND AT RE), Peace Station, Veturitori, 00520 Helsinki (+358-9-7568 2828) (fax 147297) (rauhanliitto@rauhanliitto.fi).

Physicians for Social Responsibility / Lääkärin Sosiaalinen Vastuu / Läkarens Sociala Ansvar [PSR/LSV] (IP HR PA EL), Caloniuksenkatu 9 D 64, 00100 Helsinki (+358-45-350 8516) (lsv@lsv.fi) (www.lsv.fi).

SaferGlobe (RE AT CR), Siltasaarenkatu 4 – 7th floor, 00530 Helsinki (+358-40-778 8523) (toimisto@saferglobe.fi) (www.saferglobe.fi). *Peace and security think-tank.*

Sitoutumaton Vasemmisto / Independent Left (WR EL HR), Mannerheimintie 5B 7krs, 00100 Helsinki (sitvas-hallitus@helsinki.fi) (sitvasfi.wordpress.com).

Suomen Luonnonsuojeluliitto / Finnish Association for Nature Conservation [FANC] (EL), Itälahdenkatu 22-b A, 00210 Helsinki (+358-9-2280 8224) (toimisto@sll.fi) (www.sll.fi).

Suomen Rauhanpuolustajat / Finnish Peace Committee (IB WP TW), Hämeentie 48, 00500 Helsinki (+358-50-358 1441) (pulut@rauhanpuolustajat.fi) (www.rauhanpuolustajat.fi). *Rauhan Puolesta.*

Union of Conscientious Objectors / Aseistakieltäytyjäliitto [AKL] (WR), Rauhanasema, Veturitori 3, 00520 Helsinki (+358-40-836 2786) (toimisto@akl-web.fi) (www.akl-web.fi).

Women's International League for Peace and Freedom – Finnish Section [WILPF] (WL), PL 1174, 00101 Helsinki (wilpf@wilpf.fi) (wilpf.fi).

FRANCE

Action des Chrétiens pour l'Abolition de la Torture [ACAT] (HR), 7 rue Georges Lardennois, 75019 Paris (+33-14040 4243) (fax 14040 4244) (acat@acatfrance.fr) (www.acatfrance.fr).

Action des Citoyens pour le Désarmement Nucléaire [ACDN] (ND), 31 Rue du Cormier, 17100 Saintes (+33-673 507661) (contact@acdn.net) (www.acdn.net). *Opposes both military and civilian nukes.*

Alternatives Non-Violentes [ANV] (PA RE CR), Centre 308, 82 rue Jeanne d'Arc, 76000 Rouen (+33-235 752344) (contact@alternatives-non-violentes.org) (alternatives-non-violentes.org).

For explanation of codes and abbreviations, see introduction

Amis de la Terre – France (FE), Mundo M, 47 ave Pasteur, 93100 Montreuil (+33-14851 3222) (fax 14851 9512) (france@amisdelaterre.org) (www.amisdelaterre.org).

Association des Médecins Français pour la Prévention de la Guerre Nucléaire [AMF-PGN] (IP), 5 Rue Las Cases, 75007 Paris (+33-14336 7781) (revue@amfpgn.org) (amfpgn.org). *Médecine et Guerre Nucléaire.*

Association française pour les Nations Unies (UN), 26 Av Charles Floquet, 75007 Paris (+33-17716 2454) (contact@afnu.fr) (afnu.fr).

Brigades de Paix Internationales [PBI-France] (HR PO RE CD), 21 ter, rue Voltaire, 75011 Paris (+33-14373 4960) (pbi.france@free.fr) (www.pbi-france.org).

Centre de Ressources sur la Non-violence de Midi-Pyrénées (RE CR), 2 Allée du Limousin, 31770 Colomiers (+33-561 786680) (crnv.midi-pyrenees@wanadoo.fr) (www.non-violence-mp.org).

Centre Français d'Enregistrement des Citoyens du Monde (WF), 15 rue Victor Duruy, 75015 Paris (+33-14531 2999) (contact@citoyensdumonde.net) (www.citoyensdumonde.net). *Citoyens du Monde.*

Centre mondial de la Paix, des Libertés et des Droits de l'Homme (RE), Place Monseigneur, BP 10183, 55100 Verdun (+33-329 865500) (contact@cmpaix.eu) (www.cmpaix.eu).

Cesser d'Alimenter la Guerre / Stop Fuelling War [SFW] (AT RA), c/o Centre Quaker de Paris, 114 rue de Vaugirard, 75006 Paris (stopfuellingwar@gmail.com) (stopfuellingwar.org). *Countering the normalisation of the trade in arms.*

Coordination pour l'Éducation à la Non-violence et la Paix (RE), 148 rue du Faubourg Saint-Denis, 75010 Paris (+33-14633 4156) (education-nvp.org).

Greenpeace (GP), 13 rue d'Enghien, 75010 Paris (+33-18096 9696) (fax) (contact.fr@greenpeace.org) (www.greenpeace.org/france).

Groupement pour les Droits des Minorités [GDM] (HR), 212 rue St-Martin, 75003 Paris (+33-14575 0137) (fax 14579 8046) (yplasseraud@wanadoo.fr). *La Lettre du GDM.*

Institut de Recherche sur la Résolution Non-violente des Conflits [IRNC] (RE SD CR PA), 14 rue des Meuniers, 93100 Montreuil-sous-Bois (+33-14287 9469) (fax) (irnc@irnc.org) (www.irnc.org). *Alternatives Non-violentes.*

Ligue d'Amitié Internationale (CD), Les Champs Fleuris – Nº 4, 14 rue Maurice Boyau, 91220 Bretigny-sur-Orge (+33-160 853407) (www.ifl-france.org). *Affiliate of the International Friendship League.*

Ligue Internationale des Femmes pour la Paix et la Liberté – Section française [LIFPL/WILPF] (WL ND RE), 114 rue de Vaugirard, 75006 Paris (+33-14844 6711) (wilpf-france.net).

Mémorial de Caen Museum – Cité de l'Histoire pour la Paix / Centre for History and Peace (PO RE), Esplanade Eisenhower, BP 55026, 14050 Caen Cedex 4 (+33-231 060644) (fax 231 060670) (contact@memorial-caen.fr) (www.memorial-caen.fr).

Mouvement de la Paix (IB WP ND RE AT), 9 Rue Dulcie September, 93400 Saint-Ouen (+33-14012 0912) (national@mvtpaix.org) (www.mvtpaix.org). *Planète Paix; La Paix en Mouvement.*

Mouvement International de la Réconciliation [MIR] (FR WR), 68 rue de Babylone, 75007 Paris (+33-14753 8405) (mirfr@club-internet.fr) (www.mirfrance.org). *Cahiers de la Réconciliation.*

Mouvement pour une Alternative Non-violente [MAN] (WR SD CR AT RA), 47 ave Pasteur, 93100 Montreuil (+33-14544 4825) (man@nonviolence.fr) (www.nonviolence.fr).

Non-Violence Actualité **[NVA]** (CR HR RE), Centre de Ressources sur la Gestion non-violente des Relations et des Conflits, BP 241, 45202 Montargis cedex (+33-238 936722) (fax 975 385985) (Nonviolence.Actualite@wanadoo.fr) (www.nonviolence-actualite.org). 6 yrly, Eu43 pa.

Non-Violence XXI (PA RE), 47 Ave Pasteur, 93100 Montreuil (+33-14548 3762) (fax 14544 4825) (coordination@nonviolence21.org) (www.nonviolence21.org).

Pax Christi France (PC), 5 rue Morère, 75014 Paris (+33-14449 0636) (accueil@paxchristi.cef.fr) (www.paxchristi.cef.fr). *Journal de la Paix.*

Réseau "Sortir du Nucléaire" / Network for a Nuclear Phase-Out (EL RA PO), 9 rue Dumenge, 69317 Lyon cedex 04 (+33-47828 2922) (fax 47207 7004) (contact@sortirdunucleaire.org) (www.sortirdunucleaire.org). Network of groups in France against nuclear energy.

Religions pour la Paix (RP), 8 bis Rue Jean Bart, 75006 Paris (Religionspourlapaix@yahoo.fr) (religionspourlapaix.org).

Service Civil International [SCI-F] (SC), 75 rue du Chevalier Français, 59800 Lille (+33-320 552258) (sci@sci-france.org) (www.sci-france.org).

Silence (EL AL PA PO), 9 rue Dumenge, 69317 Lyon cedex 04 (+33-478 395533) (www.revuesilence.net). Mthly, Eu55 pa.

Société Religieuse des Amis (SF), Centre Quaker International, 114 Rue de Vaugirard, 75006 Paris (+33-14548 7423) (assembleedefrance@gmail.com) (www.QuakersEnFrance.org). *Lettre des Amis.*

Solidarités Jeunesses (WC CD), 10 Rue du 8 Mai 1945, 75010 Paris (+33-15526 8877) (fax 15326 0326) (secretariat@solidaritesjeunesses.org) (www.solidaritesjeunesses.org).

Sortir de la Violence – France (FR CR RE), 11 rue de la Chaise, 75007 Paris (sdv-France@sortirdelaviolence.org) (www.sortirdelaviolence.org).

Union Pacifiste de France [UPF] (WR AT), BP 40196, 75624 Paris cédex 13 (+33-14586 0875) (union.pacifiste@orange.fr) (www.unionpacifiste.org). *Union Pacifiste.*

FRENCH POLYNESIA

Ligue Internationale des Femmes pour la Paix et la Liberté – Section Polynésienne [LIFPL] (WL), Faaone pk 49.2, Côté Montagne, 98713 Faaone, Tahiti (+689-264729) (wilpf.polynesie@gmail.com).

GEORGIA

Sakhartvelos Mtsvaneta Modzraoba / Green Movement of Georgia (FE). 55 Kandelaki St, 0160 Tbilisi (+995-32-386978) (info@greens.ge) (www.greens.ge).

War Resisters' International – Georgian Section (WR), 45 Kavtaradze St – Apt 45, Tbilisi 0186 (+995-577-117878) (uchananua@yahoo.com).

GERMANY

Aktion Sühnezeichen Friedensdienste [ASF] (WC RP HR CD), Auguststr 80, 10117 Berlin-Mitte (+49-30-2839 5184) (fax 2839 5135) (asf@asf-ev.de) (www.asf-ev.de). *Zeichen.*

Aktion Völkerrecht / International Law Campaign (WF ND CD), c/o Peter Kolbe, Werderstr 36, 69120 Heidelberg (buero@a-vr.org) (www.aktion-voelkerrecht.de).

Aktionsgemeinschaft Dienst für den Frieden [AGDF] (WC PA RP), Endenicher Str 41, 53115 Bonn (+49-228-249990) (fax 249 9920) (agdf@friedensdienst.de) (www.friedensdienst.de). Voluntary service co-ordination agency.

Amnesty International (AI), Zinnowitzer Str, 10115 Berlin (+49-30-420 2480) (fax 4202 48448) (info@amnesty.de) (www.amnesty.de). *ai-Journal.*

Anti-Kriegs-Museum / Anti-War Museum (WR), Brüsseler Str 21, 13353 Berlin (+49-30-4549 0110) (Anti-Kriegs-Museum@gmx.de) (www.anti-kriegs-museum.de).

For explanation of codes and abbreviations, see introduction

GERMANY

Arbeitsgemeinschaft für Friedens- und Konfliktforschung / German Association for Peace and Conflict Studies [AFK] (RE), c/o Fakultät Gesellschaft und Ökonomie, Hochschule Rhein-Waal, 47533 Kleve (+49-2821-806739793) (fax 8067 3162) (afk-gf@afk-web.de) (afk-web.de).

Archiv Aktiv für gewaltfreie Bewegungen (WR RE EL), Normannenweg 17-21, 20537 Hamburg (+49-40-430 2046) (email@archiv-aktiv.de) (www.archiv-aktiv.de).

ausgestrahlt (EL RA ND), Grosse Bergstr 189, 22767 Hamburg (+49-40-2531 8940) (fax 2531 8944) (info@ausgestrahlt.de) (www.ausgestrahlt.de). .ausgestrahlt-magazin. Anti-nuclear direct action network.

Bürgermeister für den Frieden in Deutschland und Österreich (CD ND DA), c/o Landeshauptstadt Hannover, Büro Oberbürgermeister, Trammplatz 2, 30159 Hannover (+49-511-1684 1446) (fax 1684 4025) (mayorsforpeace@hannover-stadt.de) (www.mayorsforpeace.de).

Berghof Foundation (CR RE), Altensteinstr 48a, 14195 Berlin (+49-30-844 1540) (fax 8441 5499) (info@berghof-conflictresearch.org) (www.berghof-conflictresearch.org). Works to prevent political and social violence.

Bund für Soziale Verteidigung [BSV] (WR SD CD), Schwarzer Weg 8, 32423 Minden (+49-571-29456) (fax 23019) (office@soziale-verteidigung.de) (www.soziale-verteidigung.de). *Soziale Verteidigung.*

Bund für Umwelt und Naturschutz Deutschland [BUND] (FE), Am Köllnischen Park 1, 10179 Berlin (+49-30-275 8640) (fax 2758 6440) (info@bund.net) (www.bund.net).

Connection eV (PA HR), Von-Behring-Str 110, 63075 Offenbach (+49-69-8237 5534) (fax 8237 5535) (office@Connection-eV.org) (www.Connection-eV.org). *KDV im Krieg.* International network for COs and deserters.

Deutsch-Russischer Austausch / Nyemyetsko-Russkiy Obmyen [DRA] (CD), Badstr 44, 13357 Berlin (+49-30-446 6800) (fax 4466 8010) (info@austausch.org) (www.austausch.org). German-Russian Exchange.

Deutsche Friedens-Bücherei (RE PA EL), Postfach 101361, 66013 Saarbrücken (+33-387 950018).

Deutsche Friedensgesellschaft – Internationale der Kriegsdienstgegner [DFG-IdK] (WR DA), Jungfrauenthal 37, 20149 Hamburg (+49-40-453433) (fax 4440 5270) (mail@dfg-idk.de) (www.dfg-idk.de). *Rundbrief.*

Deutsche Friedensgesellschaft – Vereinigte Kriegsdienstgegner [DFG-VK] (WR IB RE), Werastr 10, 70182 Stuttgart (+49-711-5189 2626) (fax 2486 9622) (office@dfg-vk.de) (www.dfg-vk.de).

Deutsche Gesellschaft für die Vereinten Nationen [DGVN] (UN), Zimmerstr 26/27, 10969 Berlin (+49-30-259 3750) (fax 2593 7529) (info@dgvn.de) (www.dgvn.de). *Vereinte Nationen.*

Deutsche Sektion der IPPNW / Ärzte in sozialer Verantwortung (IPPNW Germany) (IP AT DA), Körtestr 10, 10967 Berlin (+49-30-698 0740) (fax 693 8166) (kontakt@ippnw.de) (www.ippnw.de). *Forum.*

Deutscher Friedensrat / German Peace Council (WP), Platz der Vereinten Nationen 7, 10249 Berlin (+49-30-426 5290) (fax 4201 7338) (saefkow-berlin@t-online.de) (www.deutscher-friedensrat.de).

Deutsches Bündnis Kindersoldaten (HR PA), c/o Kindernothilfe, Düsseldorfer Landstr 180, 47249 Duisburg (+49-203-778 9111) (fax 778 9118) (info@kindernothilfe.de) (www.kindernothilfe.de). Campaigns against use of child soldiers.

DFG-VK Hessen (WR), Mühlgasse 13, 60486 Frankfurt/Main (+49-69-431440) (dfgvkhessen@t-online.de) (www.dfg-vk-hessen.de).

Forum Ziviler Friedensdienst / Civil Peace Service Forum [forumZFD] (SF CR RE), Am Kölner Brett 8, 50825 Köln (+49-221-912 7320) (fax 9127 3299) (kontakt@forumZFD.de) (www.forumZFD.de). Offers conflict transformation training & courses.

Friedensausschuss der Religiösen Gesellschaft der Freunde (Quäker) (SF PA CR DA RA), via Helga Tempel, Föhrenstieg 8, 22926 Ahrensburg (+49-4102-53337) (helga.tempel@gmx.de). *Quäker.*

Gandhi Information Centre (PA RE), Postfach 210109, 10501 Berlin (mkgandhi@snafu.de) (www.nonviolent-resistance.info). Previously Gandhi-Informations-Zentrum.

GandhiServe Foundation (RE HR), Rathausstr 51a, 12105 Berlin (+49-1523-398 7220) (fax 3212-100 3676) (mail@gandhimail.org) (www.gandhiservefoundation.org).

Gewaltfreie Aktion Atomwaffen Abschaffen / Nonviolent Action to Abolish Nuclear Weapons [GAAA] (ND RA), c/o Marion Küpker, Beckstr 14, 20357 Hamburg (+49-40-430 7332) (marion.kuepker@gaaa.org) (www.gaaa.org).

Graswurzelrevolution (WR AL RA), Breul 43, 48143 Münster (+49-251-482 9057) (fax 482 9032) (redaktion@graswurzel.net) (www.graswurzel.net).

Greenpeace (GP), Hongkongstr 10, 20457 Hamburg (+49-40-306180) (fax 3061 8100) (mail@greenpeace.de) (www.greenpeace.de). Berlin: +49-30-308 8990.

Heidelberger Institut für Internationale Konfliktforschung [HIIK] (RE), Bergheimer Str 58, 69115 Heidelberg (+49-6221-542863) (info@hiik.de). *Conflict Barometer.*

Initiative Musiker/innen gegen Auftritte der Bundeswehrmusikkorps (PA), c/o Dietmar Parchow, Austr 77, 72669 Unterensingen (musikergegenmilitaermusik@idk-berlin.de) (musiker-gegen-militaermusik.jimdo.com). Against public and church use of military bands.

Institut für Friedensarbeit und Gewaltfreie Konfliktaustragung [IFGK] (WR RE CR), Hauptstr 35, 55491 Wahlenau/Hunsrück (+49-6543-980096) (info@dr-barbara-mueller.com) (www.ifgk.de). *IFGK Working Papers.*

Institut für Friedenspädagogik Tübingen/ Institute for Peace Education Tübingen (RE CR), Corrensstr 12, 72076 Tübingen (+49-7071-920510) (fax 920 5111) (info-tuebingen@berghof-foundation.org) (www.friedenspaedagogik.de). A branch of the Berghof Foundation.

Institute for International Assistance and Solidarity [IFIAS] (IB CD HR ND), Postfach 170420, 53027 Bonn (+49-228-721 6864) (fax 721 6866) (drake@ifias.eu) (www.ifias.eu). Also in Belgium.

Internationale der Kriegsdienstgegner/innen [IDK] (WR AL), Postfach 280312, 13443 Berlin (info@idk-berlin.de) (www.idk-info.net).

Internationale Frauenliga für Frieden und Freiheit [IFFF] (WL), Haus der Demokratie und Menschenrechte, Greifswalder Str 4, 10405 Berlin (info@wilpf.de) (wilpf.de).

Internationale Jugendgemeinschaftsdienste [IJGD] (WC EL CD), Kasernenstr 48, 53111 Bonn (+49-228-228 0014) (fax 228 0010) (workcamps@ijgd.de) (www.ijgd.de). Workcamps and volunteering in Germany and abroad.

Juristen und Juristinnen gegan Atomare, Biologische und Chemische Waffen – IALANA Deutschland (ND), Marienstr 19-20, 10117 Berlin (+49-30-2065 4857) (fax 2065 4858) (info@ialana.de) (www.ialana.de).

Kampagne gegen Wehrpflicht, Zwangsdienste und Militär (PA RA SD), Kopenhagener Str 71, 10437 Berlin (+49-30-4401 3025) (fax 4401 3029) (info@kampagne.de) (www.kampagne.de).

Komitee für Grundrechte und Demokratie (HR CD RA PA), Aquinostr 7-11 (HH), 50670 Köln (+49-221-972 6920) (fax 972 6931) (info@grundrechtekomitee.de) (www.grundrechtekomitee.de).

Kooperation für den Frieden (DA ND RE), Römerstr 88, 53111 Bonn (+49-228-692905) (fax 692906) (info@koop-frieden.de) (www.koop-frieden.de). Networking organisation in German peace movement.

KURVE Wustrow – Bildungs- und Begegnungsstätte für gewaltfreie Aktion (FR PA CR HR RE), Kirchstr 14, 29462 Wustrow (+49-5843-98710) (fax 987111) (info@kurvewustrow.org) (www.kurvewustrow.org).

Netzwerk Friedenskooperative (ND PA AT), Römerstr 88, 53111 Bonn (+49-228-692904) (fax 692906) (friekoop@friedenskooperative.de) (www.friedenskooperative.de). *Friedensforum.*

Netzwerk Friedenssteuer [NWFS] (TR), Krennerweg 12, 81479 München (+49-8062-725 2395) (fax 725 2396) (info@netzwerk-friedenssteuer.de) (www.netzwerk-friedenssteuer.de). *Friedenssteuer-Nachrichten.*

Ohne Rüstung Leben (AT CR PA ND DA), Arndtstr 31, 70197 Stuttgart (+49-711-608396) (fax 608357) (orl@gaia.de) (www.ohne-ruestung-leben.de). *Ohne Rüstung Leben-Informationen.*

Pax Christi Deutsche Sektion (PC), Hedwigskirchgasse 3, 10117 Berlin (+49-30-2007 6780) (fax 2007 67819) (sekretariat@paxchristi.de) (www.paxchristi.de).

Peace Brigades International Deutscher Zweig [PBI] (CR HR PA), Bahrenfelder Str 101 A, 22765 Hamburg (+49-40-3890 4370) (fax 3890 43729) (info@pbi-deutschland.de) (www.pbideutschland.de).

Pestizid Aktions-Netzwerk [PAN Germany] (EL), Nernstweg 32, 22765 Hamburg (+49-40-3991 9100) (fax 3991 91030) (info@pan-germany.org) (www.pan-germany.org).

Projekt Alternativen zur Gewalt / AVP Germany [PAG] (CR), Kaliweg 31, 30952 Ronnenberg (+49-5109-7695) (fax 1014) (info@pag.de) (www.pag.de). Part of Alternatives to Violence network.

RüstungsInformationsBüro [RIB-Büro] (AT PA RE), Stühlinger Str 7, 79016 Freiburg (+49-761-767 8088) (fax 767 8089) (rib@rib-ev.de) (www.rib-ev.de). Campaign against small arms.

RfP Deutschland / Religions for Peace (RP), c/o Franz Brendle, Im Schellenkönig 61, 70184 Stuttgart (+49-711-539 0209) (fax 505 8648) (rfp@r-f-p.de) (www.religionsforpeace.de). *Informationen.*

Servas Germany (SE), O'Swaldtstr 32, 22111 Hamburg (mail@servas.de) (www.servas.de).

Stiftung die schwelle / Schwelle Foundation – Beiträge zum Frieden (CR TW RE HR), Wachmannstr 79, 28209 Bremen (+49-421-303 2575) (stiftung@dieschwelle.de) (www.dieschwelle.de).

Terre des Femmes – Menschenrechte für die Frau eV (HR), Brunnenstr 128, 13355 Berlin (+49-30-4050 46990) (fax 4050 469999) (info@frauenrechte.de) (www.frauenrechte.de).

GERMANY

Versöhnungsbund [VB] (FR IB PA),
Schwarzer Weg 8, 32423 Minden
(+49-571-850875) (fax 829 2387)
(vb@versoehnungsbund.de)
(www.versoehnungsbund.de).

GHANA

**Anam Foundation for Peacebuilding
[AF4PB]** (CR PO), Box TL 392, Tamale
(+233-20-276 8844) (info@anam4peace.org)
(www.anam4peace.org).
United Nations Association of Ghana (UN),
Private Mail Bag, Ministries Post Office,
Accra (+233-30-376 8858)
(office@unaghana.org) (www.unaghana.org).

GREECE

Diethnis Amnistia / Amnesty International
(AI), 30 Sina Street, 10672 Athinai
(+30-210 3600 628) (fax 210 3638 016)
(athens@amnesty.org.gr)
(www.amnesty.org.gr). *Martyries.*
**Elliniki Epitropi gia ti Thiethni Yphesi kai
Eirene / Greek Committee for International
Detente and Peace [EEDYE]** (WP),
Themistokleous 48, 10681 Athinai
(+30-210 3844 853) (fax 210 3844 879)
(eedye@otenet.gr) (eedye.gr).
**Enomenes Koinonies ton Valkanion /
United Societies of the Balkans [USB]** (CD
CR HR PO), Adamanas 9, Agios Paulos,
55438 Thessaloniki (+30-231 0215 629) (fax)
(info@usbngo.gr) (www.usbngo.gr).
Greenpeace Greece (GP), Kolonou 78, 10437
Athinai (+30-210 3840 774)
(fax 210 3804 008)
(gpgreece@greenpeace.org)
(www.greenpeace.org/greece).
**Kinisi Ethelonton / Volunteer Movement
[SCI-Hellas]** (SC), Pythagora 12, Neos
Kosmos, 11743 Athinai (+30-215 5406 504)
(info@sci.gr) (www.sci.gr).
Oikologoi Prasinoi / Ecologist Greens (EL),
Plateia Eleftherias 14, 10553 Athinai
(+30-210 3306 301) (fax 210 3241 825)
(ecogreen@otenet.gr) (www.ecogreens.gr).
Green Party.
**Syndhesmos Antirrision Syneidhisis /
Association of Greek Conscientious
Objectors [SAS]** (WR), Tsamadou 13A,
10683 Athinai (+30-694 4542 228)
(fax 210 4622 753) (greekCO@hotmail.com)
(www.antirrisies.gr).

HONG KONG

**Alternatives to Violence Project – AVP
Hong Kong** (CR PO), 12a Shun Ho Tower,
24-30 Ice House St, Central
(avphongkong@gmail.com)
(www.avphongkong.org).
Amnesty International Hong Kong (AI), Unit
3D, Best-O-Best Commercial Centre, 32-36
Ferry St, Kowloon (+852-2300 1250)
(fax 2782 0583) (admin-hk@amnesty.org.hk)
(www.amnesty.org.hk).
**Association for the Advancement of
Feminism [AAF]** (HR), Flats 119-120, Lai
Yeung House, Lei Cheng Uk Estate, Kowloon
(+852-2720 0891) (fax 2720 0205)
(aaf@aaf.org.hk) (www.aaf.org.hk). *Nuliu.*
Greenpeace China (GP), 8/F Pacific Plaza,
410-418 Des Voeux Rd West
(+852-2854 8300) (fax 2745 2426)
(enquiry.hk@greenpeace.org)
(www.greenpeace.org/china).
Also Beijing office: see under China.
**Human Rights in China – Hong Kong Office
[HRIC]** (HR), GPO, PO Box 1778
(+852-2701 8021) (hrichk@hrichina.org)
(www.hrichina.org).
Main office in New York (+1-212-239 4495).

HUNGARY

ACAT-Hungary (HR), c/o Csaba Kabódi,
Eötvös University, Egyetem Tér 1-3, 1364
Budapest (+36-1-252 5961) (fax)
(kabodi@ajk.elte.hu).
Bocs Foundation (FR EL TW), Pf 7, 8003
Székesfehérvár (m@bocs.hu)
(www.bocs.hu). *Bocsmagazin.*
**Magyar Orvosmozgalom a Nukleáris
Háború Megelőzéséért** (IP), c/o Zita Makoi,
Hegedus Gy u 48, 1133 Budapest
(zita.makoi@gmail.com).
**Magyar Természetvédők Szövetsége
[MTVSZ]** (FE), Ulloi U 91B – III/21, 1091
Budapest (info@mtvsz.hu) (www.mtvsz.hu).

ICELAND

Amnesty International (AI), Thingholtsstraeti
27, 101 Reykjavík (+354-511 7900)
(fax 511 7901) (amnesty@amnesty.is)
(www.amnesty.is).
Peace 2000 Institute (CR RE), Vogasel 1,
109 Reykjavík (+354-557 1000) (fax 496
2005) (info@peace2000.org)
(peace2000.org). Offices also in Britain, USA.
**Samtök Hernadarandstaedinga / Campaign
Against Militarism** (WR ND DA), Njalsgata
87, 101 Reykjavík (+354-554 0900)
(sha@fridur.is) (fridur.is). *Dagfari.*

INDIA

**All India Peace and Solidarity Organisation
[AIPSO]** (WP), c/o AIPSO West Bengal, 5
Sarat Ghosh St (behind Entally Market),
Kolkota 700014 (bengalaipso@gmail.com)
(www.aipsowb.org).
Anglican Pacifist Fellowship [APF] (RP), c/o
John Nagella, Opp SBI Colony, AT
Agraharam, Guntur 552004, Andhra Pradesh.
Anuvrat Global Organisation [ANUVIBHA]
(IB EL ND PO CR), B01-02, Anuvibha Jaipur
Kendra, opp Gaurav Tower, Malviya Nagar
302017, Rajasthan (+91-141-404 9714)
(slgandhi@hotmail.com) (www.anuvibha.in).

For explanation of codes and abbreviations,
see introduction

Atheist Centre (HR RA), Benz Circle, Patamata, Vijayawada 520010, AP (+91-866-247 2330) (fax 248 4850) (atheistcentre@yahoo.com) (www.atheistcentre.in). *Atheist.*

Bombay Sarvodaya Friendship Centre (FR WC SF), 701 Sainath Estate, Opp Lokmanya Vidyalaya, Nilam Nagar-II, Mulund East, Mumbai 400081 (+91-22-2563 1022) (danielm@mtnl.net.in).

Centre for Peace and Development (AT ND RE TW EL), 12/1 BT Rd "A" Cross, Chamarajapet, Bangalore 560018 (+91-80-4153 8790).

Coalition for Nuclear Disarmament and Peace [CNDP] (ND), A-124/6 – First Floor, Katwaria Sarai, New Delhi 110016 (+91-11-6566 3958) (fax 2651 7814) (cndpindia@gmail.com) (www.cndpindia.com). Network of 200 organisations.

Ekta Parishad (HR PO TW), 2/3A – Second Floor – Jungpura-A, New Delhi 10014 (+91-11-2437 3998) (ektaparishad@gmail.com) (www.ektaparishad.com). Federation of thousands of community organisations.

Friends of the Gandhi Museum (RE EL PO), B-4 Puru Society, Airport Rd, Lohegaon, Pune 411032 (+91-937 120 1138) (satyagrahi2000@gmail.com).

Gandhi Book Centre / Mumbai Sarvodaya Mandal (PO), 299 Tardeo Rd, Nana Chowk, Mumbai 400007 (+91-22-2387 2061) (info@mkgandhi.org) (www.mkgandhi.org).

Gandhi Research Foundation (RE), Gandhi Teerth, Jain Hills PO Box 118, Jalgaon 425001, Maharashtra (+91-257-226 0011) (fax 226 1133) (gandhiexam@gandhifoundation.net) (www.gandhifoundation.net).

Gandhian Society Villages Association (WR), Amaravathy Pudur PO, Pasumpon District, Tamil Nadu 623301 (+91-8645-83234).

Greenpeace India (GP), 60 Wellington Rd, Richmond Town, Bangalore 560025, Karnataka (+91-80-2213 1899) (fax 4115 4862) (supporter.services.in@greenpeace.org) (www.greenpeace.org/india). Regional Office in Delhi (+91-11-6666 5000).

Gujarat Vidyapeeth (RE), Ashram Rd (near Income tax), Ahmedabad 380014 (+91-79-2754 0746) (fax 2754 2547) (registrar@gujaratvidyapith.org) (www.gujaratvidyapith.org). Gandhian study centre.

Indian Doctors for Peace and Development [IDPD] (IP), 139-E Kitchlu Nagar, Ludhiana 141001, Punjab (+91-161-230 0252) (fax 230 4360) (idpd2001@yahoo.com) (www.idpd.org).

Nagaland Peace Centre (PA CR), D Block, Kohima Town, PO Kohima 797001, Nagaland (+91-370-229 1400).

National Gandhi Museum and Library (RE), Rajghat, New Delhi 110002 (+91-11-2331 1793) (fax 2332 8310) (gandhimuseumdelhi@gmail.com) (www.gandhimuseum.org). Has collection of original relics, books, etc.

Organisation for Nuclear Disarmament, World Peace and Environment [ONDAW-PE] (ND EL), 11 Gautam Palli, Lucknow 226001, UP (+91-522-223 5659) (ammarrizvi505@yahoo.com).

People's Movement Against Nuclear Energy – WISE India [PMANE] (EL ND), 42/27 Esankai Mani Veethy, Prakkai Road Jn, Nagercoil 629002, Tamil Nadu (drspudayakumar@yahoo.com). Linked to World Information Service on Energy.

Swadhina / Independence (WR), 34/C Bondel Rd, Ballygunge, Kolkata 700019 (+91-33-3245 1730) (mainoffice.swadhina@gmail.com) (www.swadhina.org.in).

Tibetan Centre for Human Rights and Democracy (FR HR), Narthang Building – Top Floor, Gangchen Kyishong, Dharamsala, HP 176215 (+91-1892-223363) (fax 225874) (office@tchrd.org) (www.tchrd.org). Works for human rights of Tibetans in Tibet.

Vikas Adhyayan Kendra / Centre for Development Studies (HR TW), D-1 Shivdham, 62 Link Rd. Malad (West), Mumbai 400064 (+91-22-2882 2850) (fax 2889 8941) (vak@bom3.vsnl.net.in) (www.vakindia.org). *Facts Against Myths.*

War Resisters of India/West (WR), c/o Swati & Michael, Juna Mozda, Dediapada, Dt Narmada, Gujarat 393040 (+91-2649-290249) (mozdam@gmail.com).

Women's International League for Peace and Freedom – India [WILPF] (WL), c/o Peace Research Centre, Gujatat Vidyapith, Ahmedabad 380014.

IRAN

Iranian Physicians for Social Responsibility [PSR-Iran] (IP), PO Box 11155-18747, Tehran Peace Museum, Parke shahr, Tehran (+98-21-6675 6945) (fax 6693 9992) (info@irpsr.org).

IRELAND, NORTHERN

NOTE: Organisations working on an all-Ireland basis (ie covering both the Republic of Ireland and Northern Ireland), with their office address in the Irish Republic, will be found listed there. Similarly, groups operating on a United Kingdom-wide basis (ie covering both Britain and Northern Ireland), with a British-based office, will be found listed under Britain.

Amnesty International – NI Region [AI-NI] (AI), 397 Ormeau Rd, Belfast BT7 (+44-28-9064 3000) (fax 9069 0989) (nireland@amnesty.org.uk) (www.amnesty.org.uk).

IRELAND, Northern

Bahá'í Council for Northern Ireland (RP), Apt 4, 2 Lower Windsor Ave, Belfast BT9 (+44-28-9016 0457) (bcni@bahai.org.uk) (www.bahaicouncil-ni.org.uk).

Centre for Democracy and PeaceBuilding [CDPB] (HR CR), 46 Hill St, Belfast BT1 2LB (info@democracyandpeace.org) (democracyandpeace.org). Sharing peace-building expertise internationally.

Children are Unbeatable! Alliance (HR), Unit 9, 40 Montgomery Rd, Belfast BT6 (+44-28-9040 1290) (carolconlin@btinternet.com) (www.childrenareunbeatable.org.uk). For abolition of all physical punishment.

Christian Aid Ireland (TW), Linden House, Beechill Business Park, 96 Beechill Rd, Belfast BT8 7QN (+44-28-9064 8133) (belfast@christian-aid.org) (www.christianaid.ie).

Co-operation Ireland (CD), 5 Weavers Court Business Park, Linfield Rd, Belfast BT12 (+44-28-9032 1462) (info@cooperationireland.org) (www.cooperationireland.org). Works for tolerance and acceptance of differences.

Committee on the Administration of Justice [CAJ] (HR), Community House, Citylink Business Park, 6A Albert St, Belfast BT12 (+44-28-9031 6000) (info@caj.org.uk) (www.caj.org.uk). *Just News.*

Corrymeela Community (RP), 83 University St, Belfast BT7 1HP (+44-28-9050 8080) (fax 9050 8070) (belfast@corrymeela.org) (www.corrymeela.org). *Corrymeela.*

Friends of the Earth – NI (FE), 7 Donegall Street Place, Belfast BT1 2FN (+44-28-9023 3488) (fax 9024 7556) (foe-ni@foe.co.uk) (www.foe.co.uk/ni).

Global Peacebuilders (CR), c/o Springboard Opportunities, 2nd Floor, 7 North St, Belfast BT1 1NH (+44-28-9031 5111) (fax 9031 3171) (james@springboard-opps.org) (www.globalpeacebuilders.org).

Green Party in Northern Ireland (EL), 1st Floor, 76 Abbey St, Bangor BT20 4JB (+44-28-9145 9110) (info@greenpartyni.org) (www.greenpartyni.org).

Healing Through Remembering [HTR] (RE), Unit 2.2, Bryson House, 28 Bedford St, Belfast BT2 7FE (+44-28-9023 8844) (info@healingthroughremembering.org) (www.healingthroughremembering.org).

Institute for Conflict Research [ICR] (RE CR HR), North City Business Centre – Unit 12-14, 2 Duncairn Gdns, Belfast BT15 2GG (+44-28-9074 2682) (info@conflictresearch.org.uk) (www.conflictresearch.org.uk).

Institute for the Study of Conflict Transformation and Social Justice [ISCT-SJ] (RE CR), Queen's University Belfast, 19 University Sq, Belfast BT7 (+44-28-9097 3609) (ctsj@qub.ac.uk).

Irish Network for Nonviolent Action Training and Education [INNATE] (WR RA FR), c/o 16 Ravensdene Park, Belfast BT6 0DA (+44-28-9064 7106) (fax) (innate@ntlworld.com) (www.innatenonviolence.org). *Nonviolent News.*

Northern Ireland Community Relations Council [CRC] (CR PO RE), 2nd Floor, Equality House, 7-9 Shaftesbury Sq, Belfast BT2 7DP (+44-28-9022 7500) (info@nicrc.org.uk) (www.community-relations.org.uk).

Northern Ireland Council for Integrated Education [NICIE] (PO HR CD RE), 25 College Gdns, Belfast BT9 (+44-28-9097 2910) (fax 9097 2919) (info@nicie.org.uk) (www.nicie.org.uk).

Oxfam Ireland (TW), 115 North St, Belfast (+44-28-9023 0220) (fax 9023 7771) (info@oxfamireland.org) (www.oxfamireland.org).

Peace People (FR CD HR), 224 Lisburn Rd, Belfast BT9 6GE (+44-28-9066 3465) (info@peacepeople.com) (www.peacepeople.com).

Quaker Service (SF), 541 Lisburn Rd, Belfast BT9 7GQ (+44-28-9020 1444) (info@quakerservice.com) (www.quakerservice.com).

The Junction (CR PO), 8-14 Bishop St, Derry/Londonderry BT48 6PW (+44-28-7136 1942) (info@thejunction-ni.org) (thejunction-ni.org). Community relations, civic empowerment.

TIDES Training (CR), 174 Trust, Duncairn Complex, Duncairn Ave, Belfast BT14 6BP (+44-28-9075 1686) (info@tidestraining.org) (www.tidestraining.org).

Tools for Solidarity – Ireland (TW PO), 55A Sunnyside St, Belfast BT7 (+44-28-9543 5972) (fax) (tools.belfast@myphone.coop) (www.toolsforsolidarity.com). *Solidarity.*

Transitional Justice Institute [TJI] (RE), Ulster University – Jordanstown Campus, Shore Rd, Newtownabbey BT37 (+44-28-9036 6202) (fax 9036 8962) (transitionaljustice@ulster.ac.uk) (www.transitionaljustice.ulster.ac.uk). Also Magee Campus, Londonderry.

IRELAND, REPUBLIC OF

Amnesty International Ireland (AI), Sean MacBride House, 48 Fleet St, Dublin 2 (+353-1-863 8300) (fax 671 9338) (info@amnesty.ie) (www.amnesty.ie). *Amnesty Ireland.*

Chernobyl Children International (PO EL HR), 1A The Stables, Alfred St, Cork City (+353-21-455 8774) (fax 450 5564) (info@chernobyl-ireland.com) (www.chernobyl-international.com).

Co-operation Ireland [CI] (CD), Port Centre, Alexandra Rd, Dublin 1 (+353-1-819 7692) (fax 894 4962) (info@cooperationireland.org) (www.cooperationireland.org). Works for tolerance and acceptance of differences.

Comhlámh – Development Workers and Volunteers in Global Solidarity (TW HR), 12 Parliament St, Dublin 2 (+353-1-478 3490) (info@comhlamh.org) (www.comhlamh.org). Action and education for global justice.

Dublin Quaker Peace Committee (SF), c/o Quaker House, Stocking Lane, Rathfarnham, Dublin 16 (info@dublinquakerpeace.org) (www.dublinquakerpeace.org).

Educate Together (HR RE PO CR), 11-12 Hogan Place, Dublin 2 (+353-1-429 2500) (fax 429 2502) (info@educatetogether.ie) (www.educatetogether.ie).

Friends of the Earth (FE), 9 Upper Mount St, Dublin 2 (+353-1-639 4652) (info@foe.ie) (www.foe.ie).

Friends of the Irish Environment (EL), Kilcatherine, Eyeries, Co Cork (+353-27-74771) (admin@friendsoftheirishenvironment.org) (www.friendsoftheirishenvironment.org).

Ireland Palestine Solidarity Campaign [IPSC] (HR), 35 North Lotts, Dublin 1, D01 A3E0, Co Offaly (+353-1-872 7798) (info@ipsc.ie) (www.ipsc.ie).

Irish Anti-War Movement, PO Box 9260, Dublin 1 (+353-1-872 7912) (info@irishantiwar.org) (www.irishantiwar.org).

Irish Campaign for Nuclear Disarmament / Feachtas um Dhí-armáil Eithneach [ICND] (IB ND), PO Box 6327, Dublin 6 (irishcnd@gmail.com) (www.irishcnd.org). *Peacework.*

Irish Centre for Human Rights (HR), National University of Ireland, University Rd, Galway (+353-91-493948) (fax 494575) (humanrights@nuigalway.ie) (www.nuigalway.ie/human_rights).

Irish United Nations Association [IUNA] (UN), 14 Lower Pembroke St, Dublin 2 (+353-1-661 6920) (irelandun@gmail.com).

Pax Christi Ireland (PC HR AT), 52 Lower Rathmines Rd, Dublin 6 (+353-1-496 5293) (www.paxchristi.ie).

Peace and Neutrality Alliance / Comhaontas na Síochána is Neodrachta [PANA] (ND CD), 17 Castle St, Dalkey, Co Dublin (+353-1-235 1512) (info@pana.ie) (www.pana.ie).

Peace Brigades International – Ireland [PBI] (HR), 12 Parliament St, Temple Bar, Dublin 2 (pbiireland@peacebrigades.org) (www.pbi-ireland.org).

Programme for International Peace Studies (RE), Irish School of Ecumenics – Loyola Institute Building, TCD – Main Campus, Dublin 2 (+353-1-896 4770) (fax 672 5024) (peacesec@tcd.ie) (www.tcd.ie/ise). *Unity.*

Servas (SE), c/o Donal Coleman, 53 Glengara Park, Glenageary, Co Dublin A96 TOF6

(+353-87-915 9635) (ireland@servas.org) (www.servas.org).

ShannonWatch (DA HR), PO Box 476, Limerick DSU, Dock Rd, Limerick (+353-87-822 5087) (shannonwatch@gmail.com) (www.shannonwatch.org). Monitors foreign military use of Shannon Airport.

Vegetarian Society of Ireland [VSI] (EL PO), c/o Dublin Food Coop, 12 Newmarket, Dublin 8 (info@vegetarian.ie) (www.vegetarian.ie). *The Irish Vegetarian.*

Voluntary Service International [VSI] (SC), 30 Mountjoy Sq, Dublin 1 (+353-1-855 1011) (fax 855 1012) (info@vsi.ie) (www.vsi.ie). *VSI News.*

ISLE OF MAN

Shee Nish! / Peace Now! (AT PA DA), c/o Stuart Hartill, Eskdale Apartments – Apt 10, Queens Drive West, Ramsey IM8 2JD (+44-1624-803157) (stuarth@manx.net). Widely-based coalition of peace campaigners.

ISRAEL (see also Palestine)

NOTE: Territories allocated to Israel in the United Nations partition of Palestine in 1947, together with further areas annexed by Israel prior to 1967, are included here. Other parts of Palestine occupied by Israel in 1967 or later are listed under Palestine.

Al-Beit – Association for the Defence of Human Rights in Israel (HR CD TW), PO Box 650, Arara 30026 (+972-6-635 4370) (fax 635 4367) (uridavis@actcom.co.il). Concentrates on right of residence and housing.

Alternative Information Centre [AIC] (HR RE TW AL AT), POB 31417, West Jerusalem 91313 (+972-2-624 1159) (fax 3-762 4664) (connie.hackbarth@alternativenews.org) (www.alternativenews.org). *Economy of the Occupation.* See also Palestine.

Amnesty International Israel (AI), PO Box 5239, Tel-Aviv 66550 (+972-3-525 0005) (fax 525 0001) (info@amnesty.org.il) (amnesty.org.il).

B'Tselem – Israeli Information Centre for Human Rights in the Occupied Territories (HR), PO Box 53132, West Jerusalem 9153002 (+972-2-673 5599) (fax 674 9111) (mail@btselem.org) (www.btselem.org).

Bimkom – Planners for Planning Rights (HR), 13 Ebenezra St – PO Box 7154, West Jerusalem 9107101 (+972-2-566 9655) (fax 566 0551) (bimkom@bimkom.org) (www.bimkom.org).

Coalition of Women for Peace [CWP] (HR CD), POB 29214, Tel Aviv – Jaffa 61292 (+972-3-528 1005) (fax) (cwp@coalitionof-women.org) (www.coalitionofwomen.org).

Combatants for Peace (CD), PO Box 3049, Beit Yehushua 40591 (office@cfpeace.org) (www.cfpeace.org). Israeli and Palestinian ex-fighters for peace.

ISRAEL

Defence for Children International – Israel
[DCI-Israel] (HR), PO Box 2533, West
Jerusalem 91024 (+972-2-563 3003)
(fax 563 1241) (dci@dci-il.org).

Geneva Initiative (CD CR), c/o HL Education
for Peace, 33 Jabotinsky Rd, Ramat-Gan
525108 (+972-3-693 8780) (fax 691 1306)
(www.geneva-accord.org).
See also Palestine.

Givat Haviva Jewish-Arab Centre for Peace
[JACP] (CR HR RE), MP Menashe 37850
(+972-4-630 9289) (fax 630 9305)
(givathaviva@givathaviva.org.il)
(www.givathaviva.org.il).

Greenpeace Mediterranean – Israel (GP
HR), PO Box 20079, Tel Aviv 61200
(+972-3-561 4014) (fax 561 0415)
(gpmedisr@greenpeace.org)
(www.greenpeace.org/israel).

Gush Shalom / Peace Bloc (CD CR HR RE
RA), PO Box 2542, Holon 58125
(+972-3-556 5804) (info@gush-shalom.org)
(www.gush-shalom.org).

Hamerkaz Hamishpati L'zkhuyot Hami-ut
Ha'aravi Beyisrael / Legal Centre for Arab
Minority Rights in Israel [Adalah] (HR), 94
Yaffa St, PO Box 8921, Haifa 31090
(+972-4-950 1610) (fax 950 3140)
(adalah@adalah.org) (www.adalah.org).
Works for equal rights for Arab citizens in
Israel.

HaMoked – Centre for the Defence of the
Individual (HR), 4 Abu Obeidah St,
Jerusalem 97200 (+972-2-627 1698)
(mail@hamoked.org.il) (www.hamoked.org.il).

Hand in Hand – Centre for Jewish-Arab
Education in Israel (PO CD RE), PO Box
10339, Jerusalem 91102 (+972-2-673 5356)
(info@handinhand.org)
(www.handinhandk12.org).
Supports integrated, bilingual education.

Interfaith Encounter Association [IEA] (RP
CD), PO Box 3814, West Jerusalem 91037
(+972-2-651 0520) (fax 651 0557)
(yehuda@interfaith-encounter.org)
(www.interfaith-encounter.org).
IEA Stories.

Israel-Palestine Creative Regional
Initiatives [IPCRI] (RE CR EL CD), see
under Palestine (+972-52-238 1715)
(www.ipcri.org).

Israeli Committee for a Middle East Free
from Atomic, Biological and Chemical
Weapons (ND HR), PO Box 16202, Tel Aviv
61161 (+972-3-522 2869) (fax)
(spiro@bezeqint.net).

Mossawa Center – Advocacy Center for
Arab Citizens in Israel (HR), 5 Saint Lucas
St, PO Box 4471, Haifa 31043
(+972-4-855 5901) (fax 855 2772)
(programs.mossawa@gmail.com)
(www.mossawa.org).

New Profile – Movement for the
Demilitarisation of Israeli Society (WR), c/o
Sergeiy Sandler, POB 48005, Tel Aviv 61480
(+972-3-696 1137) (newprofile@speedy.co.il)
(www.newprofile.org).
Feminist movement of women and men.

Ometz Le'sarev / Courage to Refuse, PO
Box 16238, Tel Aviv (+972-3-523 3103)
(info@seruv.org.il) (www.seruv.org.il).
(Zionists) refusing deployment in the
Territories.

OneVoice Movement – Israel [OVI] (CD CR),
PO Box 29695, Tel Aviv 66881
(+972-3-516 8005) (info@OneVoice.org.il)
(www.onevoicemovement.org).
See also Palestine.

Palestinian-Israeli Peace NGO Forum
(Israeli Office) (CD), c/o The Peres Center
for Peace, 132 Kedem St, Jaffa 68066
(+972-3-568 0646) (fax 562 7265)
(info@peres-center.org)
(www.peacengo.org).
See also under Palestine.

Parents' Circle – Families' Forum:
Bereaved Israeli and Palestinian Families
Supporting Peace and Tolerance (CD CR),
1 Hayasmin St, Ramat-Efal 52960
(+972-3-535 5089) (fax 635 8367)
(contact@theparentscircle.org)
(www.theparentscircle.com).
See also under Palestine.

Public Committee Against Torture in Israel
[PCATI] (HR), POB 4634, West Jerusalem
91046 (+972-2-642 9825) (fax 643 2847)
(pcati@stoptorture.org.il)
(www.stoptorture.org.il).

Rabbis for Human Rights [RHR] (HR), 9
HaRechavim St, West Jerusalem 9346209
(+972-2-648 2757) (fax 678 3611)
(info@rhr.israel.net) (www.rhr.israel.net).

Sadaka-Reut – Arab-Jewish Partnership
(CR RE HR CD), 35 Shivtey Israel St, PO
Box 8523, Jaffa – Tel-Aviv 61084
(+972-3-518 2336) (fax)
(info@reutsadaka.org)
(www.reutsadaka.org).

Shalom Achshav / Peace Now, PO Box
22651, Tel Aviv 62032 (+972-3-602 3300)
(fax 602 3301) (info@peacenow.org.il)
(www.peacenow.org.il).

Shatil (CD HR), PO Box 53395, West
Jerusalem 91533 (+972-2-672 3597)
(fax 673 5149) (shatil@shatil.nif.org.il)
(www.shatil.org.il).
Also 4 other regional offices.

Shovrim Shtika / Breaking the Silence (HR),
PO Box 51027, 6713206 Tel Aviv
(info@breakingthesilence.org.il)
(www.shovrimshtika.org).
Also www.breakingthesilence.org.il.

Wahat al-Salam – Neve Shalom [WAS-NS]
(HR RE CR PO CD), Doar Na / Mobile Post,
Shimshon 9976100 (+972-2-999 6305)
(fax 991 1072) (info@wasns.info)
(wasns.info). "Oasis of Peace".

Windows – Israeli-Palestinian Friendship Centre (CD), PO Box 5195, Tel Aviv – Jaffa (+972-3-620 8324) (fax 629 2570) (office@win-peace.org) (www.win-peace.org). *Windows*. Chlenov 41. See also in Palestine.

ITALY

Amnesty International – Sezione Italiana (AI), Via Magenta 5, 00185 Roma (+39-06 4490210) (fax 06 449 0222) (infoamnesty@amnesty.it) (www.amnesty.it).

Archivio Disarmo [IRIAD] (IB RE AT), Via Paolo Mercuri 8, 00193 Roma (+39-06 3600 0343) (fax 06 3600 0345) (archiviodisarmo@pec.it) (www.archiviodisarmo.org).

Associazione Italiana Medicina per la Prevenzione della Guerra Nucleare [AIMPGN] (IP), Via Bari 4, 64029 Silvi Marina (TE) (+39-085 935 1350) (fax 085 935 3333) (mdipaolantonio55@gmail.com) (www.ippnw-italy.org).

Associazione Memoria Condivisa (CR), Viale 1º Maggio 32, 71100 Foggia (+39-0881 637775) (fax (info@memoriacondivisa.it) (www.memoriacondivisa.it). Supports non-violence as a response to terrorism.

Associazione Museo Italiano per la Pace / Association of Italian Museums for Peace (RE), Via Ezio Andolfato 1, 20126 Milano (museoitalianoperlapace@gmail.com). Promotes culture of peace in schools.

Azione dei Cristiani per l'Abolizione della Tortura [ACAT] (HR), c/o Rinascita Cristiana, Via della Traspontina 15, 00193 Roma (+39-06 686 5358) (posta@acatitalia.it) (www.acatitalia.it).

Centro Studi Sereno Regis – Italian Peace Research Institute / Rete CCP [IPRI] (RE CR EL), Via Garibaldi 13, 10122 Torino (+39-011 532824) (fax 011 515 8000) (www.serenoregis.org). *IPRI Newsletter*.

Eirene Centro studi per la pace (RE SD), Via Enrico Scuri 1, 24128 Bergamo (+39-035 260073) (fax 035 432 9224) (info@eirene.it) (www.eirene.it).

Gesellschaft für Bedrohte Völker / Associazione per i Popoli Minacciati / Lia por i Popui Manacês (HR), CP 233, 39100 Bozen/Bolzano, Südtirol (+39-0471 972240) (fax) (gfbv.bz@ines.com) (www.gfbv.it). Part of international GFBV network.

Green Cross Italy (EL TW DA HR), Via dei Gracchi 187, 00192 Roma (+39-06 3600 4300) (fax 06 3600 4364) (info@greencross.it) (www.greencrossitalia.org).

Greenpeace (GP), Via Della Cordonata 7, 00187 Roma (+39-06 6813 6061) (fax 06 4543 9793) (info.it@greenpeace.org) (www.greenpeace.org/italy). *GP News*.

International School on Disarmament and Research on Conflicts [ISODARCO] (RE CR DA), c/o Prof Carlo Schaerf, via della Rotonda 4, 00186 Roma (+39-06 689 2340) (isodarco@gmail.com) (www.isodarco.it).

Lega degli Obiettori di Coscienza [LOC] (WR), Via Mario Pichi 1, 20143 Milano (+39-02 837 8817) (fax 02 5810 1220) (locosm@tin.it) (ospiti.peacelink.it/loc/).

Movimento Internazionale della Riconciliazione [MIR] (FR), via Garibaldi 13, 10122 Torino (+39-011 532824) (fax 011 515 8000) (segretaria@miritalia.org) (www.miritalia.org).

Movimento Nonviolento [MN] (WR TR EL), Via Spagna 8, 37123 Verona (+39-045 800 9803) (fax) (azionenonviolenta@sis.it) (www.nonviolenti.org). *Azione Nonviolenta*.

Operazione Colomba / Operation Dove (RP CD CR), Via Mameli 5, 47921 Rimini (+39-0541 29005) (fax) (info@operazionecolomba@it) (www.operationdove.org). A project of Associazione Papa Giovanni XXIII.

Pax Christi Italia (PC), via Quintole per le Rose 131, 50029 Tavarnuzze, Firenze (+39-055 202 0375) (fax) (info@paxchristi.it) (www.paxchristi.it). *Mosaico di Pace*.

PBI Italia (PA RA HR), Via Asiago 5/a, 35010 Cadoneghe (PD) (+39-345 269 0132) (info@pbi-italy.org) (www.pbi-italy.org).

Religioni per la Pace Italia (RP), Via Pio VIII 38-D-2, 00165 Roma (+39-333 273 1245) (info@religioniperlapaceitalia.org) (www.religioniperlapaceitalia.org).

Servas Italia (SE), c/o Centro Studi Sereno Regis, Via Garibaldi 13, 10122 Torino (segretario@servas.it) (www.servas.it).

Società Italiana per l'Organizzazione Internazionale [SIOI] (UN), Piazza di San Marco 51, 00186 Roma (+39-06 692 0781) (fax 06 678 9102) (sioi@sioi.org) (www.sioi.org). *La Comunità Internazionale*.

IVORY COAST

Centre de Recherche et d'Action pour la Paix [CERAP] (RE HR), 15 Ave Jean Mermoz Cocody, 08 BP 2088, Abidjan 08 (+225-2240 4720) (fax 2244 8438) (info@cerap-inades.org) (www.cerap-inades.org).

JAPAN

Chikyu no Tomo / Friends of the Earth (FE), 1-21-9 Komone, Itabashi-ku, Tokyo 173-0037 (+81-3-6909 5983) (fax 6909 5986) (info@foejapan.org) (www.foejapan.org).

Goi Peace Foundation / May Peace Prevail on Earth International – Japan Office (CD PO), Heiwa-Daiichi Bldg, 1-4-5 Hirakawa-Cho, Chiyoda-ku, Tokyo 102-0093 (+81-3-3265 2071) (fax 3239 0919) (info@goipeace.or.jp) (www.goipeace.or.jp).

Green Action (EL), Suite 103, 22-75 Tanaka Sekiden-cho, Sakyo-ku, Kyoto 606-8203 (+81-75-701 7223) (fax 702 1952) (info@greenaction-japan.org) (www.greenaction-japan.org). Campaigns especially against nuclear fuel cycle.

JAPAN

Greenpeace Japan (GP), N F Bldg 2F 8-13-11, Nishi-Shinjuku, Shinjuku, Tokyo 160-0023 (+81-3-5338 9800) (fax 5338 9817) (www.greenpeace.or.jp).

Himeyuri Peace Museum (RE), 671-1 Ihara, Itoman-shi, Okinawa 901-0344 (+81-98-997 2100) (fax 997 2102) (himeyuri1@himeyuri.or.jp) (www.himeyuri.or.jp).

Hiroshima Peace Culture Foundation [HPCF] (PA ND RE), 1-2 Nakajima-cho, Naka-ku, Hiroshima 730-0811 (+81-82-241 5246) (fax 542 7941) (p-soumu@pcf.city.hiroshima.jp) (www.pcf.city.hiroshima.jp/hpcf). *Peace Culture*.

Hiroshima Peace Memorial Museum (RE), 1-2 Nakajima-cho, Naka-ku, Hiroshima 730-0811 (+81-82-241 4004) (fax 542 7941) (hpcf@pcf.city.hiroshima.jp) (www.pcf.city.hiroshima.jp).

Japan Council Against A & H Bombs – Gensuikyo (IB ND PA), 2-4-4 Yushima, Bunkyo-ku, Tokyo 113-8464 (+81-3-5842 6034) (fax 5842 6033) (antiatom@topaz.plala.or.jp) (www.antiatom.org). *No More Hiroshimas; Gensuikyo Tsushin.* National federation.

Japanese Physicians for the Prevention of Nuclear War [JPPNW] (IP), c/o Hiroshima Prefectural Medical Association, 3-2-3 Futabanosato, Higashi-ku, Hiroshima 732-0057 (+81-82-568 1511) (fax 568 2112) (ippnw-japan@hiroshima.med.or.jp) (www.hiroshima.med.or.jp).

Kyoto Museum for World Peace (RE), Ritsumeikan University, 56-1 Kitamachi, Tojiin, Kyoto 603-8577 (+81-75-465 8151) (fax 465 7899) (peacelib@st.ritsumei.ac.jp) (www.ritsumei.ac.jp/mng/er/wp-museum).

Network Against Japan Arms Trade [NAJAT] (AT), 311 Shimin Plaza – 302 Heisei Building – 3-12, Shimomiyabi Cho, Shinjuku, Tokyo 162-0822 (anti.arms.export@gmail.com) (najat2016.wordpress.com).

Nihon Hidankyo / Japan Confederation of A- and H-Bomb Sufferers' Organisations (ND CR HR), Gable Bldg 902, 1-3-5 Shiba Daimon, Minato-ku, Tokyo 105-0012 (+81-3-3438 1897) (fax 3431 2113) (kj3t-tnk@asahi-net.or.jp) (www.ne.jp/asahi/hidankyo/nihon). *Hidankyo*.

Nipponzan Myohoji (WR), 7-8 Shinsen-Cho, Shibuya-ku, Tokyo 150-0045 (+81-3-3461 9363) (fax 3461 9367) (info@nipponzanmyohoji.org) (nipponzanmyohoji.org).

Organising Committee – World Conference Against A and H bombs (ND), 2-4-4 Yushima, Bunkyo-ku, Tokyo 113-8464 (+81-3-5842 6034) (fax 5842 6033) (intl@antiatom.org).

Peace Depot – Peace Resources Cooperative (ND PA RE), Hiyoshi Gruene 1st Floor, 1-30-27-4 Hiyoshi Hon-cho, Kohoku-ku, Yokohama 223-0062 (+81-45-563 5101) (fax 563 9907) (office@peacedepot.org) (www.peacedepot.org). *Nuclear Weapon & Nuclear Test Monitor.*

Toda Peace Institute (RE CR PA WF ND), Samon Eleven Bldg – 5th floor, 3-1 Samoncho, Shinjuku-ku, Tokyo 160-0017 (contact@toda.org) (www.toda.org).

United Nations Association (UN), Nippon Building – Rm 427, 2-6-2 Ohtemachi, Chiyoda-ku, Tokyo 100-8699 (+81-3-3270 4731) (info@unaj.or.jp) (www.unaj.or.jp).

WRI Japan (WR HR AL), 666 Ukai-cho, Inuyama-shi, Aichi-ken 468-0085 (+81-568-615850).

KAZAKHSTAN

Chalyqaralyq qauipsizdik Zhenye Sayasat Optalyghy / Centre for International Security and Policy [CISP] (RE), PO Box 257, 37/9 Turan Ave, 010088 Astana (+7-717-225 0544) (info@cisp-astana.kz) (www.cisp-astana.kz).

Servas Kazakhstan (SE), Garibaldi Str 52, Karaganda City (+7-3212-439316) (fax 412021) (kazakhstan@servas.org) (www.servas-kazakhstan.narod.ru).

KENYA

Centre for Research and Dialogue – Somalia [CRD] (CR RE), PO Box 28832, Nairobi (www.crdsomalia.org). Based in Mogadishu, Somalia.

International Friendship League – Kenya [IFL] (CD), PO Box 9929, 00200 Nairobi. Part of international network of groups.

Sudanese Women's Voice for Peace, PO Box 21123, Nairobi.

KOREA, REPUBLIC OF

Greenpeace East Asia – Seoul Office (GP), 2/F – 358-121 Seogyo-dong, Mapo-gu, Seoul (+82-2-3144 1994) (fax 6455 1995) (greenpeace.kr@greenpeace.org) (www.greenpeace.org/eastasia).

International Peace Youth Group [IPYG] (RP), 46 Cheongpa-ro 71-gil, Yongsan-gu, Seoul 04304 (+82-2-514 1963) (info@ipyg.org) (ipyg.org).

Korea Federation for Environmental Movement [KFEM] (FE), 251 Nooha-dong, Jongno-gu, Seoul 110-806 (+82-2-735 7000) (fax 730 1240) (ma@kfem.or.kr) (www.kfem.or.kr). Anti-nuclear movement.

Pyeonghwa wa Tongil Yoneun Saramdeul / Solidarity for Peace and Re-Unification of Korea [SPARK] (PC), 3-47 Beonji 2 Cheung,

For explanation of codes and abbreviations, see introduction

Chungjeongno 3 ga, Sodaemun-gu, Seoul 120-837 (+82-2-711 7292) (fax 712 8445) (spark946@hanmail.net) (www.peaceone.org). *Pyeonghwamuri*.
World Without War (WR), 422-9 Mangwon-dong, Mapo-gu, Seoul 121-230 (+82-2-6401 0514) (fax) (peace@withoutwar.org) (www.withoutwar.org).

LATVIA
Latvijas Zemes Draugi (FE), Lapu iela 17, Zemgales Priekšpilseta, Riga 1002 (+371-6722 5112) (zemesdraugi@zemesdraugi.lv) (www.zemesdraugi.lv).

LEBANON
Greenpeace Mediterranean (GP), PO Box 13-6590, Beirut (+961-1-361255) (fax 36 1254) (supporters@greenpeace.org.lb) (www.greenpeace.org/lebanon).
See also Israel, Turkey.

LITHUANIA
United Nations Association (UN HR), Lithuanian Culture Research Institute, Saltoniskiu St 58, 08015 Vilnius (+370-5-275 1898) (jurate128@yahoo.de).

LUXEMBOURG
Action des Chrétiens pour l'Abolition de la Torture [ACAT] (HR), 5 Av Marie-Thérèse, 2132 Luxembourg (+352-4474 3558) (fax 4474 3559) (contact@acat.lu) (www.acat.lu).
Association Luxembourgeoise pour les Nations Unies [ALNU] (UN), 3 Rte d'Arlon, 8009 Strassen (+352-461468) (fax 461469) (alnu@pt.lu) (www.alnu.lu).
Greenpeace Luxembourg (GP), BP 229, 4003 Esch/Alzette (+352-546 2521) (fax 545405) (membres.lu@greenpea.org) (www.greenpeace.org/luxembourg).
Iwerliewen fir Bedreete Volleker (HR), BP 98, 6905 Niederanven (+352-2625 8687) (info@iwerliewen.org) (iwerliewen.org).
Mouvement Écologique (FE), 6 Rue Vauban, 2663 Luxembourg (+352-439 0301) (fax 4390 3043) (meco@oeko.lu) (www.meco.lu).
Servas (SE), see under Belgium.

MALAWI
Citizens for Justice – Friends of the Earth Malawi (FE), Post Dot Net, Box X100, Crossroads, Lilongwe (+265-176 1887) (fax 176 1886) (info@cfjmalawi.org) (cfjmalawi.org).
International Friendship League – Malawi [IFL] (CD), PO Box 812, Mzuzu (menardkamabga@yahoo.com).

MALAYSIA
Malaysian Physicians for Peace and Social Responsibility [MPPSR] (IP), c/o Academy of Medicine, 50480 Kuala Lumpur (+60-3-7956 8407) (rsmcoy@sternyx.com) (www.ppsr.org).

Sahabat Alam Malaysia / Friends of the Earth Malaysia [SAM] (FE), 258 Jalan Air Itam, George Town, 10460 Penang (+60-4-228 6930) (fax 228 6932) (sam_inquiry@yahoo.com) (www.foe-malaysia.org).

MALI
Amnesty International Mali [AI Mali] (AI), BP E 3885 ML, Bamako.

MALTA
John XXIII Peace Laboratory [Peacelab] (IB RP RE), Triq Hal-Far, Zurrieq ZRQ 2609 (+356-2168 9504) (fax 2164 1591) (info@peacelab.org) (www.peacelab.org). *It-Tieqa*.
Moviment ghall-Ambient / Friends of the Earth Malta (FE), PO Box 1013, South Street, Valletta VLT 1000 (+356-7996 1460) (info@foemalta.org) (www.foemalta.org).

MAURITIUS
Lalit (SF WL PA), 153 Main Rd, Grand River North West, Port-Louis (+230-208 2132) (lalitmail@intnet.mu) (www.lalitmauritius.org). Anti-militarist party and campaign.

MEXICO
Médicos Mexicanos para la Prevención de la Guerra Nuclear (IP), Antiguo Claustro – Hospital Juarez – PA, Plaza San Pablo, 06090 Mexico – DF (fromow@servidor.unam.mx).

MOLDOVA
Asociatia de Voluntariat International [AVI] (SC), 129 – 3A Vasile Alecsandri Str, 2012 Chisinau (+373-2-292 7724) (fax 293 0415) (avi@avimd.org) (www.avimd.org).

MONACO
Organisation pour la Paix par le Sport – Peace and Sport (CD), Immeuble les Mandariniers, 42ter Blvd du Jardin Exotique, 98000 (+377-9797 7800) (fax 9797 1891) (contact@peace-sport.org) (www.peace-sport.org).

MONGOLIA
Oyu Tolgoi Watch (EL HR), POB 636, Ulaanbaatar 46A (+976-9918 5828) (otwatch@gmail.com). Opposing devastation by Rio Tinto mining project.

MONTENEGRO
Nansen Dialogue Centre Montenegro (CR CD), Cetinsjki put bb 16/2, 81000 Podgorica (+382-20-290094) (fax) (ndcmontenegro@nansen-dialogue.net) (nansen-dialogue.net/ndcmontenegro).

NAMIBIA
Alternatives to Violence Project [AVP Namibia] (CR), PO Box 50617, Bachbrecht, Windhoek (+264-61-371554) (fax 371555) (vicky@peace.org.na).

NAMIBIA

Earth Life (Namibia) [ELN] (EL), PO Box 24892, Windhoek 9000 (+264-61-227913) (fax 305213) (earthl@iway.na).

NEPAL

Concern for Children and Environment – Nepal [CONCERN] (EL HR CR), Dallu Aawas, PO Box 4543, Kathmandu (+977-1-428 8253) (fax 427 7033) (concern@mos.com.np) (concern.org.np).

Human Rights and Peace Foundation [HURPEF] (HR), GPO 8975, Epc 5397, Kathmandu (+977-1-438 5231) (hurpef@hons.com.np) (www.hurpef.org.np).

Human Rights Without Frontiers – Nepal (WR HR), PO Box 10660, Maitidevi-33, Kathmandu (+977-1-444 2367) (fax 443 5331) (hrwfnepal@mail.com.np) (www.hrwfnepal.net.np). *Human Rights Monitor.*

National Land Rights Forum (WR HR), Bhumi-Ghar, Tokha-10, Dhapasi Kathmandu (+977-1-691 4586) (fax 435 7033) (land@nlrfnepal.org) (www.nlrfnepal.org).

Nepal Physicians for Social Responsibility (IP), PO Box 19624, Bagbazar, Kathmandu (psrn@healthnet.org.np).

People's Forum for Human Rights – Bhutan (HR), Anarmani 4, Birtamod, Jhapa (+977-23-540824) (rizal_pfhrb@ntc.net.np).

WILPF (WL), PO Box 13613, Chabahill 7, Mirmire Tole, Kathmandu (+977-11-448 6280) (wilpfnepalsectiom@gmail.com).

NETHERLANDS

Amsterdamse Catholic Worker / Ploughshares Support Group (PA AT RP HR RA), Postbus 12622, 1100 AP Amsterdam (+31-20-699 8996) (noelhuis@antenna.nl) (noelhuis.nl). *A Pinch of Salt.*

Anti-Militaristies Onderzoekskollectief – VD AMOK (WR RE AT ND), Lauwerecht 55, 3515 GN Utrecht (+31-30-890 1341) (info@vdamok.nl) (www.vdamok.nl).

Campagne tegen Wapenhandel (AT), Anna Spenglerstr 71, 1054 NH Amsterdam (+31-20-616 4684) (fax) (info@stopwapenhandel.org) (www.stopwapenhandel.org). *Campaign against arms trade.*

Centre for International Conflict Analysis and Management [CICAM] (RE), Postbus 9108, 6500 HK Nijmegen (+31-24-361 5687) (cicam@fm.ru.nl) (www.ru.nl/cicam).

Christian Peacemaker Teams – Nederland [CPT-NL] (RP RA PA), c/o Irene van Setten, Bredasingel 70, 6843 RE Arnhem (+31-26-848 1706) (info@cpt-nl.org) (www.cpt-nl.org).

Greenpeace Nederland (GP), NDSM-Plein 32, 1033 WB Amsterdam (+31-20-626 1877)

(fax 622 1272) (info@greenpeace.nl) (www.greenpeace.nl).

Kerk en Vrede (FR PA RE), Joseph Haydnlaan 2a, 3533 AE Utrecht (+31-30-231 6666) (secretariaat@kerkenvrede.nl) (kerkenvrede.nl).

Milieudefensie – FoE Netherlands (FE), Postbus 19199, 1000 GD Amsterdam (+31-20-626 2620) (fax 550 7310) (service@milieudefensie.nl) (www.milieudefensie.nl). *Down to Earth.*

Museum voor Vrede en Geweldloosheid [MVG] (RE PA), Ezelsveldlaan 212, 2611 DK Delft (+31-15-785 0137) (info@vredesmuseum.nl) (www.vredesmuseum.nl). *De Vredesboot.*

Musicians without Borders (RP), Kloveniersburgwal 87, 1011 KA Amsterdam (+31-20-330 5012) (info@musicianswithoutborders.org) (www.musicianswithoutborders.org).

Nederlands Expertisecentrum Alternatieven voor Gewald / Netherlands Expertise Centre Alternatives to Violence [NEAG] (CR), Vossiusstr 20, 1071 AD Amsterdam (+31-20-670 5295) (info@neag.nl) (www.neag.nl). Affiliated to Nonviolent Peaceforce.

Nederlandse Vereniging voor Medische Polemologie [NVMP] (IP), PO Box 199, 4190 CD Geldermalsen (+31-6-4200 9559) (office@nvmp.org) (nvmp.org).

Pax (PC AT RE CD), Sint Jacobsstr 12, 3511 BS Utrecht (+31-30-233 3346) (info@paxforpeace.nl) (www.paxforpeace.nl). Also www.paxforpeace.nl.

Peace Brigades Nederland [PBI] (RA PO CR RE), de Kargadoor, Oudegracht 36, 3511 AP Utrecht (+31-6-1649 8221) (info@peacebrigades.nl) (www.peacebrigades.nl).

Religieus Genootschap der Vrienden – Quakers Nederland (SF), Postbus 2167, 7420 AD Deventer (+31-570-655229) (secretariaat@dequakers.nl) (www.quakers.nu). *De Vriendenkring.*

Stichting Voor Aktieve Geweldloosheid [SVAG] (SD PO RE), Postbus 288, 5280 AG Boxtel (info@geweldloosactief.nl) (www.geweldlozekracht.nl). *Geweldloze Kracht.*

Stichting Vredesburo Eindhoven (PA RE), Grote Berg 41, 5611 KH Eindhoven (+31-40-244 4707) (info@vredesburo.nl) (www.vredesburo.nl). *Vredesburo Nieuwsbrief.*

Upact (PO RE), Postbus 19, 3500 AA Utrecht (+31-30-223 8724) (info@upact.nl) (www.upact.nl). *Upact Nieuws.*

Vredesbeweging Pais (WR EL), Ezelsveldlaan 212, 2611 DK Delft (+31-15-785 0137) (info@vredesbeweging.nl) (www.vredesbeweging.nl). *vredesmagazine.*

Vrouwen en Duurzame Vrede (CR ND SD), Haaksbergstr 317, 7545 GJ Enschede (+31-53-434 0559) (info@vrouwenenduurzamevrede.nl) (www.vrouwenenduurzamevrede.nl).

Women's International League for Peace and Freedom – Netherlands [WILPF-IVVV] (WL), Laan van Nieuw Oost Indië 252, 2593 CD Den Haag (+31-345-615105) (info@wilpf.nl) (www.wilpf.nl).

NEW ZEALAND / AOTEAROA

Abolition 2000 Aotearoa New Zealand [A2000 ANZ] (ND), c/o Pax Christi, PO Box 68419, Newton, Aukland 1145 (+64-9-377 5541) (abolition2000@ymail.com) (www.a2000.org.nz).

Amnesty International (AI), PO Box 5300, Wellesley St, Auckland 1141 (+64-9-303 4520) (fax 303 4528) (info@amnesty.org.nz) (www.amnesty.org.nz).

Anabaptist Association of Australia and New Zealand (RP), see under Australia (anabaptist.asn.au).

Anglican Pacifist Fellowship [APF] (RP AT TR), c/o Indrea Alexander, 9 Holmes St, Waimate 7924 (apfnzsecretary@gmail.com) (converge.org.nz/pma/apf). *The Anglican Pacifist of Aotearoa New Zealand.*

Anti-Bases Campaign [ABC] (PA RE), Box 2258, Christchurch 8140 (abc@chch.planet.org.nz) (www.converge.org.nz/abc). 2 yrly.

Campaign Against Foreign Control of Aotearoa [CAFCA], PO Box 2258, Christchurch 8140 (cafca@chch.planet.org.nz) (www.cafca.org.nz). *Foreign Control Watchdog.*

Disarmament and Security Centre [DSC] (IB WL RE ND CR), PO Box 8390, Christchurch 8440 (+64-22-067 3517) (lucy@disarmsecure.org) (www.disarmsecure.org).

Engineers for Social Responsibility [ESR] (EL ND AT), PO Box 6208, Wellesley Street, Auckland 1141 (www.esr.org.nz).

Green Party of Aotearoa/NZ (EL), PO Box 11652, Wellington 6142 (+64-4-801 5102) (fax 801 5104) (greenparty@greens.org.nz) (www.greens.org.nz). *Te Awa.*

Greenpeace Aotearoa New Zealand (GP), 11 Akiraho St, Mount Eden, Auckland (+64-9-630 6317) (fax 630 7121) (info@greenpeace.org.nz) (www.greenpeace.org/new-zealand). *Kakariki.*

New Zealand Burma Support Group (HR EL), 14 Waitati Pl, Mt Albert, Auckland (+64-9-828 4855) (nzburma@xtra.co.nz). *Newsletter.*

Pax Christi Aotearoa/NZ (PC), PO Box 68419, Newton, Aukland (paxnz@xtra.co.nz) (nzpaxchristi.wordpress.com).

Peace Action Wellington (DA AT RA), PO Box 9263, Wellington (peacewellington@riseup.net) (peacewellington.org). Work includes direct action against arms fairs.

Peace Foundation (CR RE), PO Box 8055, Symonds Street, Auckland 1150 (+64-9-373 2379) (fax 379 2668) (peace@peacefoundation.org.nz) (kiaora.peace.net.nz).

Peace Movement Aotearoa [PMA] (AT HR PA RE), PO Box 9314, Wellington 6141 (+64-4-382 8129) (fax 382 8173) (pma@xtra.co.nz) (www.converge.org.nz/pma). National networking body.

Quaker Peace and Service Aotearoa/New Zealand [QPSANZ] (SF), Quaker Meeting House, 72 Cresswell Ave, Christchurch 8061 (+64-3-980 4884) (www.quaker.org.nz/groups/qpsanz).

Stop the Arms Trade NZ (AT DA), PO Box 9843, Wellington (stop-the-arms-trade@riseup.net) (www.stoptheatrmstrade.nz). Actions against weapons expos.

Women's International League for Peace and Freedom [WILPF] (WL), PO Box 2054, Wellington (wilpfaotearoa@gmail.com) (www.wilpf.org.nz).

NICARAGUA

Centro de Prevención de la Violencia [CEPREV] (HR PO DA), Villa Fontana – casa 23, Club Terraza 1/2 c al lago, Managua (fax +505-2278 1637) (www.ceprev.org). Promotes a culture of peace.

NIGERIA

Alternatives to Violence Project [AVP Nigeria] (WR), 5 Ogunlesi St, off Bode Thomas Rd, Onipanu, Lagos (+234-1-497 1359) (avp@linkserve.com.ng).

Anglican Pacifist Fellowship – Nigeria [APF] (RP), c/o Peter U James, Akwa Ibom Peace Group, PO Box 269, Abak, Akwa Ibom State.

United Nations Association of Nigeria (UN), PO Box 54423, Falomo, Ikoyi, Lagos (+234-802-319 8698).

NORTH MACEDONIA

Dvizenje na ekologistitje na Makedonija / Ecologists' Movement of Macedonia [DEM] (FE), Ul Vasil Gjorgov 39 – 6, 1000 Skopje (+389-2-220518) (fax) (dem@dem.org.mk) (www.dem.org.mk).

Mirovna Aktsiya / Aksioni Paqësor / Peace Action (WR), Joseski Ice, Ul Andon Slabejko Br 138, 75000 Prilep (+389-48-22616) (office@mirovnaakcija.org) (www.mirovnaakcija).

For explanation to codes and abbreviations, see introduction

North MACEDONIA

Nansen Dialogue Centre Skopje [NDC Skopje] (CR CD), Str Bahar Mois No 4, 1000 Skopje (+389-2-320 9905) (fax 320 9906) (ndcskopje@nansen-dialogue.net) (ndc.net.mk).

United Nations Association of Macedonia (UN), St Zorz Bize 9-b, 1000 Skopje (+389-2-244 3751) (fpesevi@mt.net.mk) (www.sunamk.org).

NORWAY

Amnesty International (AI), PO Box 702, Sentrum, 0106 Oslo (+47-2240 2200) (fax 2240 2250) (info@amnesty.no) (www.amnesty.no).

Folkereisning Mot Krig [FMK] (WR AT), PO Box 2779, Solli, 0204 Oslo (+47-2246 4670) (fax) (fmk@ikkevold.no) (www.ikkevold.no). *Ikkevold.*

Fred og Forsoning – IFOR Norge (FR), Fredshuset, Møllergata 12, 0179 Oslo (contact@ifor.no) (www.ifor.no).

Informasjonsarbeidere for Fred [IF] (IB AT ND DA), c/o Heffermehl, Stensgaten 24B, 0358 Oslo (+47-9174 4783) (fredpax@online.no) (peacesispossible.info).

Internasjonal Dugnad [ID] (SC), Nordahl Brunsgt 22, 0165 Oslo (+47-2211 3123) (info@internasjonaldugnad.org) (www.internasjonaldugnad.org). *Dugnad Nytt.*

Narviksenteret – Nordnorsk Fredssenter (IB), Postboks 700, 8509 Narvik (+47-9154 7078) (fax 7694 4560) (fred.no).

Nei til Atomvåpen / No to Nuclear Weapons (ND), Postboks 8838, Youngstorget, 0028 Oslo (post@neitilatomvapen.org) (www.neitilatomvapen.no).

Nobels Fredssenter / Nobel Peace Centre (RE), PO Box 1894 Vika, 0124 Oslo (+47-4830 1000) (fax 9142 9238) (post@nobelpeacecenter.org) (www.nobelpeacecenter.org).

Norges Fredslag (DA AT ND RE), Grensen 9B, Postboks 8922, Youngstorget, 0028 Oslo (www.fredslaget.no). *Norwegian Peace Association.*

Norges Fredsråd / Norwegian Peace Council (IB), Postboks 8940 Youngstorget, 0028 Oslo (+47-9527 4822) (fax 2286 8401) (post@norgesfredsrad.no) (norgesfredsrad.no).

Norwegian Nobel Institute / Det Norske Nobelinstitutt (RE DA CR), Henrik Ibsens gate 51, 0255 Oslo (+47-2212 9300) (fax 9476 1117) (postmaster@nobel.no) (nobelpeaceprize.org).

Peace Brigades Norge [PBI-Norge] (CR HR PA), Fredshuset, Møllergata 12, 0172 Oslo (kontakt@pbi.no) (www.pbi.no).

WILPF Norge – Internasjonal Kvinneliga for Fred og Frihet [IKFF] (WL), Storgata 11, 0155 Oslo (+47-9308 9644) (ikff@ikff.no) (www.ikff.no). *Fred og Frihet.*

PAKISTAN

Human Rights Commission of Pakistan [HRCP] (HR), Aiwan-i-Jamhoor, 107 Tipu Block, New Garden Town, Lahore 54600 (+92-42-3586 4994) (fax 3588 3582) (hrcp@hrcp-web.org) (hrcp-web.org).

Revolutionary Association of the Women of Afghanistan [RAWA] (HR), PO Box 374, Quetta (+92-300-554 1258) (rawa@rawa.org) (www.rawa.org).

Servas Pakistan [SE-PK] (SE), c/o Muhammad Naseem, GPO Box 516, Lahore 54000 (+92-321-444 4516) (fax 42-3532 2223) (servaspakistan@yahoo.com) (pages.intnet.mu/servas/Pakistan). *Servas Pakistan Newsletter.*

Women's Internationl League for Peace and Freedom (WL), Sharah-e-Kashmir, Gulab Nagar, nr Darbar Saeen Mircho, Sector H-13, Islamabad (+92-51-250 6521) (mossarat_coco@yahoo.com).

PALESTINE (see also Israel)

NOTE: Because all of Palestine is under Israeli control (including areas not under day-to-day occupation), it is advisable to add 'via Israel' to addresses here (as well as 'Palestine').

Al-Haq (HR), PO Box 1413, Ramallah, West Bank (+970-2-295 4646) (fax 295 4903) (www.alhaq.org).

Al-Watan Centre (CR HR RE), PO Box 158, Hebron, West Bank (+970-2-222 3777) (fax 222 0907) (info@alwatan.org) (www.alwatan.org). *Supports popular resistance and nonviolence.*

Alternative Information Centre [AIC] (HR RE TW AL AT), Building 111, Main Street, Beit Sahour, West Bank (+972-2-277 5444) (fax 277 5445) (www.alternativenews.org). *See also Israel.*

Arab Educational Institute – Open Windows [AEI] (RE PC), Paul VI Street, Bethlehem, West Bank (+970-2-274 4030) (fax 277 7554) (info@aeicenter.org) (www.aeicenter.org).

Christian Peacemaker Teams [CPT] (RP), c/o Redeemer Church, PO Box 14076, Muristan Rd, Jerusalem 91140 (+972-2-222 8485) (cptheb@cpt.org) (www.cpt.org).

Combatants for Peace (CD), Ramallah (for postal address, see under Israel) (office@cfpeace.org) (www.cfpeace.org). *Palestinian and Israeli ex-fighters for peace.*

Ecumenical Accompaniment Programme in Palestine and Israel – Jerusalem Office [EAPPI] (RP HR CD CR), PO Box 741, East Jerusalem 91000 (+972-2-628 9402) (communications@eappi.org) (eappi.org).

Geneva Initiative (CD CR), c/o Palestinian
Peace Coalition, PO Box 4252, Ramallah
(+972-2-297 2535) (fax 297 2538)
(www.geneva-accord.org). See also Israel.

Good Shepherd Collective (HR RA CR), Um
al-Khair, South Hebron Hills, Hebron
Governate, West Bank (+972-58-438 1133)
(info@goodshepherdcollective.org)
(goodshepherdcollective.org).
Collective resisting military occupation.

**International Peace and Co-operation
Centre [IPCC]** (TW CR), PO Box 24162,
Jerusalem 91240 (+972-2-581 1992)
(fax 540 0522) (info@ipcc-jerusalem.org)
(home.ipcc-jerusalem.org).

**Israel-Palestine Creative Regional
Initiatives [IPCRI]** (RE CR EL CD), PO Box
9321, Jerusalem 91092 (+970-59-856 7287)
(ipcri@ipcri.org) (www.ipcri.org).
Office is in Ammunition Hill, East Jerusalem.

**Middle East Non-violence and Democracy –
FOR Palestine [MEND]** (FR HR CR), PO
Box 66558, Beit Hanina, East Jerusalem
(+970-2-656 7310) (fax 656 7311)
(lucynusseibeh@gmail.com)
(www.mendonline.org).

**Miftah – Palestinian Initiative for the
Promotion of Global Dialogue and
Democracy** (HR), PO Box 69647, Jerusalem
95908 (+970-2-298 9490) (fax 298 9492)
(administration@miftah.org)
(www.miftah.org).

**Movement Against Israeli Apartheid in
Palestine [MAIAP]** (HR), see under Israel.

OneVoice Movement – Palestine (CD CR),
PO Box 2401, Ramallah, West Bank
(+970-2-295 2076) (info@OneVoice.ps)
(www.onevoicemovement.org).
See also Israel.

Palestine-Israel Journal (RE CD RE), PO
Box 19839, East Jerusalem (+972-2-628
2115) (fax 627 3388) (pij@pij.org)
(www.pij.org). 4 yrly.

Palestinian BDS National Committee (HR
RA), c/o PACBI, PO Box 1701, Ramallah,
West Bank (pacbi@bdsmovement.net)
(bdsmovement.net/bnc).

**Palestinian Centre for Human Rights
[PCHR]** (HR), PO Box 1328, Gaza City,
Gaza Strip (+970-8-282 4776) (fax)
(pchr@pchrgaza.org) (www.pchrgaza.org).

**Palestinian Human Rights Monitoring
Group [PHRMG]** (HR), PO Box 19918, East
Jerusalem 91198 (+970-2-583 8189) (fax 583
7197) (admin@phrmg.org) (www.phrmg.org).
Office: Ahmad Jaber House, Beit Hanina.

**Palestinian Physicians for the Prevention of
Nuclear War [PPPNW]** (IP), PO Box 51681,
East Jerusalem (azizlabadi@yahoo.com).

**Palestinian-Israeli Peace NGO Forum
(Palestinian Office)** (CD), c/o Panorama, Al
Ahliya St, Ramallah 2045 (+970-2-295 9618)
(fax 298 1824)
(panorama@panoramacenter.org)
(www.peacengo.org). See also under Israel.

**Parents' Circle – Families' Forum:
Bereaved Palestinian and Israeli Families
Supporting Peace and Tolerance** (CD CR),
13 Jamal Abed Al-Nasser St, Al-Ram, East
Jerusalem (+972-2-234 4554) (fax 234 4553)
(alquds@theparentscircle.com)
(www.theparentscircle.com).
See also under Israel.

**Wi'am – Palestinian Conflict Resolution
Centre** (FR CR), PO Box 1039, Bethlehem,
West Bank (+970-2-277 7333) (fax)
(hope@alaslah.org) (www.alaslah.org).

**Windows – Israeli-Palestinian Friendship
Centre** (CD), PO Box 352, Ramallah
(office@win-peace.org) (www.win-peace.org).
See also in Israel.

PARAGUAY

Amnistía Internacional Paraguay (AI), Dr
Hassler 5229 – e/ Cruz del Defensor y Cruz
del Chaco, Bsrrio Villa Mora, Asunción
(+595-21-604822) (fax 663272)
(ai-info@py.amnesty.org)
(www.amnesty.org).

**Movimiento Objeción de Conciencia –
Paraguay [MOC-PY]** (WR), Calle Iture Nº
1324 – entre Primera e Secunda Proyectada,
Asunción (+598-981-415586)
(moc_py@yahoo.com) (moc_py.org).

SERPAJ-Paraguay (HR PA), Calle Teniente
Prieto 354 – entre Dr Facundo Insfran y Tte
Rodi, Asunción (+595-21-481333)
(serpajpy@serpajpy.org.py)
(www.serpajpy.org.py).

PHILIPPINES

**Aksyon para sa Kapayapaan at Katarungan
(Action for Peace and Justice) – Center
for Active Non-Violence [AKKAPKA-
CANV]** (FR TW HR EL), Rm 222,
Administration Bldg, Pius XII Catholic Centre,
1175 UN Avenue, Paco, 1007 Manila
(+63-2-526 0103) (fax 400 0823)
(akkapka.canv84@gmail.com).

**Task Force Detainees of the Philippines
[TFDP]** (HR), 45 Saint Mary St, Cubao, 1109
Quezon City (+63-2-437 8054) (fax 911 3643)
(main.tfdp.net).

POLAND

**Lekarze Przeciw Wojnie Nuklearnej –
Sekcja Polska IPPNW** (IP), Ul Mokotowska
3 – lok 6, 02640 Warszawa
(+48-22-845 5784) (b.wasilewski@ips.pl).

Servas Polska (SE), c/o Joanna Mozga, Ul
Kasprzaka 24A m 39, 01211 Warszawa
(joanna@servas.pl) (servas.pl).

**Stowarzyszenie "Nigdy Wiecej" / "Never
Again" Association** (HR PO), PO Box 6,
03700 Warszawa 4
(redakcja@nigdywiecej.org)
(www.nigdywiecej.org). Works for genocide
commemoration, anti-racism.

For explanation of codes and abbreviations,
see introduction

PORTUGAL

Amnistia Internacional Portugal (AI), Av Infante Santo 42 – 2º, 1350-179 Lisboa (+351-21 386 1652) (fax 21 386 1782) (aiportugal@amnistia-internacional.pt) (www.amnistia-internacional.pt).

Associação das Nações Unidas Portugal (UN), Rua do Almada 679 – 1º – S 103, 4050-039 Porto (+351-22 200 7767) (fax 22 200 7868) (anuportugal@gmail.com) (www.anup.pt).

Associação Livre dos Objectores e Objectoras de Consciência [ALOOC] (WR AL), Rua D Aleixo Corte-Real 394 – 3º D, 1800-166 Lisboa (alooc.portugal@gmail.om).

Conselho Português para a Paz e Cooperação [CPPC] (WP ND DA), Rua Rodrigo da Fonseca 56-2º, 1250-193 Lisboa (+351-21 386 3375) (fax 21 386 3221) (conselhopaz@cppc.pt) (www.cppc.pt). Portuguese Council for Peace and Co-operation.

Observatório Género e Violência Armada / Observatory on Gender and Armed Violence [OGIVA] (DA HR), Centro Estudos Sociais, Colégio de S Jerónimo, Apartado 3087, 3000-995 Coimbra (+351-239 855593) (fax 239 855589) (ogiva@ces.uc.pt) (www.ces.uc.pt/ogiva).

PUERTO RICO

Pax Christi Puerto Rico (PC), c/o Randolph Rivera Cuevas, HC 3 Box 9695, Gurabo 00778 (+1787-761 1355) (fax) (clidin@bppr.com).

RUSSIA

Bellona Russia – St Petersburg (EL), Suvorovskiy Pr 59, 191015 Sankt-Peterburg (+7-812-275 7761) (fax 719 8843) (mail@bellona.ru) (www.bellona.ru). *Environment and Rights.* Environmental Rights Centre. Main office in Norway.

Dom Druzeiy v Moskvye / Friends' House Moscow (SF), Sukharevskaya M – pl 6 – str 1, 127051 Moskva (+7-903-664 1075) (dd.moskva@gmail.com) (friendshousemoscow.org).

Dom Mira i Nyenasiliya / House of Peace and Nonviolence (PC), a/ya 33, 191002 Sankt-Peterburg (+7-951-644 8052) (peacehouse.spb@gmail.com) (www.peacehouse.ru).

Federatsiya Mira i Soglasiya / International Federation for Peace and Conciliation [IFPC] (WP), 36 Prospekt Mira, 129090 Moskva (+7-495-680 3576) (fax 688 9587) (vik@ifpc.ru) (www.ifpc.ru). *Mir i Soglasie.*

Greenpeace Russia (GP), Lyeningradskii prospect – d 26 – k 1, 125040 Moskva (+7-495-988 7460) (fax) (info@greenpeace.ru) (www.greenpeace.org/russia).

Interchurch Partnership – Peace Resarch Centre (PC RE), PO Box 31, 191002 Sankt-Peterburg (+7-812-764 0423) (fax 764 6695) (mshishova@yahoo.com).

Memorial (HR CD), Malyi Karetnyi pereulok 12, 127051 Moskva (+7-495-650 7883) (fax 609 0694) (info@memo.ru) (www.memo.ru).

Nyemyetsko-Russkiy Obmyen / Deutscher-Russischer Austausch [NRO] (CD), Ligovski Pr 87 – Ofis 300, 191040 Sankt-Peterburg (+7-812-718 3793) (fax 718 3791) (nro@obmen.org) (www.obmen.org). German-Russian Exchange.

Soldatskiye Matyeri Sankt-Peterburg / Soldiers' Mothers of St Petersburg (HR PA PC), Ul Razyezzhaya 9, 191002 Sankt-Peterburg (+7-812-712 4199) (fax 712 5058) (soldiersmothers@yandex.ru) (www.soldiersmothers.ru).

Tsentr Mezhnatsionalnovo Sotrudnichestva / Centre for Interethnic Co-operation (CR CD), a/ya 8, 127055 Moskva (+7-499-972 6807) (center@interethnic.org) (www.interethnic.org).

RWANDA

Life & Peace Institute – DR Congo (RE RP), PO Box 64, Cyangugu (+243-81-249 4489) (pieter.vanholder@life-peace.org) (www.life-peace.org).

Peace & Conflict Resolution Project (of Bukavu, DR Congo) [PCR] (CR), PO Box 37, Cyangugu (+243-993-463279) (peacecpr@yahoo.com) (www.peaceconflictresolutionproject.webs.com). Operates in Bukavu, eastern Congo.

SERBIA

Beogradski Forum za Svet Ravnopravih / Belgrade Forum for a World of Equals [Beoforum] (WP), Sremska Broj 6 – IV sprat, 11000 Beograd (+381-11-328 3778) (beoforum@gmail.com) (www.beoforum.rs).

Centar za Nenasilnu Akciju – Beograd / Centre for Nonviolent Action – Belgrade [CNA] (CR PA RE CD), Cika Ljubina 6, 11000 Beograd (+381-11-263 7603) (fax) (cna.beograd@nenasilje.org) (www.nenasilje.org). See also in Bosnia-Herzegovina.

Centre for Applied NonViolent Action and Strategies [CANVAS], Gandijeva 76a, 11070 Novi Beograd (+381-11-222 8331) (fax 222 8336) (office@canvasopedia.org) (www.canvasopedia.org).

Žene U Crnom Protiv Rata / Women in Black Against War (WR), Jug Bogdanova 18/V, 11000 Beograd (+381-11-262 3225) (zeneucrnombeograd@gmail.com) (www.zeneucrnom.org).

For explanation of codes and abbreviations, see introduction

SINGAPORE

Inter-Religious Organisation – Singapore (RP), Palmer House, 70 Palmer Rd – 05-01/02, Singapore 079427 (+65-6221 9858) (fax 6221 9212) (irosingapore@gmail.com) (iro.sg).
Affiliate of Religions for Peace International.

United Nations Association of Singapore [UNAS] (UN), PO Box 351, Tanglin Post Office, Singapore 912412 (+65-6792 0026) (sctham@unas.org.sg) (www.unas.org.sg).
World Forum.

SLOVAKIA

Pax Christi Bratislava-Pezinok (PC), Kpt Jaroša 15, 90201 Pezinok (+421-33-640 1284) (fax) (molnars@nextra.sk).

Priatelia Zeme Slovensko / Friends of the Earth Slovakia (FE), Komenského 21, 97401 Banská Bystrica (+421-48-412 3859) (fax) (foe@priateliazeme.sk) (www.priateliazeme.sk).

SOMALIA

Centre for Research and Dialogue [CRD] (CR RE), (for postal address see under Kenya (+252-1-658666) (fax 5-932355) (crd@crdsomalia.org) (www.crdsomalia.org). Street address: K4 Airport Rd, Mogadishu.

SOUTH AFRICA

Action Support Centre [ASC] (CR), Postnet Suite No 145, Private Bag X9, Melville 2109 (+27-11 482 7442) (fax 11 482 2484) (info@asc.org.za) (www.asc.org.za).

African Centre for the Constructive Resolution of Disputes [ACCORD] (RE CD CR), 2 Golf Course Drive, Mount Edgecombe, Durban 4320, Kwazulu-Natal (+27-31 502 3908) (fax 31 502 4160) (info@accord.org.za) (www.accord.org.za).
Conflict Trends.

Anglican Pacifist Fellowship [APF] (RP), c/o Victor Spencer, PO Box 54, Ficksburg 9730 (+27-51-922700) (victor.spencer@cpsanet.co.za).

Boycott, Disinvestment and Sanctions Against Israel in South Africa [BDS SA] (HR RA), PO Box 2318, Houghton 2041, Johannesburg (+27-11 403 2097) (fax 86 650 4836) (administrator@bdssouthafrica.com) (www.bdssouthafrica.com).

Centre for the Study of Violence and Reconciliation (RE CR HR), PO Box 30778, Braamfontein, Johannesburg 2017 (+27-11 403 5650) (fax 11 339 6785) (info@csvr.org.za) (www.csvr.org.za).
Also in Cape Town (+27-21 447 2470).

Earthlife Africa [ELA] (EL), PO Box 32131, Braamfontein 2107 (+27-11 339 3662) (fax 11 339 3270) (seccp@earthlife.org.za) (www.earthlife.org.za).

GroundWork / Friends of the Earth South Africa (FE), PO Box 2375, Pietermaritzburg 3200 (+27-33 342 5662) (fax 33 342 5665) (team@groundwork.org.za) (www.groundwork.org.za).

GunFree South Africa [GFSA] (AT PA RE), PO Box 12988, Mowbray 7705 (+27-72 544 0573) (fax 86 545 0094) (info@gfsa.org.za) (www.gunfree.org.za).

Institute for Healing of Memories (CR), PO Box 36069, Glosderry 7702 (+27-21 683 6231) (fax 21 683 5747) (info@healingofmemories.co.za) (www.healing-memories.org.za).

International Centre of Nonviolence [ICON] (RE HR), ML Sultan Campus, Durban University of Technology, PO Box 1334, Durban 4000 (+27-31 373 5499) (icon@dut.ac.za) (www.icon.org.za).
Works for a culture of nonviolence.

Trauma Centre for Survivors of Violence and Torture (CR HR), Cowley House, 126 Chapel St, Woodstock, Cape Town 7925 (+27-21 465 7373) (info@trauma.org.za) (www.trauma.org.za).

United Nations Association of South Africa [UNA-SA] (UN), c/o The Coachman's Cottage Museum, PO Box 1256, Somerset West 7129 (+27-21 850 0509) (fax 800 981771) (admin@unasa.org.za) (www.unasa.org.za).

SOUTH SUDAN

Organisation for Nonviolence and Development [ONAD] (WR CR HR), PO Box 508, Juba (+211-921-352592) (onadjuba2011@gmail.com) (www.onadev.org).

SPAIN

Alternativa Antimilitarista – Movimiento de Objeción de Conciencia [AA-MOC] (WR RA TR), C/San Cosme y San Damián 24-2º, 28012 Madrid (+34-91 475 3782) (moc.lavapies@nodo50.org) (www.antimilitaristas.org).

Amnistía Internacional España (AI), C/ Fernando VI – 8 – 1º Izda, 28004 Madrid (+34-91 310 1277) (fax 91 319 5334) (info@madrid.es.amnesty.org) (www.es.amnesty.org).

Antimilitaristes – MOC València (WR RA TR), C/ Roger de Flor 8 – baix-dta, 46001 València (+34-96 391 6702) (retirada@pangea.org) (mocvalencia.org).

Brigadas Internacionales de Paz – Estado Español [PBI] (CR HR TW), C/ Ballesta 9 – 3º E, Madrid (www.pbi-ee.org).

Centre d'Estudis per la Pau JM Delàs (WR RE AT RP IB), Rivadeneyra 6 – 10è, 08002 Barcelona, Catalunya (+34-93 317 6177) (fax 93 412 5384) (info@centredelas.org) (www.centredelas.org).
Materiales de Trabajo.

SPAIN

Centro de Investigación para la Paz (RE), Duque de Sesto 40, 28009 Madrid (+34-91 576 3299) (fax 91 577 4726) (cip@fuhem.es) (www.cip-ecosocial.fuhem.es).
Papeles de Relaciones Ecosociales y Cambio Global.

Ekologistak Martxan Bizkaia (ND EL TW), c/ Pelota 5 – Behea, 48005 Bilbo, Euskadi (+34-94 479 0119) (fax) (bizkaia@ekologistakmartxan.org) (www.ekologistakmartxan.org). *Eco Boletin.*

Escola de Cultura de Pau (RE), Plaça del Coneixement – Edifici MRA (Mòdul Recerca A), UAB, 08193 Bellaterra (+34-93 586 8848) (fax 93 581 3294) (escolapau@uab.cat) (escolapau.uab.cat).

Fundación Cultura de Paz [FCP] (IB WP RE), Calle Velázquez 14 – 3º dcha, 28001 Madrid (+34-91 426 1555) (fax 91 431 6387) (info@fund-culturadepaz.org) (www.fund-culturadepaz.org).

Fundación Seminario de Investigación para la Paz [SIP] (RE), Centro Pignatelli, Pº de la Constitución 6, 50008 Zaragoza (+34-976 217215) (fax 976 230113) (sipp@seipaz.org) (www.seipaz.org).

Gernika Gogoratuz – Peace Research Centre [GGG] (IB RE), Artekale 1-1, 48300 Gernika-Lumo, Bizkaia (+34-94 625 3558) (fax 94 625 6765) (gernikag@gernikagogoratuz.org) (www.gernikagogoratuz.org).

Gesto por la Paz de Euskal Herria – Euskal Herriko Bakearen Aldeko (PA HR RE), Apdo 10152, 48080 Bilbao (+34-94 416 3929) (fax 94 415 3285) (gesto@gesto.org) (www.gesto.org).
Association for peace in the Basque Country.

Grup Antimilitarista Tortuga (PA), C/ Ametler 26 – 7ª, 03203 Elx, Alacant (tortuga@nodo50.org) (www.grupotortuga.com). Part of network Alternativa Antimilitarista – MOC.

Justicia y Paz – España [CGJP] (RP), Rafael de Riego 16 – 3º dcha, 28045 Madrid (+34-91 506 1828) (juspax@juspax-es.org) (www.juspax-es.org).

Kontzientzi Eragozpen Mugimendua / MOC Euskal Herria [KEM-MOC] (WR AL RA TR), Calle Fika Nº 4 – lonja derecha, 48006 Bilbao, Euskadi (+34-94-415 3772) (mocbilbao@gmail.com) (www.sinkuartel.org). Part of network Alternativa Antimilitarista – MOC.

Liga Internacional de Mujeres por la Paz y la Libertad (WL), 26-28 bajo – Almería, Zaragoza (wilpf.espanya@gmail.com) (wilpf.es).

Moviment per la Pau (PA RE AT), C/ Providència 42, 08024 Barcelona (+34-93 219 3371) (fax 93 213 0890) (movpau@pangea.org). *Lletres de Pau.*

Paz y Cooperación / Peace and Co-operation (IB RE TW), Meléndez Valdés 68 – 4º izq, 28015 Madrid (+34-91 549 6156) (fax 91 543 5282) (pazycooperacion@hotmail.com) (www.peaceandcooperation.org).
Premio Escolar Paz y Cooperación.

Servas España (SE), Calle de la Roca 5, 08319 Dosrius (servas.spain@gmail.com) (www.servas.es).

Servei Civil Internacional – Catalunya [SCI] (SC PA), c/ Carme 95 – baixos 2a, 08001 Barcelona, Catalunya (+34-93 441 7079) (comunicacio@sci-cat.org) (www.sci-cat.org).

Servicio Civil Internacional [SCI] (SC), c/Ronda de Segovia 55 – oficina 2, 28005 Madrid (+34-91 366 3259) (fax 91 366 2203) (oficina@ongsci.org) (www.ongsci.org).

Survival International (España) [SI] (HR), C/Príncipe 12 – 3º, 28012 Madrid (+34-91 521 7283) (fax 91 523 1420) (info@survival.es) (www.survival.es).
Boletín de Acción Urgente.

SRI LANKA

Lanka Jathika Sarvodaya Shramadana Sangamaya [Sarvodaya] (HR TW), Damsak Mandira, 98 Rawatawatte Rd, Moratuwa (+94-11-264 7159) (fax 265 6512) (ed@sarvodaya.org) (www.sarvodaya.org).

Mahatma Gandhi Centre (PO PA RE), 22/17 Kalyani Rd, Colombo 00600 (+94-11-250 1825) (fax) (power2people@gandhiswaraj.com) (gandhiswaraj.con).

National Peace Council of Sri Lanka [NPC] (CR RE CD), 12/14 Purana Vihara Rd, Colombo 6 (+94-11-281 8344) (fax 281 9064) (npc@sltnet.lk) (www.peace-srilanka.org).
Paths to Peace.

Nonviolent Direct Action Group [NVDAG] (FR WR IB), PO Box 2, 29 Kandy Rd, Kaithady-Nunavil, Chavakachcheri (del-smskr@eureka.lk). *NVDAG Report.*

SCI Sri Lanka (SC), 18/A/4 Deveni Rajasinghe, Mawatha, Kandy (+94-81-238 7188) (fax) (scisl@sltnet.lk).

SUDAN

Peace Desk of New Sudan Council of Churches (RP CD CR HR), see under Kenya.

Sudanese Women's Voice for Peace, see under Kenya.

SWEDEN

Göteborgs Ickevåldsnätverk / Nonviolence Network of Gothenburg (AL PA CR RA), c/o Elisabet Ahlin, Norra Krokslättsgatan 17A, 41264 Göteborg (+46-31-832187) (elisabet.ahlin@gmail.com).

Greenpeace (GP), Rosenlundsgatan 29 B, 11863 Stockholm (+46-8-702 7070) (info.se@greenpeace.org) (www.greenpeace.se).

Internationella Kvinnoförbundet för Fred och Frihet [IKFF] (WL), Norrtullsgatan 45 – 1 tr, 11345 Stockholm (+46-8-702 9810) (info@ikff.se) (www.ikff.se).

Jordens Vänner / Friends of the Earth Sweden (FE TW), Box 7048, 40231 Göteborg (+46-31-121808) (fax 121817) (info@jordensvanner.se) (www.jordensvanner.se).

Kristna Fredsrörelsen (FR), Ekumeniska Centret, Box 14038, 16714 Bromma (+46-8-453 6840) (fax 453 6829) (info@krf.se) (krf.se). *Fredsnytt*.

Life & Peace Institute [LPI] (RP AT RE TW CR), Säbygatan 4, 75323 Uppsala (+46-18-660130) (info@life-peace.org) (www.life-peace.org). *Horn of Africa Bulletin*. Projects in East Africa and Central Africa.

Ofog (WR RA AT ND AL), c/o Göteborgs Fredskommitté, Linnégatan 21, 41304 Göteborg (+46-733-815361) (info@ofog.org) (www.ofog.org).

PBI-Sverige (HR CR), Blixtåsvägen 6, 42437 Angered (+46-31-330 7509) (info@pbi-sweden.org) (www.pbi-sweden.org).

PeaceQuest International (CD CR RE), Box 55913, 10216 Stockholm (+46-8-5592 1180) (info@peacequest.eu) (www.peacequest.eu).

Servas Sverige (SE), c/o Eva Hartman-Juhlin, Svankärrsvägen 3B, 75653 Upsalla (sweden@servas.se) (www.servas.se).

Stockholm Centre for the Ethics of War and Peace [SCEWP] (RE), Universitetsvägen 10, 11418 Stockholm (stockholmcentre.org).

Svenska FN-Förbundet (UN), Box 15115, 10465 Stockholm (+46-8-462 2540) (fax 641 8876) (info@fn.se) (www.fn.se). *Världshorisont*.

Svenska Fredskommittén / Swedish Peace Committee [SFK] (DA ND), Tegelviksgatan 40, 11641 Stockholm (info@svenskafredskommitten.nu) (www.svenskafredskommitten.nu).

Sveriges Fredsråd / Swedish Peace Council (IB), Tegelviksgatan 40, 11641 Stockholm (info@FredNu.se) (frednu.se). National federation.

Swedish Peace and Arbitration Society / Svenska Freds- och Skiljedomsföreningen [SPAS] (WR IB AT), Polhemsgatan 4, 11236 Stockholm (+46-8-5580 3180) (info@svenskafreds.se) (www.svenskafreds.se). *Pax*.

Vännernas Samfund (Kväkarna) (SF), Box 9166, 10272 Stockholm (+46-8-668 6816) (fax) (info@kvakare.se).

SWITZERLAND

Action des Chrétiens pour l'Abolition de la Torture / Aktion der Christen für die Abschaffung der Folter [ACAT-Suisse] (HR), Speichergasse 29, 3001 Berne (+41-31 312 2044) (info@acat.ch) (www.acat.ch). *acatnews*.

Amnesty International (AI), Speichergasse 33, 3011 Bern (+41-31 307 2222) (fax 31 307 2233) (info@amnesty.ch) (www.amnesty.ch). Amnesty Magazin(e).

APRED – Participative Institute for the Progress of Peace (RE CD HR), Route des Siernes Picaz 46, 1659 Flendruz (+41-79 524 3574) (info@demilitarisation.org) (www.apred.org).

Ärzte/Ärztinnen für Soziale Verantwortung / Médecins pour une Résponsibilité Sociale [PSR/IPPNW] (IP), Bireggstr 36, 6003 Luzern (+41-41 240 6349) (fax) (sekretariat@ippnw.ch) (www.ippnw.ch).

Basel Peace Office (RE ND), Universität Basel, Petersgraben 27, 4051 Basel (info@baselpeaceoffice.org) (www.baselpeaceoffice.org).

Centre pour l'Action Non-Violente [CENAC] (WR RP IB), 52 rue de Genève, 1004 Lausanne (+41-21 661 2434) (fax 21 661 2436) (info@non-violence.ch) (www.non-violence.ch).

cfd – the feminist peace organisation (PA CR HR), Postfach, 3001 Berne (+41-31 300 5060) (info@cfd-ch.org) (www.cfd-ch.org). *cfd-Zeitung*.

Eirene Suisse (RP TW EL CR), 9 Rue du Valais, 1202 Genève (+41-22 321 8556) (fax) (info@eirenesuisse.ch) (eirenesuisse.ch).

Gender and Mine Action Programme (AT CR RE HR), c/o Geneva International Centre for Humanitarian Demining, PO Box 1300, 1211 Genève 1 (+41-22 730 9335) (fax 22 730 9362) (info@gmap.ch) (www.gmap.ch).

Gesellschaft für bedrohte Völker / Société pour les Peuples menacés (HR), Schermenweg 154, 3072 Ostermunigen (+41-31 939 0000) (fax 31 939 0019) (info@gfbv.ch) (www.gfbv.ch).

Grüne Partei der Schweiz / Parti écologiste suisse / Partito ecologista svizzero (EL IB), Waisenhausplatz 21, 3011 Bern (+41-31 326 6660) (fax 31 326 6662) (gruene@gruene.ch) (www.gruene.ch). *Greenfo*. Green party. Grüne / Les Verts / I Verdi.

Greenpeace (GP), Badenerstr 171, Postfach 9320, 8036 Zürich (+41-44 447 4141) (fax 44 447 4199) (gp@greenpeace.ch) (www.greenpeace.org/switzerland).

Groupe pour une Suisse sans Armée / Gruppe für eine Schweiz ohne Armee [GSsA/GSoA] (WR DA ND), Case Postale 151, 1211 Genève 8 (+41-22 320 4676) (gssa@gssa.ch) (www.gssa.ch). *Une Suisse sans Armée*.

Institute for Peace and Dialogue [IPD] (CR CD RE), Hegenheimerstr 175, 4055 Basel (+41-76 431 6170) (fhuseynli@ipdinstitute.ch) (www.idpinstitute.ch).

MIR Suisse / IFOR Schweiz (FR), Brue 4, 2613 Villeret (+41-32 940 7237) (secretariat@ifor-mir.ch) (ifor-mir.ch).

SWITZERLAND

Neuer Israel Fonds Schweiz – NIF Switzerland (HR), Winkelriedplatz 4, 4053 Basel (+41-61 272 1455) (fax 61 361 2972) (info@nif.ch) (www.mif.ch).

Peace Brigades International – Schweiz/Suisse [PBI] (CD HR CR RE), Gutenbergstr 35, 3011 Bern (+41-31 372 4444) (info@peacebrigades.ch) (www.peacebrigades.ch).

Pro Natura (FE), Postfach, 4018 Basel (+41-61-317 9191) (fax 317 9266) (mailbox@pronatura.ch) (www.pronatura.ch).

Schweizerische Friedensbewegung / Moviment Svizzer da Pasch / Swiss Peace Movement (WP), Postfach 2113, 4001 Basel (+41-61 681 0363) (mail@friedensbewegung.ch) (www.friedensbewegung.ch). *Unsere Welt.*

Schweizerische Friedensstiftung [swisspeace] (RE CR), Sonnenbergstr 17, PO Box, 3001 Bern (+41-31 330 1212) (info@swisspeace.ch) (www.swisspeace.ch).

Schweizerischer Friedensrat / Consiglio Svizzera per pa Pace / Conseil Suisse pour la Paix [SFR] (IB AT EL), Gartenhofstr 7, 8004 Zürich (+41-44 242 9321) (info@friedensrat.ch) (www.friedensrat.ch). *FriZ. Swiss Peace Council.*

Service Civil International – Schweizer Zweig / Branche suisse / Sede svizzera [SCI] (SC), Monbijoustr 32, Postfach 2944, 3001 Bern (+41-31 381 4620) (info@scich.org) (www.scich.org). *Service Civil International.*

Société Religieuse des Amis, Assemblée de Suisse (Quaker) [SYM] (SF), c/o Maison Quaker, 13 Av du Mervelet, 1209 Genève (+41-22 748 4800) (fax 22 748 4819) (symclerk@swiss-quakers.ch) (www.swiss-quakers.ch). *Entre Amis.*

Société Suisse – Nations Unies / Schweizerisches Versicherungsverband (UN), Postfach 762, 6431 Schwyz (info@schweiz-uno.ch) (www.schweiz-uno.ch).

umverkehR (EL), Kalkbreitestrasse 2, Postfach 8214, 8036 Zürich (+41-44 242 7276) (info@umverkehr.ch) (www.umverkehr.ch). Working especially to cut car use.

Weltföderalisten Schweiz / Fédéralistes mondiaux Suisse (WF), c/o Hexagon AG, Graben 5, 6300 Zug (info@weltfoederalisten.ch) (www.weltfoederalisten.ch). Member of World Federalist Movement (WFM).

SYRIA

Syrian Human Rights Committee [SHRC] (HR), see under Britain. Syrian human rights group in exile in Britain.

TAIWAN

Chinese Association for Human Rights [CAHR] (HR), 4F-3 – No 23 – Sec 1 – Hangchow S Rd, Taipei 10051 (+886-2-3393 6900) (fax 2395 7399) (humanright@cahr.org.tw) (www.cahr.org.tw).

Greenpeace East Asia – Taipei Office (GP), No 10, Lane 83, Section 1, Roosevelt Rd, Zhongzheng District, Taipei City 10093 (+886-2-2321 5006) (fax 2321 3209) (inquiry.tw@greenpeace.org) (www.greenpeace.org/eastasia).

John Paul II Peace Institute / Fujen Peace Centre (RP), Fujen Catholic University, 24205 Hsinchuang, Taipei County (+886-2-2905 3111) (fax 2905 2170) (peace@mail.fju.edu.tw) (peace.fjac.fju.edu.tw). *Peace Papers.*

TANZANIA

United Nations Association of Tanzania (UN), PO Box 9182, Dar es Salaam (+255-22-219 9200) (fax 266 8749) (info@una.or.tz) (una.or.tz).

THAILAND

Asian Institute for Human Rights [AIHR] (HR), 109 Soi Sithicon, Suthisarnwinichai Road, Samsennok, Huaykwang, Bangkok 10310 (+66-2 277 6882) (fax) (kalpalatad@aihr.info) (aihr.info).

Greenway Thailand (WC), 40/1 Moo 4 Ban Vihan, Kaow Tambon Vihan, Kaow, Tha Chang district, Singburi 16140 (+66-36 521619) (info@greenwaythailand.org) (www.greenwaythailand.org).

TIBET

Tibetan Centre for Human Rights and Democracy (FR HR), see under India. Works for human rights of Tibetans in Tibet.

TOGO

Amis de la Terre – Togo [ADT] (FE), BP 20190, Lomé (+228-2222 1731) (fax 2222 1732) (adt-togo@amiterre.tg) (www.amiterre.tg).

Amnesty International Togo (AI), 2 BP 20013, Lomé 2 (+228-2222 5820) (fax) (contact@amnesty.tg) (www.amnesty.tg). *Echos d'AI; Miafé Dzena.*

TRINIDAD AND TOBAGO

United Nations Association of Trinidad & Tobago [UNATT] (UN), 106 Woodford Street, Newtown, Port of Spain (+1 868-221 7645) (info@unassociationtt.org) (unassociationtt.org).

TUNISIA

Coalition Nationale Tunisienne contre la Peine de Mort (HR), 56 Avenue de la Liberté, 1002 Tunis (+216-2168 7533) (abolitionpm@gmail.com). National Coalition Against the Death Penalty.

TURKEY

Greenpeace Mediterranean (GP), İstiklal Caddesi Kallavi Sok – No 1 Kat 2, Beyoğlu, İstanbul (+90-212-292 7619) (fax 292 7622) (bilgi.tr@greenpeace.org) (www.greenpeace.org/turkey). See also Israel, Lebanon.

İnsan Hakları Derneği / Human Rights Association [İHD] (HR), Necatibey Cad 82/11-12, Kızılay, Çankaya, 06430 Ankara (+90-312-230 3567) (fax 230 1707) (posta@ihd.org.tr) (www.ihd.org.tr).

Şiddetsizlik Eğitim ve Araştırma Denerği / Nonviolent Education and Research Association (RE WR), Kuloğlu Mah Güllabici sok no 16 – Daire 2, 34433 Cihangir, İstanbul (+90-212-244 1269) (merhaba@siddetsizlikmerkezi.org) (www.siddetsizlikmerkezi.org).

Türkiye İnsan Hakları Vakfı / Human Rights Foundation of Turkey [TİHV/HRFT] (HR), Mithatpaşa Cad – No 49/11 – 6 Kat, 06420 Kızılay / Ankara (+90-312-310 6636) (fax 310 6463) (tihv@tihv.org.tr) (www.tihv.org.tr). In Istanbul: +90-212-249 3092.

Türkiye Çevre Vakfi / Environment Foundation of Turkey [TÇV] (EL), Tunalı Hilmi Cd 50/20, Kavaklidere, 06660 Ankara (+90-312-425 5508) (fax 418 5118) (cevre@cevre.org.tr) (www.cevre.org.tr). Çevre.

Vicdani Ret Derneği / Conscientious Objector Association [VR-DER] (WR HR), Osmanağa Mah Söğütluçeşme Cad – Sevil Pasaji No 74 – Kat 5 – Ofis 108, Kadıköy, İstanbul (+90-216-345 0100) (fax) (vicdaniretdernegi@gmail.com) (vicdaniret.org). For legalising conscientious objection.

UGANDA

International Friendship League – Uganda [IFL] (CD), c/o Ismael Nyonyintono, PO Box 37692, Kampala (ismaeluk@yahoo.com).

Jamii Ya Kupatanisha [JYAK] (FR WR CR), PO Box 198, Kampala (+256-41-427 1435) (fax 434 7389) (jyak.peace@gmail.com).

Justice & Peace Commission of Gulu Archdiocese (PC HR), PO Box 200, Gulu (+256-471-32026) (fax 432860) (jpcgulu@infocom.co.ug).

Women's International League for Peace and Freedom [WILPF Uganda] (WL), PO Box 3556, Kampala (+256-77-240 5295) (wilpf.org/uganda).

UKRAINE

Mama-86 (EL), Bul Chapaeva 14 – Of 1, 01030 Kiyiv (+380-44-234 6929) (fax) (info@mama-86.org.ua) (www.mama-86.org.ua). Includes anti-nuclear campaigning.

Zeleniy Svit – Druzi Zemli (FE PA), A/C 61, 49000 Dnipropetrovsk (+380-56-370 9572) (fax 370 9573) (foeukraine@gmail.com) (www.zsfoe.org). Green World – Friends of the Earth.

UNITED STATES OF AMERICA

350.org (EL), 20 Jay St – Suite 732, Brooklyn, NY 11201 (+1-646-801 0759) (feedback@350.org) (350.org). Campaign on climate change. Formerly Step It Up.

A Rocha USA (EL), PO Box 1338, Fredricksburg, TX 78624 (+1-830-522 5319) (usa@arocha.org) (arocha.us). Christian.

About Face: Veterans Against the War [IVAW] (PA RA), PO Box 3565, New York City, NY 10008 (+1-929-430 4988) (aboutfaceveterans.org). Formerly Iraq Veterans Against the War.

Action Reconciliation Service for Peace – US [ARSP] (CD RE), 1501 Cherry St, Philadelphia, PA 19102 (+1-215-241 7249) (info@actionreconciliation.org) (actionreconciliation.org).

AJ Muste Memorial Institute (IB RE WR), 168 Canal St – 6th Flr, New York, NY 10013 (+1-212-533 4335) (info@ajmuste.org) (www.ajmuste.org). Muste Notes.

Al-Awda – The Palestine Right to Return Coalition (HR), PO Box 8812, Coral Springs, FL 33075 (+1-760-918 9441) (fax 918 9442) (info@al-awda.org) (al-awda.org).

Albert Einstein Institution (RE SD), PO Box 455, East Boston, MA 02128 (+1-617-247 4882) (fax 247 4035) (einstein@igc.org) (www.aeinstein.org).

Alliance for Global Justice (HR RA EL), 225 E 26th St – Suite 1, Tucson, AZ 85713 (+1-202-540 8336) (afgj@afgj.org) (afgj.org). Focus on changing US policy towards Latin America.

Alliance for Middle East Peace [ALLMEP] (CD), 2550 M St NW, Washington, DC 20037 (+1-202-618 4600) (fax 888-784 4530) (info@allmep.org) (www.allmep.org). Promoting people-to-people coexistence.

Alliance for Nuclear Accountability [ANA] (ND DA EL), 322 4th St NE, Washington, DC 20002 (+1-202-544 0217) (sgordon@ananuclear.org) (www.ananuclear.org).

Alternatives to Violence Project – USA [AVP/USA] (CR PC), 1050 Selby Ave, St Paul, MN 55104 (+1-888-278 7820) (info@avpusa.org) (avpusa.org).

American Civil Liberties Union [ACLU] (HR), 125 Broad St – 18th Floor, New York, NY 10004 (aclu@aclu.org) (www.aclu.org).

American Friends of Neve Shalom / Wahat al-Salam (CD HR PA RE), 229 N Central Ave – Suite 401, Glendale, CA 91203-3541 (+1-818-662 8883) (afnswas@oasisofpeace.org) (www.oasisofpeace.org). Support mixed (Jewish-Palestinian) Israeli village.

American Friends Service Committee [AFSC] (SF RE CR), 1501 Cherry St, Philadelphia, PA 19102 (+1-215-241 7000) (fax 241 7275) (afscinfo@afsc.org) (www.afsc.org).
Quaker Action.

American Jews for a Just Peace [AJJP] (RA), PO Box 1032, Arlington, MA 02474 (www.ajjp.org).

Amnesty International USA [AIUSA] (AI), 5 Penn Plaza – 16th floor, New York, NY 10001 (+1-212-807 8400) (admin-us@aiusa.org) (www.amnestyusa.org).

Anglican Pacifist Fellowship – US [APF] (RP), c/o Nathaniel W Pierce, 3864 Rumsey Dr, Trappe, MD 21673-1722 (+1-410-476 4556) (nwpierce@verizon.net).

Arkansas Coalition for Peace and Justice (DA HR), PO Box 250398, Little Rock, AR 72225 (+1-501-952 8181) (acpj@arpeaceandjustice.org) (arpeaceandjustice.org).

Arms Control Association [ACA] (AT ND RE), 1200 18th St – Ste 1175, Washington, DC 20036 (+1-202-463 8270) (fax 463 8273) (aca@armscontrol.org) (www.armscontrol.org).

Asian Pacific Environmental Network [APEN] (EL), 426 17th St – Suite 500, Oakland, CA 94612 (+1-510-834 8920) (fax 834 8926) (apen@apen4ej.org) (apen4ej.org).

Association of Christians for the Abolition of Torture [ACAT] (HR), PO Box 314, Pleasant Hill, TN 38578-0314 (revhdsmith@starpower.net).

Baptist Peace Fellowship of North America – Bautistas por la Paz [BPFNA] (RP), 300 Hawthorne Lane – Ste 205, Charlotte, NC 28204 (+1-704-521 6051) (fax 521 6053) (bpfna@bpfna.org) (www.bpfna.org).
Baptist Peacemaker.

Beyond Nuclear (EL ND), 7304 Carroll Ave – Suite 182, Takoma Park, MD 20912 (+1-301-270 2209) (info@beyondnuclear.org) (www.beyondnuclear.org).

Brady Campaign to Prevent Gun Violence (RE HR DA PO), 840 First St NE – Suite 400, Washington, DC 20002 (+1-202-370 8100) (policy@bradymail.org) (www.bradycampaign.org).

Brethren Volunteer Service (PA CD RP), Church of the Brethren, 1451 Dundee Ave, Elgin, IL 60120 (+1-847-742 5100) (fax 429 4394) (bvs@brethren.org) (www.brethrenvolunteerservice.org).

Bruderhof Communities (RP), 101 Woodcrest Dr, Rifton, NY 12471 (+1-845-658 7700) (info@bruderhof.com) (www.bruderhof.com). Also known as Church Communities International.

Buddhist Peace Fellowship [BPF] (FR IB), PO Box 3470, Berkeley, CA 94703 (+1-510-239 3764) (info@bpf.org) (www.buddhistpeacefellowship.org).

Campaign for Peace & Democracy [CPD] (IB HR RE), 2808 Broadway – No 12, New York, NY 10025 (+1-212-666 5924) (cpd@igc.org) (www.cpdweb.org).

Campaign for Peace, Disarmament & Common Security (DA ND), 2161 Massachusetts Ave, Cambridge, MA 02140 (+1-617-661 6130) (JGerson@gmail.com) (www.cpdcs.org).
For nuclear weapons abolition and common security.

Campaign to Establish a US Department of Peace (RE PO CR CD), c/o The Peace Alliance, 2108 Military Rd, Arlington, VA 22207 (1-202-684 2553) (www.thepeacealliance.org).

Cat Lovers Against the Bomb [CLAB] (ND AT HR), c/o Nebraskans for Peace, PO Box 83466, Lincoln, NE 68501-3466 (+1-402-475 4620) (fax 483 4108) (catcal@aol.com) (www.catloversagainstthebomb.org).
Calendar.

Catholic Mobilizing Network to End the Use of the Death Penalty [CMN] (RP), 415 Michigan Ave NE – Suite 210, Washington, DC 20017 (+1-202-541 5290) (info@catholicsmobilizing.org) (catholicsmobilizing.org). Formerly Catholics Against Capital Punishment.

Catholic Peace Fellowship (RP PA), PO Box 4232, South Bend, IN 46634 (+1-574-232 2811) (staff@catholicpeacefellowship.org) (www.catholicpeacefellowship.org).
Promotes conscientious objection.

Catholic Worker Movement (AL RP PA), 36 E 1st St, New York, NY 10003 (+1-212-777 9617).
The Catholic Worker.

Center for Applied Conflict Management [CACM] (RE CR), Kent State University, PO Box 5190, Kent, OH 44242-0001 (+1-330-672 3143) (fax 672 3362) (cacm@kent.edu) (www.kent.edu/cacm).

Center for Citizen Initiatives [CCI] (CD), 820 N Delaware St – Ste 405, San Mateo, CA 94401 (+1-650-458 8115) (info@ccisf.org) (ccisf.org).
Organise US-Russia citizen exchanges.

Center for Energy Research (EL CR ND), 104 Commercial St NE, Salem, OR 97301 (pbergel@igc.org).
Dedicated to breaking the nuclear chain.

Center for Genetics and Society [CGS] (EL HR), 1936 University Ave – Suite 350, Berrkeley, CA 94794 (+1-510-625 0819) (fax 665 8760) (info@geneticsandsociety.org) (www.geneticsandsociety.org).

Center for Jewish Nonviolence [CJNV] (PA RA HR), c/o T'ruah – The Rabbinic Call for

Human Rights, 266 West 37th St – Suite 803, New York, NY 10018 (CJNV.campaigns@gmail.com) (centerforjewishnonviolence.org). Organises visits to Israel for nonviolent action.

Center for Nonviolence and Peace Studies [CNPS] (RE CR PO), University of Rhode Island, 74 Lower College Rd – MCC 202, Kingston, RI 02881 (+1-401-874 2875) (fax 874 9108) (nonviolence@etal.uri.edu) (www.uri.edu/nonviolence). *Become the Change.*

Center for Nonviolent Solutions (RE CR), 901 Pleasant St, Worcester, MA 01602 (+1-774-641 1566) (inquiry@nonviolentsolution.org) (www.nonviolentsolution.org).

Center for Religious Tolerance [CRT] (RP CR), 520 Ralph St, Sarasota, FL 34242 (+1-941-312 9795) (info@c-r-t.org) (www.c-r-t.org). Supports international interfaith initiatives.

Center for Restorative Justice & Peacemaking (CR RE), University of Minnesota, 105 Peters Hall, 1404 Gortner Ave, Saint Paul, MN 55108 (+1-612-625 1220) (fax 624 3744) (www.cehd.umn.edu/ssw/rjp). For community-based response to crime and violence.

Center for the Study and Promotion of Zones of Peace (RE), 139 Kuulei Rd, Kailua, HI 96734 (+1-808-263 4015) (fax) (lop-rey.zop-hi@worldnet.att.net).

Center for Victims of Torture (HR RE), 2356 University Ave W – Suite 430, Saint Paul, MN 55114 (+1-612-436 4800) (cvt@cvt.org) (www.cvt.org).

Center on Conscience & War [CCW] (PA HR), 1830 Connecticut Ave NW, Washington, DC 20009-5706 (+1-202-483 2220) (fax 483 1246) (ccw@CenteronConscience.org) (www.centeronconscience.org). *The Reporter for Conscience' sake.*

Christian Peacemaker Teams [CPT] (RP RA), PO Box 6508, Chicago, IL 60680-6508 (+1-773-376 0550) (fax 376 0549) (peacemakers@cpt.org) (www.cpt.org).

Citizens for Peaceful Resolutions [CPR] (ND PA PO), PO Box 364, Ventura, CA 93002-0364 (www.c-p-r.net). Committed to interconnectedess of all life.

Co-operation Ireland (USA) (CD), 1501 Broadway – Suite 2600 (Attn Richard Pino), NY 10036 (www.cooperationireland.org).

Coalition to Stop Gun Violence (DA AT), 1424 L Street NW – Suite 2-1, Washington, DC 20005 (+1-202-408 0061) (csgv@csgv.org) (www.csgv.org).

CODEPINK: Women for Peace (PA), 2010 Linden Ave, Venice, CA 90291 (+1-310-827 4320) (fax 827 4547) (info@codepink.org) (www.codepink.org). A women-initiated grassroots peace campaign.

Colgate University Peace & Conflict Studies Program (RE CR), 13 Oak Dr, Hamilton, NY 13346-1398 (+1-315-228 7806) (fax 228 7121) (peace@colgate.edu) (www.colgate.edu/departments/peacestudies/).

Colombia Support Network (TW HR CD), PO Box 1505, Madison, WI 53701-1505 (+1-608-709 9817) (csn@igc.org) (www.colombiasupport.net). *Action on Colombia.*

Committee Opposed to Militarism & the Draft [COMD] (PA), PO Box 15195, San Diego, CA 92175 (+1-760-753 7518) (comd@comdsd.org) (www.comdsd.org). *Draft NOtices.*

Common Defense Campaign [CDC] (RE), c/o William Goodfellow, Centre for International Policy, 2000 M St NW – Suite 720, Washington, DC 20036-3327 (+1-202-232 3317) (wcg@ciponline.org) (www.ciponline.org). Previously the Project on Defense Alternatives.

Community of Christ Peace and Justice Ministries (RP CR TW HR), 1001 W Walnut, Independence, MO 64050-3562 (+1-816-833 1000) (fax 521 3082) (shalom@CofChrist.org) (www.CofChrist.org/peacejustice). *Herald.*

Council for Responsible Genetics [CRG] (EL HR), 5 Upland Rd – Suite 3, Cambridge, MA 02140 (+1-617-868 0870) (fax 491 5344) (crg@gene-watch.org) (www.councilforresponsiblegenetics.org). *GeneWatch.*

Courage to Resist (WR HR), 484 Lake Park Ave – No 41, Oakland, CA 94610 (+1-510-488 3559) (www.couragetoresist.org). Supports public military refusers facing court.

Creative Response to Conflict [CRC] (FR CR PO), PO Box 271, Nyack, NY 10960-0271 (+1-845-353 1796) (fax 358 4924) (inquiries@crc-global.org) (crc-global.org).

Creativity for Peace (CD), 369 Montezuma Ave – No 566, Santa Fe, NM 87501 (+1-505-982 3765) (dottie@creativityforpeace.com) (www.creativityforpeace.com).

Cultural Survival [CS] (HR), 2067 Massachusetts Ave, Cambridge, MA 02140 (+1-617-441 5400) (fax 441 5417) (culturalsurvival@cs.org) (www.cs.org).

Culture Change (EL AL PO), PO Box 3387, Santa Cruz, CA 95063 (+1-215-243 3144) (fax) (info@culturechange.org) (www.culturechange.org). 4 yrly. Supports immediate cut in petrol cosumption.

Culture of Peace Corporation / Culture of Peace News Network (RE), 95 Lyon St, New Haven, CT 06511 (coordinator@cpnn-world.org) (cpnn-world.org).

Death Penalty Information Center (HR RE), 1015 18th St NW – Suite 704, Washington, DC 20036 (+1-202-289 2275) (dpic@deathpenaltyinfo.org) (www.deathpenaltyinfo.org).

Democratic World Federalists (WF), 55 New Montgomery St – Suite 55, San Francisco, CA 94105 (+1-415-227 4880) (dwfed@dwfed.org) (www.dwfed.org).

Earth First! Journal (EL RA), PO Box 1112, Grants Pass, OR 97528 (+1-541-244 1533) (collective@earthfirstjournal.org) (www.earthfirstjournal.org). 4 yrly.

Earthworks (EL HR), 1612 K St NW – Suite 904, Washington, DC 20006 (+1-202-887 1872) (fax 887 1875) (info@earthworksaction.org) (www.earthworksaction.org). Protecting communities from mining etc.

East Timor and Indonesia Action Network [ETAN] (HR TW), PO Box 1663, New York, NY 10035-1663 (+1-917-690 4391) (etan@etan.org) (www.etan.org).

Ecumenical Accompaniment Programme in Palestine and Israel – USA [EAPPI-USA] (RP HR), c/o Steve Weaver, Church World Service, 475 Riverside Dr – Suite 700, New York, NY 10115 (info@eappi-us.org) (www.eappi-us.org).

Ecumenical Peace Institute / Clergy and Laity Concerned [EPI/CALC] (RP HR TW), PO Box 9334, Berkeley, CA 94709 (+1-510-990 0374) (epicalc@gmail.com) (www.epicalc.org).

Education for Peace in Iraq Center [EPIC] (CD HR RE), 1140 3rd St NE – Space 2138, Washington, DC 20002 (+1-202-747 6454) (info@epic-usa.org) (www.epic-usa.org). Founded by war veterans.

Educators for Peaceful Classrooms and Communities [EPCC] (RE), 520 Calabasas Rd, Watsonville, CA 95076 (www.educatorsforpeacefulclassroomsand-communities.org)

Environmentalists Against War (EL DA ND PA AT), PO Box 27, Berkeley, CA 94701 (+1-510-843 3343) (info@envirosagainstwar.org) (www.envirosagainstwar.org).

Episcopal Peace Fellowship [EPF] (FR CD), PO Box 15, Claysburg, PA 16625 (+1-312-922 8628) (epf@epfnational.org) (epfnation-al.org).

Equal Justice USA (HR), 81 Prospect St, Brooklyn, NYC, NY 11201 (+1-718-801 8940) (fax 801 8947) (info@ejusa.org) (ejusa.org). Against executions.

Esperanto-USA [E-USA] (HR), 91-J Auburn St – 1248, Portland, ME 04103 (+1-510-653 0998) (fax 866-200 1108) (eusa@esperanto-usa.org) (www.esperanto-usa.org). *Usona Esperantisto.*

Everytown for Gun Safety (DA), PO Box 4184, New York, NY 10163 (+1-646-324 8250) (info@everytown.org) (everytown.org). Working to end gun violence.

Farms Not Arms – Peace Roots Alliance [PRA] (DA EL), 425 Farm Rd – Suite 5, Summertown, TN 38483 (+1-931-964 2119) (fna_info@farmsnotarms.org) (www.farmsnotarms.org). Also West Coast office (+1-415-218 9021).

Fellowship for Intentional Community [FIC] (PO CR AL), 23 Dancing Rabbit Lane, Rutledge, MO 63563 (+1-660-883 5545) (fic@ic.org) (www.ic.org). *Communities.*

Fellowship of Reconciliation [FOR] (FR WR), 521 N Broaday, Nyack, NY 10960-0271 (+1-845-358 4601) (fax 358 4924) (communications@forusa.org) (www.forusa.org). *Fellowship.*

Food Not Bombs [FnB-US] (PA PO RA), PO Box 424, Arroyo Seco, NM 87514 (+1-575-770 3377) (menu@foodnotbombs.net) (www.foodnotbombs.net).

Footprints for Peace (ND EL), 1225 North Bend Rd, Cincinnati, OH 45224 (jim@footprintsforpeace.org) (www.footprintsforpeace.org).

Foundation for Middle East Peace [FMEP], 1319 18th St NW, Washington, DC 20036 (+1-202-835 3650) (fax 835 3651) (info@fmep.org) (fmep.org).

Franciscan Action Network (RP EL HR), PO Box 29106, Washington, DC 20017 (+1-202-527 7575) (fax 527 7576) (info@franciscanaction.org) (franciscanaction.org).

Free Palestine Movement (HR), 405 Vista Heights Rd, El Cerrito, CA 94530 (+1-510-232 2500) (info@freepalestinemovement.org) (www.freepalestinemovement.org). Formerly Free Gaza Movement.

Fresno Center for Nonviolence (PA PO), 1584 N Van Ness Ave, Fresno, CA 93728 (+1-559-237 3223) (info@centerfornonviolence.org) (centerfornonviolence.org).

Friends for a Nonviolent World (PA PO CR), 1050 Selby Ave, Saint Paul, MN 55104 (+1-651-917 0383) (info@fnvw.org) (www.fnvw.org).

Friends of Peace Pilgrim (PO CR), PO Box 2207, Shelton, CT 06484-1841 (+1-203-926 1581) (friends@peacepilgrim.org) (www.peacepilgrim.org).

Friends of the Earth (FE), 1100 15th St NW – 11th Floor, Washington, DC 20005 (+1-202-783 7400) (fax 783 0444) (foe@foe.org) (www.foe.org).

Friends Peace Teams [FPT] (SF CR), 1001 Park Ave, St Louis, MO 63104 (+1-314-588 1122) (Office@FriendsPeaceTeams.org) (friendspeaceteams.org). *PeaceWays.*

Genocide Watch (HR RE), 1405 Cola Drive, McLean, VA 22101 (+1-202-643 1405) (communications@genocidewatch.org) (www.genocidewatch.com).

Global Exchange (HR RE CD TW), 2017 Mission St – 2nd floor, San Francisco, CA 94110 (+1-415-255 7296) (fax 255 7498) (www.globalexchange.org). *Global Exchange.*

Global Family (CD WF RP), 17738 Minnow Way, Penn Valley, CA 95946 (www.globalfamily.org).

Global Green USA (EL AT CR), 1617 Broadway – 2nd floor, Santa Monica, CA 90404 (+1-310-581 2700) (fax 581 2702) (social@globalgreen.org) (www.globalgreen.org).

Global Majority (CR RE), 411 Pacific St – Suite 318, Monterey, CA 93940 (+1-831-372 5518) (fax 372 5519) (info@globalmajority.net) (globalmajority.org). Promoting peace through dialogue.

Global Meditations Network (CR PO), c/o Barbara Wolf, 218 Dartmouth St, Rochester, NY 14607 (bjwolf@globalmeditations.com) (www.globalmeditations.com).

Global Peace Foundation [GPF] (RP), 9320 Annapolis Rd – Suite 100, Lanham, MD 20706 (+1-202-643 4733) (fax -240-667 1709) (info@globalpeace.org) (www.globalpeace.org).

Global Security Institute [GSI] (ND RE WF), 220 East 49th St – Suite 1B, New York, NY 10017 (+1-646-289 5170) (fax 289 5171) (info@gsinstitute.org) (gsinstitute.org).

Global Witness (EL HR RW TW CR), 1100 17th St NW – Suite 501, Washington, DC 20036 (+1-202-827 8673) (www.globalwitness.org). Also in Britain.

GMO Free USA (EL), PO Box 458, Unionville, CT 06085 (info@gmofreeusa.org) (www.gmofreeusa.org).

Green Party of the United States (EL HR CD), PO Box 75075, Washington, DC 20013 (+1-202-319 7191) (info@gp.org) (www.gp.org).

Greenpeace USA (GP), 702 H St NW – Suite 300, Washington, DC 20001 (+1-202-462 1177) (fax 462 4507) (info@wdc.greenpeace.org) (www.greenpeace.org/usa). *Greenpeace.*

Ground Zero Center for Nonviolent Action (ND PA RA), 16159 Clear Creek Rd NW, Poulsbo, WA 98370 (+1-360-930 8697) (info@gzcenter.org) (gzcenter.org). *Ground Zero.*

Guatemala Human Rights Commission USA [GHRC] (HR), 3321 12th St NE, Washington, DC 20017 (+1-202-529 6599) (fax 526 4611) (ghrc-usa@ghrc-usa.org) (www.ghrc-usa.org). *El Quetzal.*

Hand in Hand (PO CD RE), PO Box 80102, Portland, OR 97280 (+1-503-892 2962) (info@handinhandk12.org) (www.handinhandk12.org). Supports integrated education in Israel.

Harmony for Peace Foundation (PO CD ND), PO Box 2165, Southeastern, PA 19399 (+1-484-885 8539) (info@harmonyforpeace.org) (harmonyforpeace.org). Music for peace. Works with group in Japan.

Historians for Peace and Democracy [H-PAD] (DA HR CR), c/o Van Gosse, Department of History, PO Box 3003, Franklin & Marshall College, Lancaster, PA 17604-3003 (www.historiansforpeace.org). Formerly Historians Against the War.

ICAHD-USA (HR), PO Box 81252, Pittsburgh, PA 15217 (info@icahdusa.org) (www.icahdusa.org).

Institute for Food and Development Policy / Food First (RE TW EL), 398 60th St, Oakland, CA 94618 (+1-510-654 4400) (fax 654 4551) (info@foodfirst.org) (www.foodfirst.org).

Institute for Inclusive Security (RE CR), 1615 M St NW – Suite 850, Washington, DC 20036 (+1-202-403 2000) (fax 808 7070) (info@inclusivesecurity.org) (www.inclusivesecurity.org). Promotes women's contributions to peace-building.

Institute for Middle East Understanding [IMEU] (RE CD), 2913 El Camino Real – No 436, Tustin, CA 92782 (+1-718-514 9662) (info@imeu.org) (imeu.org). Provides research and experts about Palestine.

Institute for Social Ecology (EL AL PO), PO Box 48, Plainfield, VT 05667 (info@social-ecology.org) (www.social-ecology.org).

Interfaith Peace-Builders (RP CD CR), 1628 16th St NW, Washington, DC 20009 (+1-202-244 0821) (fax -866-936 1650) (office@ifpb.org) (www.ifpb.org). Send delegations to Israel/Palestine.

International Center for Transitional Justice [ICTJ] (CR HR), 50 Broadway – 23rd Floor, New York, NY 10004 (+1-917-637 3800) (fax 637 3900) (info@ictj.org) (www.ictj.org). Offices in Europe, Asia, Africa, South America.

International Center on Nonviolent Conflict [ICNC] (RE SD), 1775 Pennsylvania Ave NW – Ste 1200, Washington, DC 20006 (+1-202-416 4720) (fax 466 5918) (icnc@nonviolent-conflict.org) (www.nonviolent-conflict.org).

International Rivers (FE HR), 2150 Allston Way – Suite 300, Berkeley, CA 94704-1378 (+1-510-848 1155) (fax 848 1008) (info@internationalrivers.org) (www.internationalrivers.org). *World Rivers Review.*

Iowa Peace Network (RP), PO Box 30021, Des Moines, IA 50310 (+1-515-255 7114) (iowapeacenetwork@gmail.com).

Israeli-Palestinian Confederation Committee (CR CD), 15915 Ventura Blvd – No 302, Encino, CA 91436 (+1-818-317 7110) (mail@aboutipc.org) (www.aboutipc.org).

Jeanette Rankin Peace Center [JRPC] (RE EL CR PO), 519 S Higgins Ave, Missoula, MT 59801 (+1-406-543 3955) (fax 541 3997) (peace@jrpc.org) (jrpc.org).

Jewish Peace Fellowship [JPF] (FR), PO Box 271, Nyack, NY 10960-0271 (+1-845-358 4601) (fax 358 4924) (jpf@forusa.org) (www.jewishpeacefellowship.org). *Shalom.*

Jewish Voice for Peace [JVP] (HR CR RA), PO Box 589, Berkeley, CA 94701 (+1-510-465 1777) (fax 465 1616) (info@jvp.org) (jewishvoiceforpeace.org). Promotes US policy based on human rights.

JustPeace – Center for Mediation and Conflict Transformation (CR RE RP), 100 Maryland Ave NE, Washington, DC 20002 (+1-202-488 5647) (justpeace@justpeaceumc.org) (justpeaceumc.org).

Kansas Institute for Peace and Conflict Resolution [KIPCOR] (RE CR), Bethel College, 300 E 27th St, North Newton, KS 67117 (+1-316-284 5217) (fax 284 5379) (kipcor@bethelks.edu) (www.kipcor.org). Formerly Kansas Peace Institute.

Karuna Center for Peacebuilding [KCP] (CR HR RE), 447 West St, Amherst, MA 01002 (+1-413-256 3800) (fax 256 3802) (info@karunacenter.org) (www.karunacenter.org).

Korea Peace Network [KPN], 8630 Fenton St – Ste 604, Silver Spring, MD 20910 (fax +1-301-565 0850) (www.peaceaction.org/korea-peace-network). Network campaigning for peace on Korean peninsula.

Law Center to Prevent Gun Violence (DA), 268 Bush St – No 555, San Francisco, CA 94104 (+1-415-433 2062) (fax 433 3357) (smartgunlaws.org).

Lawyers Committee on Nuclear Policy [LCNP] (ND AT DA), 220 E 49th St – Suite 1B, New York, NY 10017-1527 (+1-212-818 1861) (fax 818 1857) (contact@lcnp.org) (www.lcnp.org).

Los Angeles Peace Council [LAPC] (WP), PO Box 741104, Los Angeles, CA 90004 (+1-323-498 0973) (lapeacecouncil@outlook.com) (www.lapeacecouncil.org).

Lutheran Peace Fellowship [LPF] (RP), 1710 11th Ave, Seattle, WA 98122-2420 (+1-206-349 2501) (lpf@ecunet.org) (www.lutheranpeace.org).

Mahatma Gandhi Center for Global Nonviolence (RE), James Madison University, MSC 2604, The Annex, 725 S Mason St, Harrisonburg, VA 22807 (+1-540-568 4060) (fax 568 7251) (GandhiCenter@jmu.edu) (www.jmu.edu/gandhicenter).

Mahatma Gandhi Library (RE), c/o Atul Kothari, 4526 Bermuda Dr, Sugar Land, TX 77479 (+1-281-531 1977) (fax 713-785 6252) (info@gandhilibrary.org) (www.gandhilibrary.org).

Maryknoll Office for Global Concerns (PC EL RE), 200 New York Ave NW, Washington, DC 20001 (+1-202-832 1780) (fax 832 5195) (ogc@maryknoll.org) (www.maryknoll.org).

Maryland United for Peace and Justice [MUPJ] (DA HR CR), c/o Tony Langbehn, 327 E 25th St, Baltimore, MD 21218 (+1-301-390 9684) (tonylang4peace@gmail.com) (www.mupj.org).

Matsunaga Institute for Peace and Conflict Resolution (RE CR), University of Hawaii, 2424 Maile Way – Saunders 723, Honolulu, HI 96822 (+1-808-956 4237) (fax 956 0950) (uhip@hawaii.edu) (peaceinstitute.hawaii.edu).

Megiddo Peace Project (PO Box 7213), Ann Arbor, MI 48107 (megiddo@umich.edu) (www.peacetable.org). Calls for co-operation against the war system.

Metta Center for Nonviolence (RE), 205 Keller St – Suite 202D, Petaluma, CA 94952 (+1-707-774 6299) (info@mettacenter.org) (mettacenter.org).

Mid-South Peace & Justice Center (IB ND EL), 3573 Southern Ave, Memphis, TN 38111 (+1-901-725 4990) (centre@midsouthpeace.org) (midsouthpeace.org).

Middle East Research & Information Project [MERIP] (TW HR AT), 1344 T St NW – No 1, Washington, DC 20009 (+1-202-223 3677) (fax 223 3604) (www.merip.org). *Middle East Report.*

Minds of Peace (CR), PO Box 11494, St Louis, MO 63105-9998 (peace.public@gmail.com) (mindsofpeace.org). Helps discussions in divided communities.

Minnesota Alliance of Peacemakers (FR UN WL PC), PO Box 19573, Minneapolis, MN 55419 (info@mapm.org) (www.mapm.org). Umbrella group of many local organisations.

MK Gandhi Institute for Nonviolence (RE), 929 S Plymouth Ave, Rochester, NY 14608 (+1-585-463 3266) (fax 276 0203) (kmiller@admin.rochester.edu) (www.gandhiinstitute.org).

Murder Victims' Families for Human Rights (HR CR RE PO), 2161 Massachusetts Ave, Cambridge, MA 02140 (+1-617-491 9600) (info@murdervictimsfamilies.org) (www.mvfhr.org). Oppose death penalty.

National Campaign for a Peace Tax Fund [NCPTF] (TR), 2121 Decatur Pl NW, Washington, DC 20008 (+1-202-483 3751) (info@peacetaxfund.org) (www.peacetaxfund.org). *Peace Tax Fund Update.*

National Campaign for Nonviolent Resistance (RA), 431 Notre Dame Lane – Apt 206, Baltimore, MD 21212 (+1-410-323 1607) (mobuszewski2001@comcast.net). Co-ordinates anti-war trainings and actions.

National Coalition Against Censorship [NCAC] (HR), 19 Fulton St – Suite 407, New York, NY 10038 (+1-212-807 6222) (fax 807 6245) (ncac@ncac.org) (ncac.org). Alliance of over 50 national organisations.

National Coalition to Abolish the Death Penalty [NCADP] (HR), 1620 L St NW – Suite 250, Washington, DC 20036 (+1-202-331 4090) (info@ncadp.org) (www.ncadp.org).

National Network Opposing the Militarization of Youth [NNOMY] (DA PO), c/o AFSC Wage Peace Program, 65 Ninth St, San Francisco, CA 94103 (+1-760-634 3604) (admin@nnomy.org) (www.nnomy.org).

National Peace Academy [NPA] (RE), PO Box 2024, San Mateo, CA 94401 (+1-650-918 6901) (nationalpeaceacademy.us).

National War Tax Resistance Coordinating Committee [NWTRCC] (TR RA PA), PO Box 5616, Milwaukee, WI 53205-5616 (+1-262-399 8217) (nwtrcc@nwtrcc.org) (www.nwtrcc.org). *More Than a Paycheck.*

Natural Resources Defense Council [NRDC] (EL), 40 West 20th St, New York, NY 10011 (+1-212-727 2700) (fax 727 1773) (nrdcinfo@nrdc.org) (www.nrdc.org). Works to protect planet's wildlife and wild places.

Network of Spiritual Progressives [NSP] (RP PO), 2342 Shattuck Ave – Suite 1200, Berkeley, CA 94704 (+1-510-644 1200) (fax 644 1255) (www.tikkun.org). *Tikkun.*

Nevada Desert Experience [NDE] (RP ND DA RA), 1420 West Bartlett Ave, Las Vegas, NV 89106-2226 (+1-702-646 4814) (info@nevadadesertexperience.org) (www.nevadadesertexperience.org). *Desert Voices.*

New Israel Fund (HR), 6 East 39th St, New York, NY 10016-0112 (+1-212-613 4400) (fax 714 2153) (info@nif.org) (www.nif.org). Supports progressive civil society in Israel.

Nobel Peace Laureate Project (RE), PO Box 21201, Eugene, OR 97402 (+1-541-485 1604) (info@nobelpeacelaureates.org) (www.nobelpeacelaureates). Promote peace by honouring peacemakers.

North American Congress on Latin America [NACLA] (TW HR), c/o NYU CLACS, 53 Washington Sq South – Fl 4W, New York, NY 10012 (+1-646-535 9085) (nacla.org). *Report on the Americas.*

North American Vegetarian Society (EL PO), PO Box 72, Dolgeville, NY 13329 (+1-518-568 7970) (fax 568 7979) (navs@telenet.net). *Vegetarian Voice.*

Nuclear Age Peace Foundation [NAPF] (PA ND IB RE), PMB 121, 1187 Coast Village Rd – Suite 1, Santa Barbara, CA 93108-2794 (+1-805-965 3443) (fax 568 0466) (wagingpeace@napf.org) (www.wagingpeace.org). *The Sunflower.*

Nuclear Ban – Treaty Compliance Campaign (ND), 59 Gleason Rd, Northampton, MA 01060 (+1-413-727 3704) (info@nuclearban.us) (www.nuclearban.us). Supportintg 2017 UN nuclear weapons ban treaty.

Nuclear Energy Information Service [NEIS] (EL RA), 3411 W Diversey Ave – No 13, Chicago, IL 60647 (+1-773-342 7650) (neis@neis.org) (neis.org). Educates about and campaigns against nuclear power.

Nuclear Information and Resource Service [NIRS] (EL ND), 6930 Carroll Ave – Suite 340, Takoma Park, MD 20912 (+1-301-270 6477) (fax 270 4291) (timj@nirs.org) (www.nirs.org). *WISE/NIRS Nuclear Monitor.* Works with WISE, Amsterdam, to produce information.

Nuclear Resister (ND RA TR PA), PO Box 43383, Tucson, AZ 85733 (+1-520-323 8697) (fax) (nukeresister@igc.org) (www.nukeresister.org). 4 yrly, $25 ($35 abroad) pa.

Nuclear Threat Initiative [NTI] (ND), 1776 Eye St NW – Suite 600, Washington, DC 20006 (+1-202-296 4810) (fax 296 4811) (contact@nti.org) (www.nti.org).

Nuclear Watch South (EL ND), PO Box 8574, Atlanta, GA 31106 (+1-404-378 4263) (info@nonukesyall.org) (www.nonukesyall.crg). *Nuclear Watch Tower.*

Nukewatch (EL ND RA PA RE), 740A Round Lake Rd, Luck, WI 54853 (+1-715-472 4185) (nukewatch1@lakeland.ws) (www.nukewatchinfo.org). *Nukewatch Quarterly.*

Oak Ridge Environmental Peace Alliance (ND RA), PO Box 5743, Oak Ridge, TN 37831 (+1-865-483 8202) (orep@earthlink.net) (www.orepa.org).

On Earth Peace (RP), PO Box 188, 500 Main St, New Windsor, MD 21776 (+1-410-635 8704) (onearthpeace.org). Linked to Church of the Brethren.

OneVoice Movement – USA (CD CR), PO Box 1577-OCS, New York, NY 10113 (+1-212-897 3985) (info@OneVoiceMovement.org) (www.onevoicemovement.org). See also under Israel, Palestine, and Britain.

Oregon Peace Institute [OPI] (RE EL), Whitefeather Peace Community, 3315 N Russet St, Portland, OR 97217 (+1-503-327 8250) (Oregon.Peace.Institute@gmail.com) (orpeace.us). Also www.peacevoice.info.

Orthodox Peace Fellowship [OPF] (RP), PO Box 76609, Washingtgon, DC 20013 (opfnorthamerica@gmail.com) (incommunion.org).

Pace e Bene (RP PA), PO Box 2460, Athens, OH 45701-5260 (+1-510-268 8765) (fax 702-648 2281) (info@paceebene.org) (www.paceebene.org).
For nonviolence and cultural transformation.

Pastors for Peace / IFCO (RP CD), 418 West 145th St, New York, NY 10031 (+1-212-926 5757) (fax 926 5842) (ifco@ifconews.org) (www.ifconews.org).

Pathways to Peace (CD RE), PO Box 1057, Larkspur, CA 94977 (+1-415-461 0500) (fax 925 0330) (info@pathwaystopeace.org) (www.pathwaystopeace.org).

Pax Christi USA (PC CD EL), 415 Michigan Ave NE – Suite 240, Washington, DC 20017-4503 (+1-202-635 2741) (info@paxchristiusa.org) (www.paxchristiusa.org).

Peace & Justice Center (DA HR), 60 Lake St, Burlington, VT 05401 (+1-802-863 2345) (info@pjcvt.org) (www.pjcvt.org).

Peace & Justice Program of the United Methodist Church (RP), c/o General Board of Global Ministries, 475 Riverside Drive, New York, NY 10115 (info@gbgm-umc.org) (new.gbgm-umc.org).

Peace Abbey Foundation (RP PA RE), 16 Lavender St, Millis, MA 02054 (+1-508-655 2143) (administration@peaceabbey.org) (www.peaceabbey.org).
Includes Pacifist Living History Museum.

Peace Action (IB ND AT), Montgomery Center, 8630 Fenton St – Suite 934, Silver Spring, MD 20910 (+1-301-565 4050) (fax 565 0850) (kmartin@peace-action.org) (www.peaceaction.org).

Peace Action West (ND DA), 2201 Broadway – Suite 604, Oakland, CA 94612 (+1-510-849 2272) (www.peaceactionwest.org). Main office in Maryland (+1-301-565 4050).

Peace and Justice Studies Association [PJSA] (RE), 1421 37th St NW – Suite 130, Poulton Hall, Georgetown University, Washington, DC 20057 (+1-202-681 2057) (info@peacejusticestudies.org) (www.peacejusticestudies.org).

Peace Brigades International [PBI-USA] (PA RA CR), PO Box 75880, Washington, DC 20013 (+1-202-232 0142) (fax 232 0143) (info@pbiusa.org) (pbiusa.org).

Peace Development Fund [PDF] (HR EL PA), PO Box 40250, San Francisco, CA 94140-0250 (+1-415-642 0900) (peacedevfund@pdf.org) (www.peacedevelopmentfund.org). *Peace Developments.* Also PDF Center for Peace and Justice, Amherst, MA.

Peace Education and Action Centre of Eastern Iowa (RE DA), Old Brick, 26 East Market St, Iowa City, IA 52245 (+1-319-354 1925) (information@PEACEIowa.net) (peaceiowa.org).

Peace Educators Allied for Children Everywhere [PEACE] (WR RE EL CR), c/o Lucy Stroock, 55 Frost St, Cambridge, MA 02140 (+1-617-661 8374) (1peaceeducators@gmail.com) (www.peaceeducators.org).
Network of parents, teachers and others.

PeaceJam Foundation (RE CR HR), 11200 Ralston Rd, Arvada, CO 80004 (+1-303-455 2099) (rockymoutain@peacejam.org) (peacejam@peacejam.org). Also in Maine (maine@peacejam.org).

Peaceworkers (CR CD PA RA SD), 721 Shrader St, San Francisco, CA 94117 (+1-415-751 0302) (fax) (davidrhartsough@gmail.com) (www.peaceworkersus.org).
Promote international peace teams.

Physicians for Human Rights [PHR] (HR), 256 W 38th St – 9th Floor, New York, NY 10018 (+1-646-564 3720) (fax 564 3750) (communications@phrusa.org) (physiciansforhumanrights.org).
Also offices in Washington DC amd Boston.

Physicians for Social Responsibility [PSR] (IP), 1111 14th St NW – Suite 700, Washington, DC 20005 (+1-202-667 4260) (fax 667 4201) (psrnatl@psr.org) (www.psr.org).

Ploughshares Fund (ND), 1808 Wedemeyer St – Suite 200, The Presidio of San Francisco, San Francisco, CA 94129 (+1-415-668 2244) (fax 668 2214) (ploughshares@ploughshares.org) (www.ploughshares.org).
Promoting elimination of nuclear weapons.

Plowshares Network (RP RA ND PA), c/o Jonah House, 1301 Moreland Av, Baltimore, MD 21216 (+1-410-233 6238) (disarmnow@verizon.net) (www.jonahhouse.org).

Popular Resistance (RA HR EL), c/o Alliance for Global Justice, 225 E 26th St – Suite 1, Tucson, AZ 85713 (info@popularresistance.org) (popularresistance.org).
Against corporate takeover of government.

Portland State University Conflict Resolution Department (RE), 1600 SW 4th Av – Neuberger 131, Portland, OR 97201 (+1-503-725 9173) (fax 725 9174) (conflict_resolution@pdx.edu) (www.conflictresolution.pdx.edu).
Specialisation in Peace and Nonviolence Studies.

Positive Futures Network, 284 Madrona Way NE – Suite 116, Bainbridge Island, WA 98110-2870 (+1-206-842 0216) (fax 842 5208) (info@yesmagazine.org) (www.yesmagazine.org). *Yes!.*

Presbyterian Peace Fellowship [PPF] (FR), 17 Cricketown Rd, Stony Point, NY 10980 (+1-845-786 6743) (info@presbypeacefellowship.org) (www.presbypeacefellowship.org).

Project on Youth and Non-Military Opportunities [Project YANO] (RE PA), PO Box 230157, Encinitas, CA 92023 (+1-760-634 3604) (projyano@aol.com) (www.projectyano.com)

Promoting Enduring Peace [PEP] (DA EL PA), 323 Temple St, New Haven, CT 06511-6602 (+1-202-573 7322) (coordinator@pepeace.org) (www.pepeace.org).

Proposition One Campaign (ND AT), 401 Wilcox Rd, Tryon, NC 28782 (+1-202-210 3886) (et@prop1.org) (prop1.org). For nuclear weapons abolition.

Psychologists for Social Responsibility [PsySR] (ND RE CR), c/o Brad Olsen, 122 S Michigan Ave, National Louis University, Chicago, IL 60603 (+1-917-626 7571) (fax 312-261 3464) (info@psysr.org) (psysr.org).

Quaker House (SF RE), 223 Hillside Ave, Fayetteville, NC 28301 (+1-910-323 3912) (qpr@quaker.org) (www.quakerhouse.org). Work includes counselling disaffected soldiers.

Rainforest Action Network [RAN] (FE RA HR), 425 Bush St – Ste 300, San Francisco, CA 94108 (+1-415-398 4404) (fax 398 2732) (answers@ran.org) (www.ran.org).

Random Acts of Kindness Foundation [RAK] (CD CR PO), 1727 Tremont Pl, Denver, CO 80202 (+1-303-297 1964) (fax 297 2919) (info@randomactsofkindness.org) (www.randomactsofkindness.org).

Refuser Solidarity Network (PA HR), PO Box 75392, Washington, DC 20013 (+1-202-232 1100) (info@refusersolidarity.net) (www.refusersolidarity.net). Supports Israeli COs and resisters.

Religions for Peace USA (RE RP CR HR), 777 UN Plaza – 9th Floor, New York, NY 10017 (+1-212-338 9140) (fax 983 0098) (rfpusa@rfpusa.org) (www.rfpusa.org).

Renounce War Projects (RP PA), 8001 Geary Blvd, San Francisco, CA 94121 (+1-415-307 1213) (peacematters@renouncewarprojects.org) (renouncewarprojects.org). Promotes Gandhian ideals.

Reprieve US (HR), PO Box 3627, New York, NY 10163 (+1-917-855 8064) (info@reprieve.org) (www.reprieve.org). Supports people facing death penalty.

Resistance Studies Initiative – Critical Support of People Power and Social Change (RE RA WR), University of Massachusetts Department of Sociology, 200 Hicks Way – Thompson Hall, Amherst, MA 01003-9277 (+1-413-545 5957) (fax 545 3204) (resist@umass.edu) (www.umass.edu/resistancestudies).

Resource Center for Nonviolence [RCNV] (WR FR HR), 612 Ocean St, Santa Cruz, CA (+1-831-423 1626) (rcnvinfo@gmail.com) (rcnv.org).

Rising Tide North America [RTA] (EL RA), 268 Bush St – Box 3717, San Francisco, CA 94101 (+1-503-438 4697) (networking@risingtidenorthamerica.org) (risingtidenorthamerica.org). Network of groups working on climate change.

Rocky Mountain Peace and Justice Centre (ND PA RE), PO Box 1156, Boulder, CO 80306 (+1-303-444 6981) (rmpjc@earthlink.net) (www.rmpjc.org).

Ruckus Society (RA), PO Box 28741, Oakland, CA 94604 (+1-510-931 6339) (fax 866-778 6374) (ruckus@ruckus.org) (www.ruckus.org). Tools and training for direct action.

San José Peace & Justice Center, 48 South 7th St, San Jose, CA 95112 (+1-408-297 2299) (sjpjc@sanjosepeace.org) (www.sanjosepeace.org).

Satyagraha Institute (RP PA PO), c/o Carl Kline, 825 Fourth St, Brookings, SD 57006 (www.satyagrahainstitute.org). Promotes understanding of satyagraha.

School of the Americas Watch [SOA Watch] (HR), 225 E 26th St – Ste 7, Tucson, AZ 85713 (+1-202-234 3440) (info@soaw.org) (www.soaw.org).

Secular Coalition for America (HR), 1012 14th St NW – No 205, Washington, DC 20005 (+1-202-299 1091) (www.secular.org).

Seeds of Peace (CD CR PO), 370 Lexington Ave – Suite 1201, New York, NY 10017 (+1-212-573 8040) (fax 573 8047) (info@seedsofpeace.org) (www.seedsofpeace.org). Brings together teenagers from conflict areas.

September 11th Families for Peaceful Tomorrows [PT] (CD CR RE), PO Box 20145, Park West Finance Station, New York, NY 10025 (+1-212-598 0970) (info@peacefultomorrows.org) (peacefultomorrows.org). Promote nonviolent resolution of conflict.

Service Civil International / International Voluntary Service [SCI-IVS USA] (SC), PO Box 1082, Great Barrington, MA 01230 (+1-413-591 8050) (fax 434-366 3545) (sciivs.usa.ltv@gmail.com) (www.volunteersciusa.org).

Sikh Human Rights Group (HR CR), 103 Omar Ave, Evenel, NJ 07001 (shrgusa@shrg.net) (shrg.net).

States United to Prevent Gun Violence (DA RE), PO Box 1359, New York, NY 10276-1359 (info@supgv.org) (www.ceasefireusa.org). 30 affiliates.

Swarthmore College Peace Collection (RE), 500 College Ave, Swarthmore, PA 19081 (+1-610-328 8557) (fax 328 8544) (wchmiel1@swarthmore.edu) (www.swarthmore.edu/Library/peace). Also houses Global Nonviolent Action Database.

Syracuse Cultural Workers (HR PA EL PO), PO Box 6367, Syracuse, NY 13217 (+1-315-474 1132) (fax 234 0930) (scw@syracuseculturalworkers.com) (www.syracuseculturalworkers.com). *Peace Calendar*, *Women Artists Datebook*. Also posters, cards, T-shirts, books.

Syracuse Peace Council (PA EL RA), 2013 East Genesee St, Syracuse, NY 13210 (+1-315-472 5478) (spc@peacecouncil.net) (www.peacecouncil.net).

Teachers Resisting Unhealthy Children's Entertainment [TRUCE] (RE PO), 160 Lakeview Ave, Cambridge, MA 02138 (truce@truceteachers.org) (www.truceteachers.org).

The Progressive (HR), 30 W Mifflin St – Suite 703, Madison, WI 53703 (+1-608-257 4626) (editorial@progressive.org) (www.progressive.org). Mthly, $32 ($80 abroad) pa.

Torture Abolition and Survivor Support Coalition [TASSC] (HR AT CR), 4121 Harewood Rd NE – Suite B, Washington, DC 20017 (+1-202-529 2991) (fax 529 8334) (info@tassc.org) (www.tassc.org).

Training for Change (RA RE PO), PO Box 30914, Philadelphia, PA 19104 (+1-267-289 2288) (info@trainingforchange.org) (www.trainingforchange.org).

Tri-Valley CAREs (ND EL), 2582 Old First St, Livermore, CA 94550 (+1-925-443 7148) (fax 443 0177) (marylia@earthlink.net) (www.trivalleycares.org). *Citizen's Watch*. Communities Against a Radioactive Environment.

United for Peace and Justice [UFPJ] (DA), 244 Fifth Ave – Suite D55, New York, NY 10001 (+1-917-410 0119) (info.ufpj@gmail.com) (www.unitedforpeace.org). Major coalition.

United National Antiwar Coalition [UNAC] (DA), PO Box 123, Delmar, NY 12054 (+1-518-227 6947) (UNACpeace@gmail.com) (www.UNACpeace.org).

United Nations Association of the USA [UNA-USA] (UN RE), 801 Second Avenue, New York, NY 10017-4706 (fax +1-212-697 3316) (membership@unausa.org) (www.unausa.org). Also in Washington DC (+1-202-854 2360).

United States Institute of Peace [USIP] (RE), 2301 Constitution Ave NW, Washington, DC 20037 (+1-202-457 1700) (fax 429 6063) (www.usip.org). *Peace Watch*. Officially funded.

US Campaign for Burma (HR), PO Box 34126, Washington, DC 20043 (+1-202-702 1161) (fax 234 8044) (info@uscampaignforburma.org) (www.uscampaignforburma.org).

US Campaign for Palestinian Rights [USCPR] (HR), PO Box 3609, Washington, DC 20027 (uscpr.org). Formerly US Campaign to End the Israeli Occupation.

US Climate Action Network (EL RA), 50 F St NW – 8th floor, Washington, DC 20001 (+1-202-495 3046) (fax 547 6009) (www.usclimatenetwork.org)

US Peace Memorial Foundation (RE PA), 334 East Lake Rd – Unit 136, Palm Harbor, FL 34685-2427 (+1-202-455 8776) (info@USPeaceMemorial.org) (www.uspeacememorial.org). Produces US Peace Registry.

US Servas (SE), 1125 16th St – Suite 201, Arcata, CA 95521-5585 (+1-707-825 1714) (fax 825 1762) (info@usservas.org) (usservas.org). *Open Doors*.

Utah Campaign to Abolish Nuclear Weapons (ND), c/o 549 Cortez St, Salt Lake City, UT 84103 (dsawyer@xmission.com) (www.utahcan.org).

Vermonters for Justice in Palestine (HR CR), c/o Peace & Justice Center, 60 Lake St, Burlington, VT 05401 (vtjp@vtjp.org) (www.vtjp.org).

Veterans For Peace [VFP] (DA PA RA), 1404 North Broadway, St Louis, MO 63102 (+1-314-725 6005) (fax 227 1981) (vfp@veteransforpeace.org) (www.veteransforpeace.org).

Voices for Creative Nonviolence (PA), 1249 W Argyle St – No 2, Chicago, IL 60640 (+1-773-878 3815) (info@vcnv.org) (vcnv.org).

Volunteers for Peace [VFP] (WC HR PO CD EL), 7 Kilburn St – Ste 316, Burlington, VT 05410 (+1-802-540 3040) (info@vfp.org) (www.vfp.org).

Waging Nonviolence [WNV], 226 Prospect Park West – No 146, Brooklyn, New York, NY 11215 (contact@wagingnonviolence.org) (wagingnonviolence.org). Internet-based resource.

War Resisters League [WRL] (WR IB TR AT), 168 Canal St – 6th Floor, New York, NY 10013 (+1-212-228 0450) (wrl@warresisters.org) (www.warresisters.org).

War Resisters League – New England Regional Office (WR), PO Box 1093, Norwich, CT 06360 (+1-860-639 8834) (joanne@warresisters.org) (www.warresisters.org/new-england-office).

Washington Peace Center (HR PA RE), 1525 Newton St NW, Washington, DC 20010 (+1-202-234 2000) (fax 558 5685) (info@washingtonpeacecenter.org) (washingtonpeacecenter.net).

Win Without War, 2000 M St NW – Suite 720, Washington, DC 20036 (+1-202-232 3317) (info@winwithoutwar.org) (winwithoutwar.org). Coalition engaging mainstream who want a safe USA.

Witness Against Torture (RP HR), c/o New York Catholic Worker, 55 East 3rd St, New York, NY 10003 (www.witnessagainsttorture.com). Campaign to close Guantanamo and end torture.

Witness for Peace [WfP] (RP HR TW), 1616 P St NW – Suite 100, Washington, DC 20036 (+1-202-547 6112) (fax 536 4708) (witness@witnessforpeace.org) (www.witnessforpeace.org).

Women for Genuine Security (CD PA), 965 62nd St, Oakland, CA 94608 (+1-415-312 5583) (info@genuinesecurity.org) (www.genuinesecurity.org).

Women's Environment and Development Organization [WEDO] (TW EL HR), 355 Lexington Av – 3rd floor, New York, NY 10017 (+1-212-973 0325) (wedo@wedo.org) (www.wedo.org).

Women's International League for Peace and Freedom – US Section [WILPF US] (WL HR), AFSC House, PO Box 13075, Des Moines, IA 50310 (+1-617-266 0999) (info@wilpf.org) (wilpfus.org). *Peace and Freedom.*

Working Group for Peace and Demilitarization in Asia & the Pacific (DA RE), 2161 Massachusetts Ave, Cambridge, MA 02141 (+1-617-661 6130) (info@asiapacificinitiative.org) (www.asiapacificinitiative.org).

World BEYOND War (PA DA), 513 E Main St – No 1484, Charlottesville, VA 22902 (research@worldbeyondwar.org) (worldbeyondwar.org).

World Can't Wait (DA HR), 305 West Broadway – No 185, New York, NY 10013 (+1-646-807 3259) (info@worldcantwait.org) (www.worldcantwait.net). "Putting humanity and the planet first".

World Future Society (PO), 333 N LaSalle St, Chicago, IL 60654 (info@wfs.org) (wfs.site-ym.com). Clearinghouse for ideas about the future.

World Peace Now (CD ND DA), PO Box 275, Point Arena, CA 95468 (ellen.rosser@gmail.com). Formerly Friendship and Peace Society.

Worldwatch Institute (EL AT), 1400 16th St NW – Suite 430, Washington, DC 20036 (+1-202-745 8092) (fax 478 2534) (worldwatch@worldwatch.org) (www.worldwatch.org). Europe office in Copenhagen (+45-2087 1933).

URUGUAY

Amnistía Internacional Uruguay (AI), Wilson Ferreira Aldunate 1220, Montevideo 11100 (+598-2-900 7939) (fax 900 9851) (oficina@amnistia.org.uy) (www.amnistia.org.uy).

Asociación de Lucha para el Desarme Civil [ALUDEC] (CR DA), Andes 1365 – piso 10, Montevideo 11100 (+598-94-454440) (direccion@aludec.org.uy). Concerned about increased arming of "civilians".

SERPAJ-Uruguay (FR RE HR), Joaquín Requena 1642, 11200 Montevideo (+598-2-408 5301) (fax 408 5701) (serpajuy@serpaj.org.uy) (www.serpaj.org.uy).

UZBEKISTAN

"Esperanto" Xalqaro Do'stlik Klubi / International Friendship Club "Esperanto" (CD), c/o PO Box 76, 703000 Samarkand (+998-66-233 1753).

Servas (SE), c/o PO Box 76, 140100 Samarkand (+998-66-233 1753) (imps86@yahoo.com).

Xalqaro Tinchlik va Birdamlik Muzei / Internacia Muzeo de Paco kaj Solidaro (IB RE CD), PO Box 76, 140100 Samarkand (+998-66-233 1753) (fax) (imps86@yahoo.com) (peace.museum.com). International Museum of Peace and Solidarity.

VENEZUELA

Programa Venezolnao de Educación-Acción en Derechos Humanos [PROVEA] (HR), Apdo Postal 5156, Carmelitas 1010-A, Caracas (+58-212-862 1011) (fax) (www.derechos.org.ve).

VIETNAM

Vietnam Peace Committee [VPC] (WP), 105a Quan Thanh, Ba Dinh, Ha Noi (+84-4-3945 4272) (fax 3733 0201) (vietpeacecom@gmail.com).

ZAMBIA

International Friendship League – Zambia [IFL] (CD), c/o George Siluyele, PO Box 234, Chongwe, Lusaka Province (georgesiluyele@yahoo.com).

OneWorld Africa [OWA] (TW), PO Box 37011, Lusaka (+260-21-129 2740) (fax 129 4188) (priscilla.jere@oneworld.net) (africa.oneworld.net). Part of OneWorld Network, in 11 countries.

Zambian Health Workers for Social Responsibility [ZHSR] (IP), c/o Department of Medicine, School of Medicine, PO Box 50110, Lusaka (bobmtonga@hotmail.com).

ZIMBABWE

Gays and Lesbians of Zimbabwe [GALZ] (WR HR), Private Bag A6131, Avondale, Harare (+263-4-741736) (fax 778165) (director@galz.co.zw). *Galzette.*

Zimbabwe Human Rights NGO Forum (HR), PO Box 9077, 8th Floor, Bluebridge, Eastgate, Harare (+263-4-250511) (fax 250494) (admin@hrforum.co.zw) (www.hrforumzim.com).

Zimbabwe Lawyers for Human Rights [ZLHR] (HR), Box CY 1393, Causeway, Harare (+263-4-764085) (fax 705641) (info@zlhr.org.zw) (www.zlhr.org.zw).

Notes

Notes